Atle Ottesen Søvik
Free Will, Causality and the Self

Philosophische Analyse/ Philosophical Analysis

Herausgegeben von/Edited by
Herbert Hochberg, Rafael Hüntelmann,
Christian Kanzian, Richard Schantz, Erwin Tegtmeier

Band/Volume 71

Atle Ottesen Søvik

Free Will, Causality and the Self

DE GRUYTER

ISBN 978-3-11-061174-8
e-ISBN (PDF) 978-3-11-047468-8
e-ISBN (EPUB) 978-3-11-047446-6
ISSN 2198-2066

Library of Congress Cataloging-in-Publication Data
A CIP catalog record for this book has been applied for at the Library of Congress.

Bibliographic information published by the Deutsche Nationalbibliothek
The Deutsche Nationalbibliothek lists this publication in the Deutsche Nationalbibliografie;
detailed bibliographic data are available on the Internet at http://dnb.dnb.de.

© 2018 Walter de Gruyter GmbH, Berlin/Boston
This volume is text- and page-identical with the hardback published in 2016.
Printing: CPI books GmbH, Leck

♾ Printed on acid-free paper
Printed in Germany

www.degruyter.com

Foreword

This book took some years to write. The discussion on free will moves fast forward and I have been helped by many people in getting to know and think through details:

Many thanks to the following people for reading the whole manuscript at one time or another and offering many valuable comments: Robert Kane, Bob Doyle, Ragnar Mogård Bergem, Lars Fredrik Svendsen, Helen Steward, Olav Gjelsvik, Bjørn Ramberg, Michael Gisinger, and two anonymous reviewers.

Thanks to the following people for reading parts of the manuscript and offering valuable comments: Jonathan Schaffer, Oskar Skarsaune and Kristin Graff-Kallevåg.

I am grateful for brief conversations on the matter with the following people: Randolph Clarke, Alfred Mele, Michael McKenna, Chandra Sripada. Also, thanks to many of the people at CSMN/IFIKK at the University of Oslo for discussions over coffee; Einar Duenger Bøhn, Andreas Brekke Carlsson, Andreas Strand, Edmund Henden, Monica Roland and Hedda Hassel Mørch.

Thanks to the people involved at DeGruyter: Rafael Hüntelmann, Olena Gainulina and Maik Bierwirth, and to Kjetil Borgenvik at MF for great technical help with the manuscript.

Finally, I am grateful to my family who would have made my life a great joy even if free will had not existed: Andreas, Jenny, Kristian and Elise.

Oslo, February 2016.

Contents

1	Introduction —— 1
1.1	The Problem of Free Will—Main Positions and Problems —— 1
1.2	The Theory Proposed in this Book —— 10
1.3	Methodological Reflections —— 17

2	Causality —— 21
2.1	Part 1: Jonathan Schaffer's Understanding of Causality —— 21
2.1.1	To what category do causes and effects belong? —— 22
2.1.2	How many relata are there in the causal relation? —— 22
2.1.3	How are causes and effects connected? —— 23
2.1.4	How are causes selected from other conditions? —— 28
2.2	Part 2: Evaluation of Schaffer's Understanding of Causality —— 29
2.2.1	To what category do causes and effects belong? —— 31
2.2.2	How many relata are there in the causal relation? —— 33
2.2.3	How are causes and effects connected? —— 34
2.2.4	How are causes selected from other conditions? —— 49

3	The Self —— 56
3.1	Biological Background —— 59
3.2	Brain and Mind —— 62
3.3	Emotion —— 72
3.4	Memory —— 76
3.5	Consciousness —— 78
3.6	The Self —— 81
3.7	The Function of Consciousness —— 89
3.8	Thinking —— 95
3.9	Desire —— 97

4	Free Will —— 106
4.1	What Is Free Will? —— 106
4.2	Alternative Possibilities —— 114
4.3	Determinism —— 116
4.4	Independence of the Self —— 121
4.5	Responsibility —— 126
4.6	Free Will and Responsibility in Various Cases —— 139

5 Answers to Objections — 157
5.1 Main problems for Libertarians — 157
5.2 Main Problems for Compatibilists — 162
5.3 Other Problems — 163
5.4 Conclusion — 170

Bibliography — 173

Name index — 179

Subject index — 181

1 Introduction

In this chapter I first present the main positions in the free will debate—compatibilism and libertarianism. I also explore their subtypes: for compatibilism, mesh theories and reasons-responsive theories; for libertarianism, non-causal, agent-causal and event-causal theories. I then present the main problems these positions each face. For compatibilism, this includes the consequence argument, the manipulation argument and the zygote argument. Problems for libertarianism include the luck problem, the assimilation argument and the disappearing agent problem. After this, I present the theory I will propose in this book, indicating how it deals with all of these problems. I end with some methodological reflections.

1.1 The Problem of Free Will—Main Positions and Problems

There are three main questions that a theory of free will should answer: What does "free will" mean? Do we have free will? Is the proposed theory of free will coherent, given that free will seems incompatible with both determinism and indeterminism?

What does the term "free will" refer to? There are many different definitions of free will, and one should ask which understanding of free will is being considered, whether it is being affirmed or rejected. It may well be that a strong form of free will is rejected while a weaker form is affirmed. In ordinary language, a minimum requirement for what it means to have free will is to say that it is the freedom persons must have in order for it to be meaningful to hold them responsible for their actions. (Like free will, though, responsibility is understood in many different ways.) A common definition of free will is to say that (1) it is "up to us" what we choose between several alternatives, and (2) the source of the choice is in us, and not outside of us or in something else that we cannot control.[1] Even if this description does not apply to every choice, most people will say that they experience such free will at least in some of their choices. Still, both parts of even this definition are contested and can be further defined in various ways: What does it mean to be the source of a choice? Are alternative possibilities necessary for free will? How should such alternative possibilities be

---

1 Robert Kane, *The Oxford Handbook of Free Will*, 2nd ed. (Oxford: Oxford University Press, 2011), 5.

understood? Some philosophers will say that you have no free will, others will say that you have free will in a weak sense of the term, and still others will say that you have free will in a strong sense of the term. It is my goal in this book to try to find out how free your will really is.

Among those who affirm free will, compatibilists and libertarians disagree on whether free will is compatible with the idea that all events are determined. This idea, *determinism*, can be defined in many ways.[2] One common understanding refers to the belief that everything that happens must necessarily happen exactly as it does because of previous causes; therefore, at any one time, there is only one possible future.[3] Even within this definition there are many varieties, since destiny, God's predestination, logical necessities, or physical causes can be that which determines the outcome. In the free will debate today, the focus is usually on physical determinism, which is the view that previous physical causes plus the laws of nature determine one future with physical necessity.[4] At any point of time, the rest of history is then implied by the state of the world at that time. Such physical determinism will be the focus in this book as well, since I believe that is the strongest and most common challenge to the question of free will.[5] This is a metaphysical position, and this is what I mean by "determinism" in this book.

In the discussion on determinism, Compatibilists believe that determinism is compatible with having free will. For a long time the most common critique of

---

[2] According to J. H. Sobel, there are at least 90 different understandings of the term "determinism." See Bishop, in ibid., 84.

[3] Note that determinism does not necessarily mean predictability, since a system can be determined and at the same time chaotic and/or incomputable. Determinism is an ontological question; predictability is an epistemological question (Nicholas Saunders, *Divine Action and Modern Science* (Cambridge: Cambridge University Press, 2002), 87–90, 177–78). "Only one possible future" means that only one specific series of events is already determined to be the content of the future.

[4] The term "physical" is notoriously difficult to define, but a rough definition that should suffice in this context is that "physical" is that which is to some degree measurable and quantifiable.

[5] One definition is as follows: "The state of the universe at any time is wholly and unequivocally determined by the state of the universe at prior times, and the physical laws of nature." (Hodgson, in Kane, *The Oxford Handbook of Free Will* (2nd ed.), 57). This kind of physical determinism may be further divided into causal physical determinism and block universe physical determinism. My reference is to the causal version (See Bishop, in *The Oxford Handbook of Free Will* (Oxford: Oxford University Press, 2002), 113-14). We shall return to the question of how to understand causality in chapter two—for now, suffice it to say that physical causes are immanent events in the world.

compatibilism was the consequence argument. Roughly, this argument is that if determinism is true, then what happens in the future is determined by laws of nature and events that took place previously, even in the distant past. Even before any humans existed it was determined what the content of the future would be for all humans. Since the future was thus determined before our birth, it cannot be up to us what happens among different alternatives, and thus we cannot have free will.[6]

Despite this widely debated argument, compatibilists believe determinism is compatible with having free will. Compatibilists today will usually say that it does not matter that only one specific future is physically possible. Rather, they will focus instead on what the inner mental life of an agent must be like in order for the agent to be free. One strand of contemporary compatibilism is the so-called *mesh theories*, which hold that a person is free when she has the right connections or "mesh" between internal parts of her mental life.[7] Another strand is *reasons-responsive theories*. According to these theories a person is free when her actions are based on a rational response to reasons for action.[8] These different compatibilist understandings of free will do not require indeterminism, and so free will is argued to be compatible with determinism and in no need of alternative possibilities.

However, an argument other than the Consequence Argument has been in focus lately against compatibilism, and that is Derk Pereboom's four-case manipulation argument. This argument presents four cases, from a clear manipulation case to a deterministic world, where the point is to show that there are no relevant differences between the cases. Since the first case clearly seems to be a

---

[6] Peter Van Inwagen, *An Essay on Free Will* (Oxford: Clarendon Press, 1983).
[7] For example, there are hierarchical mesh theories, such as Harry Frankfurt's theory. Frankfurt argues that we have several desires whose object is an action or a state, which he calls first-order desires. But we also have desires whose object is a first-order desire, and these he calls second-order desires. The second-order desires are internal responses to the first-order desires, which one may like or dislike. According to Frankfurt, we are free when our second-order desires approve our first-order desires, because only then do we have the will we want. (Harry Frankfurt, "Freedom of the Will and the Concept of a Person," *Journal of Philosophy* 68(1971)).
[8] See for example Susan R. Wolf, *Freedom within Reason* (New York: Oxford University Press, 1990), or John Martin Fischer and Mark Ravizza, *Responsibility and Control: A Theory of Moral Responsibility*, Cambridge Studies in Philosophy and Law (Cambridge: Cambridge University Press, 1998).

case of no free will, the charge is to explain the relevant difference between case 1 and case 4.[9]

---

[9] Here are the four cases, quoted from Derk Pereboom, *Free Will, Agency, and Meaning in Life* (New York: Oxford University press, 2014), 76–79:

Case 1: A team of neuroscientists has the ability to manipulate Plum's neural states at any time by radio-like technology. In this particular case, they do so by pressing a button just before he begins to reason about his situation, which they know will produce in him a neural state that realizes a strongly egoistic reasoning process, which the neuroscientists know will deterministically result in his decision to kill White. Plum would not have killed White had the neuroscientists not intervened, since his reasoning would then not have been sufficiently egoistic to produce this decision. But at the same time, Plum's effective first-order desire to kill White conforms to his second-order desires. In addition, his process of deliberation from which the decision results is reasons-responsive; in particular, this type of process would have resulted in Plum's refraining from deciding to kill White in certain situations in which his reasons were different. His reasoning is consistent with his character because it is frequently egoistic and sometimes strongly so. Still, it is not in general exclusively egoistic, because he sometimes successfully regulates his behavior by moral reasons, especially when the egoistic reasons are relatively weak. Plum is also not constrained to act as he does, for he does not act because of an irresistible desire—the neuroscientists do not induce a desire of this sort.

Case 2: Plum is just like an ordinary human being, except that a team of neuroscientists programmed him at the beginning of his life so that his reasoning is often but not always egoistic (as in Case 1), and at times strongly so, with the intended consequence that in his current circumstances he is causally determined to engage in the egoistic reasons-responsive process of deliberation and to have the set of first- and second-order desires that result in his decision to kill White. Plum has the general ability to regulate his actions by moral reasons, but in his circumstances, due to the strongly egoistic nature of his deliberative reasoning, he is causally determined to make the decision to kill. Yet he does not decide as he does because of an irresistible desire. The neural realization of his reasoning process and of his decision is exactly the same as it is in Case 1 (although their causal histories are different).

Case 3: Plum is an ordinary human being except that the training practices of his community causally determined the nature of his deliberative reasoning processes so that they are frequently but not exclusively rationally egoistic (the resulting nature of his deliberative reasoning processes are exactly as they are in Cases 1 and 2). This training was completed before he developed the ability to prevent or alter these practices. Due to the aspect of his character produced by this training, in his present circumstances he is causally determined to engage in the strongly egoistic reasons-responsive process of deliberation that issue in his decision to kill White. While Plum does have the general ability to regulate his behavior with moral reasoning, in virtue of this aspect of his character and his circumstances he is causally determined to make his immoral decision, although he does not decide as he does due to an irresistible desire. The neural realization of his deliberative reasoning process and of the decision is just as it is in Cases 1 and 2.

Case 4: Everything that happens in our universe is causally determined by virtue of its past states together with the laws of nature. Plum is an ordinary human being, raised in normal circumstances, and again his reasoning processes are frequently but not exclusively egoistic,

Alfred Mele has a similar argument called the zygote argument: imagine a goddess creating a zygote at exactly the right time and place with the exact right structure in a deterministic universe. She does this because she knows that the zygote will then become a man (Ernie) who at an exact point of time will do something the goddess wants done—for example, kill his grandmother. Ernie will be, like any other person in a deterministic universe, considered by compatibilists to be free, but many will have the intuition that he was not responsible for killing his grandmother since the goddess had planned things so that this had to happen. Yet, since he is like any other person in our world if the world is determined, it seems that if he is not responsible, no one else is either.[10]

Even if one disagrees over how strong the manipulation argument and the zygote argument is against compatibilism, I think there can be little doubt that, if the future is already determined before we are born, we do not have a strong form of free will. It is not up to us to change the future into anything else than what was already determined before we were born. Libertarians, on the other hand, think that we do have a stronger form of free will than this. They hold that we can be the source of our choices in a more fundamental sense than what compatibilists will allow, but that requires an indeterministic world where different futures are possible and where it is up to us to influence what the future will be like.

There are three main positions among libertarians distinguished by how they understand the causality involved in free choices. Non-causalists believe that free actions are not caused at all, but are intelligible in the light of the purpose of the action. Agent causalists believe that there is a unique and irreducible kind of causation that only free agents can employ. Event causalists deny that actions have special causes, but believe instead that all causes are of the same kind: they think that events cause events, both in the mind and in the world in general.

Those who defend the strongest form of free will are the non-causalists and the agent causalists. Non-causalists argue that human action should be explained by intentions or reasons instead of causes, and that these are not reduc-

---

and sometimes strongly so (as in Cases 1–3). His decision to kill White issues from his strongly egoistic but reasons-responsive process of deliberation, and he has specified first- and second-order desire. The neural realization of Plum's reasoning process and decision is exactly as it is in Cases 1–3; he has the general ability to grasp, apply and regulate his actions with moral reasoning, and it is not because of an irresistible desire that he decides to kill.

10 Alfred R. Mele, *Free Will and Luck* (New York: Oxford University Press, 2006), 188–89.

ible to ordinary event causes.[11] A classic charge against this view was leveled by Donald Davidson.[12] He pointed out that even if a person has a reason for doing something, that does not mean that his reason is what actually caused the event to happen. People often experience having competing reasons for doing different things when they act. The challenge to non-causalists is to explain what links the personal reason to the action. Agent causalists like Timothy O'Connor hold that agents are enduring irreducible substances who have a unique ability to perform actions.[13] Agent causalists are typically criticized for appealing to both a mysterious agent and a mysterious form of causation, which does not fit into the ordinary scientific world view.[14] Nor do they explain how reasons make actions happen, for in virtue of what does the agent control her actions? Agent-causation can be argued to be an irreducible phenomenon,[15] but I shall argue later that it is superfluous to add anything to normal event-causation. This will be my main argument against non-causal and agent-causal libertarian theories—that our behavior can be explained sufficiently in event-causal terms so that there is no good reason to believe in extra agency or causation beyond that.

In my view, the most plausible of the libertarian theories are the event-causal theories. Event-causalists hold that mental events can cause free actions. There are two main event-causal theories, distinguished by where in the deliberation process they locate indeterminism.[16] The advocates of *centered* event-causal theories believe that there is indeterminism until and in the moment of choice, whereas advocates of the *deliberative* event-causal theories hold that there is indeterminism early in the deliberation process, creating different ideas in the mind (alternative possibilities), but that the rest of the deliberation process is determined.[17]

---

[11] An example of such a theory can be found in Carl Ginet, *On Action*, Cambridge Studies in Philosophy (Cambridge: Cambridge University Press, 1990).
[12] Donald Davidson, "Actions, Reasons and Causes," *The Journal of Philosophy* 60, no. 23 (1963).
[13] O'Connor, in Kane, *The Oxford Handbook of Free Will* (2nd ed.), 309–28.
[14] Pereboom, *Free Will, Agency, and Meaning in Life*, 65–69.
[15] For example, E. J. Lowe argues that both causality and agent-causality are irreducible concepts. See E. J. Lowe, *A Survey of Metaphysics* (Oxford: Oxford University Press, 2002), chapters eight to eleven.
[16] Indeterminism simply means that more than one future is possible, so when I and others I refer to speak about the location of indeterminism, the point is to speak about the source of indeterminism; where do the indeterministic effects arise?
[17] The distinction between centered and deliberative event-causal theories is from Randolph K. Clarke, *Libertarian Accounts of Free Will* (New York: Oxford University Press, 2003), 57, 71.

Since event-causal libertarian theories are close to my own theory, I shall spend a little time in presenting them here. I start with the centered event-causal libertarian theory of Robert Kane.[18] Kane thinks that free will is fundamentally about the ultimate source of action being in us.[19] More precisely, the requirement is that *"To be ultimately responsible for an action, an agent must be responsible for anything that is a sufficient cause or motive for the action's occurring."*[20] This means that the requirement of alternative possibilities is not necessary for all our actions. But it is necessary in some specific early choices in which we formed our own characters, according to Kane. He calls such actions self-forming actions, or SFAs. Even if one could not have done otherwise in some situations, one is still responsible if the reason that one could not do otherwise was earlier SFAs. For example, if you have formed your character through SFAs so that it is now impossible for you to lie, you are still free, responsible and praiseworthy for not lying in situations where you could.[21] As long as we are free to make some SFAs, we can be free, but if the world is determined, then none of our actions are SFAs and then we are not free.

But this seems to result in an infinite regress, for would not those earlier choices depend on even earlier choices, and so on indefinitely?[22] Kane's response to this criticism is that the regress is ended if there is an action in the agent's past that lacked sufficient motive.[23] There could be a situation in which the agent did not know what to do and so did not set her will before the action occurred. Then the action would set the will in the very act of choosing; Kane calls such actions "will-setting actions" (which are the same as self-forming actions). He adds that in order for such actions to provide us with free will, they must have been such that the agent could act voluntarily, intentionally and rationally in more than one way when she acted. If the action happened as an accident, it would not have made the agent the ultimate source; rather, the accident would be the source. But if the agent had a motive for both alterna-

---

18 For a detailed presentation of Kane's theory and a critique of it, see Atle O. Søvik, "A Critique of Robert Kane's Theory of Free Will," (Under review).
19 Kane, "Libertarianism," John Martin Fischer, *Four Views on Free Will*, Great Debates in Philosophy (Oxford: Blackwell Pub., 2007), 13–14.
20 Kane, "Libertarianism," ibid., 14. Emphasis in original text.
21 "Could" must here be understood in the sense that it was type physically possible.
22 Kane, in Fischer, *Four Views on Free Will*, 19–20.
23 According to Kane, we have a "sufficient motive" for doing something when our will is set one way on doing so before and when we act (Kane, ibid., 19).

tives, then she is the ultimate source of the choice no matter what she chooses, so the regress stops there.[24]

Even if such a choice is undetermined, Kane still thinks it can be a rationally willed choice. To argue this, he offers the example of a businesswoman on her way to an important meeting who witnesses an assault. In this situation she has reasons to stop and reasons to move on, and she does not know what to do. The conflicting motives stir up a chaos in the brain, which is sensitive to undetermined events at the micro level of quantum mechanics. In this situation the woman must make an effort to choose and no matter what she chooses, it will be for a reason. When she decides, that decision sets her will.[25]

The most common critique of Kane's theory is that it runs into a problem of luck. Let us say there is a 70% probability that Jack will decide to have pancakes for breakfast. If history were rolled back a hundred times and played again up to the moment of choice, Jack would decide to have pancakes 70 times and something else 30 times. But if the exact same history up to the moment of choice can give completely different choices—which Robert Kane argues it can[26]—it seems to be a matter of luck as to what Jack decides to do. The same point can be made with identical worlds up to the moment of choice, where Jack1 and Jack2 make different choices.[27]

The luck argument has been strengthened by the assimilation argument. Seth Shabo has argued a case where an indeterministic device in a person's brain determines her choices but sometimes it does not work, and then compared these situations in a rollback of histories. The argument then is that there is no relevant difference between a rollback of histories where the indeterministic device works or not—in any case there will be an undetermined outcome where the person sometimes chooses A and sometimes chooses B.[28]

Kane's theory is a *centered* event-causal theory since it locates indeterminism in the moment of choice. Deliberative event-causal theories try to reduce the luck component by locating indeterminism at an earlier point in the deliberation process. Such models are also called two-stage models, since the delibera-

---

24 Kane, ibid., 20.
25 Kane, ibid., 26–28.
26 Kane, ibid., 23.
27 Randolph Clarke distinguishes between the rollback argument with a rollback of history, and the luck-objection as the inter-world case (Clarke, in Kane, *The Oxford Handbook of Free Will* (2nd ed.), 323–24).
28 Seth Shabo, "Why Free Will Remains a Mystery," *Pacific Philosophical Quarterly* 92, no. 1 (2011), "Assimilations and Rollbacks: Two Arguments against Libertarianism Defended," *Philosophia* 42, no. 1 (2014).

tion process comprises two stages. First there is an indeterministic stage in which alternatives for actions are generated in the mind. This is followed by a deterministic stage in which one alternative for action is selected.

One of the best such proposals is Alfred Mele's *daring soft libertarianism*. Mele argues that whereas the other models shun luck and only include indeterminism to avoid determinism, this model embraces luck while still maintaining that the agent can be in control.[29] The point is that the deliberation process is indeterministic, so that it is partly a matter of luck what the agents end up choosing. But the agent learns from experiences over time and the agent's evaluations of these experiences influences how likely it is that the same choice will be made later. In this way, the agent shapes her own character over time and this also explains why we hold children less responsible than adults for what they do.[30]

Neil Levy argues that libertarians can try to reduce the luck component by making their theories almost compatibilist.[31] But he does not think that Mele's strategy with including luck in the history of an agent works, since luck has been a part of every choice, and you cannot solve the problem of luck with adding more luck.[32] Even compatibilists have a luck problem, according to Levy, since it is also a matter of luck what such agents come to think about or desire.[33]

In addition to the luck problem, the other main argument against event-causal theories is the problem of the disappearing agent. It seems that on event-causal approaches, choices reduce to desires, beliefs and bodily movement, and the agent disappears.[34] If everything is just natural causal processes occurring, where is the free agent?

As seen, the different kinds of compatibilisms and libertarianisms run into different problems. This has led various philosophers to conclude that we do not have free will, since free will is incompatible with both determinism and indeterminism.[35] But most philosophers still hold on to the idea that we have free

---

29 Mele, *Free Will and Luck*, 117.
30 Ibid., 122–23, 31–32.
31 Neil Levy, *Hard Luck: How Luck Undermines Free Will and Moral Responsibility* (New York: Oxford University Press, 2011), 77.
32 Ibid., 89.
33 Ibid., 90.
34 This is mentioned as a main objection against event-causal theories in, for example, Pereboom, *Free Will, Agency, and Meaning in Life*, 31–33, and Helen Steward, *A Metaphysics for Freedom* (Oxford: Oxford University Press, 2012), 62.
35 Pereboom, *Free Will, Agency, and Meaning in Life*, 3.

will, since this seems best to fit our experience of having free will and being responsible for our actions. Now that we have a conceptual map of the main positions and main problems, I am ready to locate my own theory as a newcomer to this map and indicate how I will relate to the different problems.

1.2 The Theory Proposed in this Book

If the compatibilists are right, we have free will only in a very limited sense since our whole future was determined before we were born. The manipulation argument and the zygote argument illustrate this well. Luck is also a real limitation to the degree of control that we can have, and I cannot see that there are good arguments in favor of non-causal or agent-causal libertarian theories. I do think, though, that we have a stronger form of free will than that which compatibilists hold, while I do not think the problem of luck is as big as it is often claimed to be.

The theory I propose in this book is a new way of navigating between compatibilism and libertarianism, and it is closest to event-causal libertarianism. It is libertarianism, since I believe that the world is indetermined at the macro level of humans, and that this is required for free will in a strong sense. I reject determinism and compatibilism, and think that we can be fundamental sources of our own choices. However, event-causal libertarianism always locates the indeterminism inside the mind of the agent. I, however, claim that there is no need for such agent-internal indeterminism. It suffices that, for free will in a strong sense, there is some indeterminism somewhere in the world making more than one future physically possible. External indeterminism is all that is required to have free will in a strong sense. Removing the internal indeterminism reduces the luck component, while still making more than one future possible, thereby avoiding the manipulation and zygote arguments.

It has been claimed that it is preposterous to base a theory of free will on external indeterminism,[36] but I shall try anyway. I will also respond to this criticism in my presentation. First, in order to show how it is possible to be the fundamental source of our choices on such conditions, it is necessary to give a detailed understanding of causation and the self. Such understandings will be presented in chapters two and three. This will clarify what it means to be an agent and what it means to be the source of a choice. I strive to give detailed

---

[36] Alfred R. Mele, *Autonomous Agents: From Self-Control to Autonomy* (New York: Oxford University Press, 1995), 195–96.

empirical content to such concepts as *agent, self, choice, cause, source,* and *control,* and will show that many problems can be solved when these are given clear empirical content.

In detail, I will structure my case as follows:

Chapter two is my understanding of causation. I argue that an agent can be the cause or ultimate source of her choices even if everything that happens in her mind is a causal process where only one thing may be token physically possible to do. In order to argue this, I must present a detailed and empirical theory about causation. I must also explain why causation should be thought of as contrastive and that we select contrasts and causes based on interests and expectations. This allows me to be clear about what it is to be the ultimate cause or source of one's actions, and to understand how agents can cause actions this way.

In chapter three, I present my theory of the self, which is informed to a large degree by the neuroscientist Antonio Damasio. His theory of the self lets me explain how a person's self can be the cause of her actions. I discuss in some detail how the mind works, and focus on giving empirical content to the concepts, trying to relate frameworks with a first-person and a third-person perspective. The work done here should be of interest to those who think about free will even if they disagree with everything else I say before that. Damasio distinguishes between the proto-self, the core self, and the autobiographical self. Especially important for me is the understanding of our autobiographical self, and how it can change the desires we feel, so that the autobiographical self then becomes the cause of the desires that cause our actions. Since the world is indetermined and causation contrastive, I shall argue that there will be cases where the autobiographical self is the ultimate cause of a person's action, and that it is the ultimate cause of its own content.

Damasio's work lets us describe a deliberation process as a causal process, where a situation triggers alternatives for action that a person desires with different degrees of strength, and activated memories from the autobiographical self mark the alternatives with feelings which change the strength of the desire for each alternative. When the strongest desire reaches a threshold for action, motor neurons are activated and the action is carried through.

With this detailed theory of the self and deliberation as background, I present my theory of free will in chapter four. I start by describing many different kinds of deliberation processes wherein an agent (which in my terminology is the same as a person, which I define as a human body with a mind and a core self) and her autobiographical self can be involved to varying degrees. I argue that a person has free will if (but not only if) her autobiographical self changes her initial desire into a different desire, which causes the choice that is made, because the person is then the cause of her choice between alternatives, and the source of the choice was within her.[37]

Concerning the requirement of alternative possibilities, in any situation there may be only one thing that it was token physically possible for a person to do. But as long as the person imagines different alternatives, the person can be rightly selected as the cause of the desire that causes the choice that is made—all the imagined alternatives need not be *token* physically possible for the person to do as long as they are *type* physically possible.[38] This presupposes that the world cannot be determined if we are to be free, for then our actions would have been determined before we were born, and it would not be right to select the autobiographical self as the cause of the choice between A and B. But if there is some indeterminism in the world, with undetermined effects at the macro level of humans, then it will often be right to select persons as the causes of the choices they make, or so I shall argue in chapter four on the basis of the discussion of causality in chapter two.

People can have more or less independent autobiographical selves, depending on how much they have changed their autobiographical selves from within

---

[37] "Choice" is an ambiguous term (Nicholas Rescher, *Free Will: A Philosophical Reappraisal* (New Brunswick, NJ: Transaction Publishers, 2009), xii). Before I choose I *have a choice*, say between alternatives A and B. A and B are possible *choices* (alternatives), and I can *make a choice* between them. When the deliberation process is over, I have *made a choice*, which means I have decided to do either A or B. There are several stages from deliberation to action. First, there is the deliberation process wherein different alternatives and desires are considered, then one of the alternatives is selected as the one to act upon, and finally an alternative is acted upon. The alternative that is acted upon is usually the one that was selected, but if there is sufficient time between the selection and action, new deliberation may take place, and a change of mind can occur. "Choice" and "decision" are ambiguous terms, but I try to clarify what I mean, and usually I mean by "choice" or "decision" the selection of the alternative that was finally acted upon. Alfred Mele suggests "intention" for the selection of the alternative to act upon, and argues that one can intend to do something without having decided it (Alfred R. Mele, *Springs of Action: Understanding Intentional Behavior* (New York: Oxford University Press, 1992), 141). It is true that "choice" suggests that several alternatives have been considered, whereas if a person only has one desire and only considers one alternative, they can act intentionally without having made a choice. All these parts of the deliberation process will be presented in detail in chapter three. I shall focus in this book on decisions about how to act, not cases where one decides what one believes to be true.

[38] Something may be *type* physically possible if it is physically possible in general. But maybe the same thing is *token* physically impossible in a certain situation, and token physically possible in other specific situations.

via a process of thinking and feeling in the light of experience.[39] But it is not only when an independent autobiographical self causes the desires of a person that the person has free will. Free will lies on a continuum, from cases where *desires alone* in the person cause the choice that is made, to cases where the *autobiographical self* causes the choice that is made, to cases where an *independent autobiographical self* causes the choice that is made. I shall argue that free will is about inner-directedness, and this means that different people can have different degrees of free will in different choices, and that we can acquire more free will throughout life. I argue that free will and self-control are the same, since self-control in my usage of the term is about how the agent causes her choices.[40] I discuss many cases of *akrasia* (weakness of the will) and find that they are easily integrated in the theory.

Is it meaningful to hold people responsible if there are many situations where only one thing is token physically possible for a person to do? I argue that responsibility is something we usually ascribe to people by comparing what they do or do not do with a moral standard for what we think they should have done in a situation. We expect people with normal emotions and normal capacities for thinking and a certain amount of life experience to come to certain conclusions about what it is good and right to do in various situations and to follow these guidelines. When they do not, we judge that as blameworthy, and we often hold them responsible in order to change their behavior for the better. Holding another person responsible is a way to make a better society, and it is not irrational, even if there is just one alternative that is token physically possible for that person to do, since holding her responsible in that situation can change what that one alternative is.

I can now indicate briefly how I will respond to the arguments against event-causal libertarianism, namely the problem of luck and the problem of the disappearing agent.[41] When it comes to the disappearing agent, we saw how Helen Steward objects that choices reduce to desires, beliefs and bodily movement, and the agent disappears.[42] But the agent does not disappear in event-causal theories. Rather, what an agent is and what it is for an agent to make a choice is explained in a more finely grained way. It is like explaining hardness by describing tension between atoms. The hardness does not disappear, it is just

---

39 I presuppose a normal capacity for feeling and thinking. Those who lack such capacity are impaired in terms of their freedom.
40 As argued by Alfred Mele, *Autonomous Agents*, 10.
41 I will reply in detail to these objections in chapter five.
42 Steward, *A Metaphysics for Freedom*, 62.

that what hardness is and what makes it hard has been explained in a more finely grained way.

In event-causal theories, the agent is reduced to a body and a set of processes within this body. Reduction here means that the same events in the world have been described in two different theoretical frameworks, where my claim is that the event-causal approach in this book is more coherent and finely grained than a theoretical framework in which an agent acts by some irreducible kind of agency. Although the agent causationist may claim that something has been omitted in the event-causal framework, I shall argue that nothing has been left out. It has just been explained in a more detailed way, including that which agent causationists leave out, namely in virtue of what agents make choices. Even if I write that agents cause their actions, that is because I then use the language from the theoretical framework of agents and actions. This can be described more precisely by referring to mind processes in a body. There is nothing wrong in talking about hardness, even if you think it can be explained more precisely in terms of tension between atoms; likewise, there is nothing wrong in talking about agents acting, although one thinks that it can be more coherently explained in another theoretical framework.

When it comes to the luck objection, I agree that different people have different degrees of luck in their life. But people also have different degrees of free will and different degrees of responsibility. Sometimes when people have very special conditions for their actions, we reduce the degree of responsibility that we ascribe to them. But, generally, people are born with standard emotions and capacity for reasoning, so that when they have grown up we think that they have had enough time to think and make experiences to realize what is fundamentally right and wrong. The standard that we compare with, when holding them responsible, is the common package of emotions and reasoning capacities that most people are born with. To a large degree, humans share a common core of capacity for emotion and reasoning. This means that luck is taken into account when we hold others responsible, both in the sense that we give them many years of experience to cancel out the effects of luck before holding them fully responsible and in the sense that we find luck to be mitigating in many ways.

On the other hand, we are more different than people can know when they hold others responsible, and luck can have played roles that few—if any—are aware of. But that is not a big problem, since I also argue that holding people responsible is something that makes it possible for them to think and feel differently about alternatives and make better choices. It is a meaningful way of giving people more freedom and responsibility.

Concerning the assimilation argument, I deny that there is indeterminism in the moment of choice. History can therefore not be rolled back and give an exact same situation with different outcomes of the choice. In a rollback of histories, external indeterminism will give different worlds with different choices, and in the cases where the agent is the ultimate cause, the agent will have free will.

My view is admittedly close to compatibilism. It is similar to compatibilist theories in its understanding of morality, alternative possibilities and focus on how the agent is the source of her action in an event-causal way. It is especially close to the compatibilist theories called *source compatibilist theories* or *quality of will theories*, where the point is that an agent in some sense is the source of the choice or that the action expresses their attitudes, and that this is what it takes to have free will.[43] A classic theory here is that of Harry Frankfurt, who argues that we have free will when we identify with our desires. Closest to my theory is probably the Deep Self theory of Chandra Sripada, in which we are morally responsible for the actions that express our deep self, and our deep self is our set of cares.[44] I think differently from Sripada when it comes to what the self is and how it causes actions. Most importantly, the difference between my theory and the Deep Self theory and other compatibilist theories lies in how I use a contrastive theory of causation to show how the self can be an ultimate cause of an agent's actions. Here I differ from all compatibilist theories in arguing that we have a stronger sense of free will than compatibilists admit, which is incompatible with determinism.

My theory is thus libertarian because it rejects that free will is compatible with only one possible future. What fundamentally makes a theory compatibilist is that it sees free will and determinism as compatible. Since I reject this, and argue that we have free will which requires indeterminism, my theory is libertarian. Nevertheless, one could argue that the common arguments against compatibilism—the consequence argument, the manipulation argument and the zygote argument—work equally well against the theory I propose. Why does it help that there is, in the world, indeterminism over which we have no control? And is not even the quantum indeterminism governed by deterministic laws?

The theory I propose depends on there being indeterminism at the macro level of humans, so that more than one future is possible. I find it quite plausi-

---

[43] See for example Angela M. Smith, "Control, Responsibility, and Moral Assessment," *Philosophical Studies* 138, no. 3 (2008), or Thomas Scanlon, *Moral Dimensions: Permissibility, Meaning, Blame* (Cambridge, MA: Belknap Press of Harvard University Press, 2008).
[44] Chandra Sripada, "Self-Expression: A Deep Self Theory of Moral Responsibility" http://sites.lsa.umich.edu/sripada/philosophy/ (Under review): 9.

ble to believe that there really is such indeterminism, especially now that we have humans interacting with indeterministic quantum devices. As James Ladyman says, a scientist may decide to go to lunch after three clicks on the Geiger counter.[45] The reason why such indeterminism is important is that it then there can be situations where it is correct to pick out the autobiographical self as the cause of why one future was actualized as opposed to another, whereas this will not be the case if the world is determined. We thus have more free will in an indeterministic world, because sometimes agents are the cause of which future becomes actualized without it being determined before they were born.

Concerning the consequence argument, I do not control the past or the laws of nature, even if the laws of nature are indeterministic. But sometimes there will be scenarios that were not determined to happen (like a storm that makes a boy fall into the water), and in this situation a woman may see it happen and imagine two alternatives: to help the boy by jumping in or not. Her immediate desire is not to jump into the cold sea, but then memories from the autobiographical self are activated about being a person who does the right thing, thoughts about what people think of those who do not help children in need, and so on—and maybe also fear of death, so that the woman has problems choosing. Finally she decides to jump into the sea because her autobiographical self causes saving the child to be the strongest desire, which then causes her to jump into the water.

Even if the process in the mind happens as if the whole world were determined, that is not important. What is important is that if the world is not determined, then it is right to select the autobiographical self as the cause of the strongest desire, which again is the cause of which alternative for action is chosen. Indeterminism in the brain is not required, but indeterminism in the world is required for it to be right to select the autobiographical self as the ultimate cause.

But is not the undetermined event that led to the storm now the cause of the person jumping in, not the person and not her autobiographical self? No, as one can see by considering contrasts. The undetermined event leading to a storm is not the cause of why the person jumps as opposed to not jumping. The undetermined event is the cause of why there is a storm as opposed to no storm. It creates a new setting in which a choice must be made, but it does not cause the choice. In the undetermined setting, the person and her autobiographical self is the cause of why she jumps, and that is why macro-level indeterminism is re-

---

45 James Ladyman et al., *Every Thing Must Go: Metaphysics Naturalized* (Oxford: Oxford University Press, 2007), 264.

quired for free will. These claims require causation to be contrastive and that contrasts are selected contextually, as I argue in chapter two.

The manipulation argument also does not work against the theory I propose, because I require the agent to be the ultimate cause of her actions in order to have free will. In the manipulation argument, either determinism or manipulation determines what the agent chooses, but in my case the agent is the ultimate cause of her own choice.

Finally, the zygote argument cannot even get off the ground against my theory, since a divine goddess cannot plan the life of a zygote in an indeterministic world. It works against compatibilist theories, but not against my theory, because I require that the agent be the ultimate cause of her actions in a stronger sense than what compatibilists do—and the sense I require presupposes indeterminism.

This is all very brief. I do not expect people to be convinced by this short introduction, but it locates what is to come on a map of other known positions, and indicates positions and arguments that will be laid out in much more detail in the rest of this book.

1.3 Methodological Reflections

By what criterion can one argue that one theory of free will is better than another theory? By 'better' I here mean 'more likely to be closer to the truth'. In this book I am guided by a specific understanding of coherence as a criterion of truth. In his book *The Coherence Theory of Truth*, Nicholas Rescher argues that coherence has three aspects.[46] The first aspect is consistency, which means lack of contradiction (and a contradiction is to state both p and not-p with respect to the same and at the same time). The second aspect is comprehensiveness, which is decided by the number of data that are integrated in the theory. Since all data are interpreted, 'data' is here understood widely as truth candidates. The third aspect is cohesiveness, which is decided by the totality of relations between the elements of the theory. The theory is more coherent when there are more connections between the elements and these are tighter and more precise. Consistency is an either-or-issue, because either the theory is consistent or not. Comprehensiveness and cohesiveness allows for degrees, since there can be

---

[46] See Nicholas Rescher, *The Coherence Theory of Truth*, Clarendon Library of Logic and Philosophy (Oxford: Clarendon Press, 1973), 31–38 and 168–175.

more elements, and more and tighter connections. For this reason one theory can be more or less coherent than another.

Rescher focuses on coherence as a *criterion* of truth, not on coherence as a part of the *definition* of truth.[47] A philosopher who has given a more precise and well-argued understanding of the criterion of coherence and its relation to ontology and truth theory is the German philosopher Lorenz B. Puntel.[48] Puntel agrees with Rescher on the aspects of the criterion of coherence, and it is not room in this book to go into the details of Puntel's systematic philosophy. I just mention it to make explicit the criteria I work by when I discuss the problem of free will, and refer to Puntel's book for those who want more information.

The practical use of the criterion of coherence will be to point out inconsistencies where they can be found; or lacks of connection between the elements of a theory; or important data that are not integrated. Then I must show how the theory I suggest deals with these problems so that my own suggestion is more coherent than the theories I criticize. There are always numerous aspects of any theory that could be discussed, and so to limit myself I have chosen to focus on the elements that are most usually discussed in the free will discourse. Important data in this discourse are the findings of neuroscience, human intuitions and experience of free will and responsibility, and of course it is also very important with precisely defined concepts.

The problem of free will is related to many questions that have no certain answers, like what is a cause, what are laws of nature, is the world determined, what is the self, what is consciousness, etc. No theory of free will is going to be totally convincing in such circumstances, and it is easy for any critic to say that more should be said or that something has been left out. However, it is interesting to ask for which theory of free will is most coherent given what we know right now. And of course, I can only answer that question on the basis of what I myself know right now. By thus participating in the discussion others can criticize my theory and inform me of important deficiencies.

It is an important problem which must be faced by any writer who wants to make a book about a huge question which is tightly connected with other huge

---

[47] In his book from 1973, Rescher defined truth as correspondence (ibid., 23–24). In 1985 he changed his mind and opted for coherence as a definition of truth (Nicholas Rescher, "Truth as Ideal Coherence," *Review of Metaphysics* 38 (1985): 796). In 2001 he leaves the question of what truth is, and defends the criterion of coherence pragmatically (see Nicholas Rescher, *Philosophical Reasoning: A Study in the Methodology of Philosophizing* (Malden, MA: Blackwell Publ., 2001), 191–194).
[48] See Lorenz B. Puntel and Alan White, *Structure and Being: A Theoretical Framework for a Systematic Philosophy* (University Park, PA: Pennsylvania State University Press, 2008).

questions. The question of free will is obviously such a question, related to other big questions of causality, determinism, laws of nature, self, mind, thinking, emotions, consciousness etc. The problem is that one can either write about everything, in which case the book becomes too long; or one can write shortly, in which case it becomes too superficial; or one can leave big questions out of the text, in which case important connections are not clarified. I have tried to find a golden mean in the following approach: the most important questions are those directly linked to what is new in my proposal and necessary to explicate what the proposal is. In this book, those are the questions of free will, causality, and the self. Concerning less important questions, I either indicate my position briefly or refer to other books that I agree with. Unfortunately, I seldom agree with everything in other books, so I will go for a combination of indicating answers and referring to others in many of the big questions that must be left out in order to stay within book length. Sometimes I just have to presuppose something since the related question is too big to defend properly. For example, I will have to presuppose a causal understanding of the mind without being able to discuss all the counterarguments. Whatever one chooses to do in these circumstances, the critic can always find something to criticize, but I believe my approach is the lesser evil.

It will be possible many places to say that more could have been written about this and that, and I agree that it could. I have nevertheless tried to say something quite thorough about causality and the self, in order to be able to suggest a new theory of free will. In defending the theory, I discuss it in light of the most common criticisms that theories of free will face. At numerous places it would have been possible to discuss what I have chosen to include and what I have chosen to leave out, but I have used the space instead on trying to argue more directly in favor of the theory proposed. Whether such a strategy is a good strategy is finally to be judged by the result, and I believe that the result has become an interesting new theory of free will.

The goal of the book is more precisely to find a coherent *naturalistic* understanding of free will. Naturalism is the view that everything is physical, but 'physical' is notoriously difficult to define, especially when it comes to consciousness. In philosophy of mind it is common to speak of physicalism instead of naturalism, where reductive physicalism holds that everything is physical, while non-reductive physicalism allows for the existence of non-physical consciousness while still giving the physical ontological priority.[49] I do not have

---

[49] Jaegwon Kim, *Philosophy of Mind*, 2nd ed. (Boulder, CO: Westview Press, 2006), 11–14.

enough space in this book to discuss the different theories of consciousness. But here I want to explain what I mean by saying that this book will present a naturalistic understanding of the mind and free will. The point is that it will be a causal understanding of the mind which is presupposed as basis for the understanding of free will. More specifically, it will be an event-causal theory of mind, so that the mind becomes a causal process like other causal processes in nature.

A brief comment should also be made on how I interpret the material I use in this book, especially the writings of Antonio Damasio and Jonathan Schaffer, since I use much material from these scholars, also texts that are written at different points of time. Since my goal is to achieve a theory as coherent as possible, I will be generally interested in interpreting these scholars as benevolently as I can in order for them efficiently to help me on the way. Nevertheless, any philosophical analysis should contain an element of self-critique to show the reader that the interpretation is fair. My main method of exerting self-critique in the analysis, is that if I find text parts which seem to contradict each other, I discuss which interpretation makes the whole theory of the scholar most coherent, and then I choose that interpretation. Of course my interpretations are still colored by my own perspective, but that does not make self-criticism any less important.

2 Causality

How should we understand the concept of a cause?[50] In this chapter I suggest a new understanding of causality in close discussion with how Jonathan Schaffer understands causality, but modified and combined with some insights from Adrian Heathcote, David Armstrong and others. In part one, I present how Jonathan Schaffer understands causality, and in part two, I criticize it and offer an alternative understanding. The alternative theory I will defend is to claim that all motion is a result of interaction between laws of nature and states of affairs, but the term "causation" is often used in theoretical frameworks at high ontological levels where causation is a short cut description of how laws of nature make complex states of affairs behave the way they do. The theory requires a narrow concept of causation where absences are left out of the concept of causation, and that selection of causes is based on setting up contrasts depending on a combination of interest and background expectation.

2.1 Part 1: Jonathan Schaffer's Understanding of Causality

According to Jonathan Schaffer, there are several key questions one needs to address in order to have a detailed understanding of what causation is. These questions can be broadly sorted into two main themes. The first theme is the relata of the causal relation, namely cause and effect. How should these be understood and individuated, and are there only two relata (cause and effect) or

---

[50] By "causality" I refer to the whole question of the relation between causes and effects, called "the causal relation." The "cause" is one side of the causal relation, whereas "causation" refers to the cause "producing" the effect. But the precise meaning of "causation," "producing" and related terms will first be defined later in this chapter following the necessary discussion. The distinction between causality and causation is inspired by Menno Hulswit´s article "Causality and causation" ((Menno Hulswit, "Causality and Causation: The Inadequacy of the Received View," *SEED* 4, no. 2 (2004)). Hulswit argues that "causation" is a *process* which is incompatible with seeing "causality" as a *relation*, which again (according to Hulswit) is because "causation" presupposes substance ontology and "causality" presupposes fact ontology. I presuppose the ontological framework of L. B. Puntel (which is a configuration ontology and not a substance ontology), where there is no contradiction in seeing a process as a relation, and so there is no contradiction in my understanding of causation as a part of the causal relation (see Lorenz B. Puntel and Alan White, *Structure and Being: A Theoretical Framework for a Systematic Philosophy* (University Park, PA: Pennsylvania State University Press, 2008)).

are there more? The second theme is the relation between the relata. How are they connected, in what direction does the connection go, and how do we select what we think of as the cause of an effect?[51] From theme one, I focus on the questions of what the relata are and how many they are.[52] From theme two, I focus on understanding the connection between cause and effect and how we select causes among all the candidates that seem causally relevant. These four questions provide the structure for both the presentation of ideas here and the following evaluation.

2.1.1 To what category do causes and effects belong?

Jonathan Schaffer addresses the first question, namely the question of what sort of entities causes and effects generally are and to what category they belong, quite briefly. The standard view is that they are events, although they can also be understood as facts, states of affairs, and other options. Schaffer agrees with the majority that causes and effects are events.[53]

2.1.2 How many relata are there in the causal relation?

It is common to answer that there are two relata in the causal relation, namely cause (C) and effect (E), so that C causes E.[54] However, some argue that there are three relata, either two on the cause side or two on the effect side. Christopher Hitchcock argues that causality should be understood as a contrastive relation on the cause side: C as opposed to C* causes E. As an argument he gives the example that moderate smoking as opposed to no smoking *causes* Jane to develop lung cancer, while moderate smoking as opposed to heavy smoking *pre-*

---

51 Jonathan Schaffer, "The Metaphysics of Causation," (Stanford Encyclopedia of Philosophy, 2007), section 1.
52 I shall also comment on the question of individuation/grainedness, but not until I have introduced certain necessary distinctions.
53 I shall return to how Schaffer defines "events" later since it will then be easier to understand what he means by defining events as "coarse-grained worldbound individuals," which is the only definition of "event" I have found in his writings ("Contrastive Causation in the Law," (2010), http://rsss.anu.edu.au/~schaffer/papers/CCLaw.pdf.).
54 Schaffer cites J. L. Mackie, Donald Davidson and David Lewis as examples of such a view, in "Contrastive Causation," *Philosophical Review* 114, no. 3 (2005): 353, n.1.

vents Jane from developing lung cancer.⁵⁵ On the other hand, Bas van Fraassen argues that the causal relation should be understood as a contrastive relation on the effect side: C causes E as opposed to E*. An example in favor of this is that syphilis causes John to have paresis as opposed to perfect health, but syphilis does not cause John to have paresis as opposed to just having syphilis.⁵⁶

Jonathan Schaffer argues that the causal relation should be understood as a contrastive relation on both sides: C as opposed to C* causes E as opposed to E*. He finds the arguments in favor of contrastivity to be good on both sides of the causal relation. Furthermore, he argues that both sides of the causal relation must be symmetrical because causes and effects are linked in causal chains where the first effect is the second cause and so on. For example, the toppling of a domino as opposed to its standing causes the next domino to topple as opposed to standing, which causes the third domino to topple as opposed to standing, and so on. Contrastivity on both sides is needed for the links in the chain to match.⁵⁷

2.1.3 How are causes and effects connected?

What makes a cause a cause? What do causal connections have in common, or what is the difference between causally related events and causally unrelated events? According to Schaffer, theories concerning what makes a cause a cause mainly fall into two categories. The first category is those who understand causation as probability-raising, and the other is those who understand causation as process-linkage.⁵⁸

---

55 Hitchcock, according to ibid., 328. But, as Douglas Ehring points out, if Jane contracts lung cancer (token event), then her smoking causes it even if it is moderate (Ehring, in Helen Beebee, Christopher Hitchcock, and Peter Charles Menzies, *The Oxford Handbook of Causation*, Oxford Handbooks in Philosophy (Oxford: Oxford University Press, 2009), 408.). So, Hitchcock's example here only works with generic causes/type events, whereas the next example from Schaffer (with dominos) also works for token events.
56 Van Fraassen, according to Schaffer, "Contrastive Causation," 328. Syphilis may lead to paresis. Even if the examples Schaffer offers on contrastivity are not very clear, we shall return to many examples on contrastivity in the discussion of selection, and then it will be clear that contrastivity is important in the causal relation.
57 Ibid.
58 Counterfactual causation is sometimes treated as a category in itself. Its most famous defender is David Lewis (see David Lewis, "Causation," ibid. 70, no. 17 (1973)). Lewis introduced probability-raising into his theory in 1986 (Christopher Hitchcock, "Probabilistic Causation," (Stanford Encyclopedia of Philosophy, 2010), section 4.1.), so Schaffer treats it as a sub-

The first view, probability-raising, holds that causation is a matter of how probable an effect is *with* a cause versus *without* that cause. The cause is understood as conditions that make something more or less likely to happen, so the focus is on conditional probability. If Pam throws a rock at a window and it breaks, her throwing the rock is the cause of the window breaking because this throw made it probable that the window would break. Other events may have been related to the window, such as the wind blowing on the window or Bob looking at the window, but these events did not make it probable that the window would break, so only the event that made it probable that the window would break (the rock being thrown) is understood as the cause of the window breaking.

Probability-raising is an alternative to a deterministic understanding of effects as necessary results of certain conditions, for if the world is not determined, effects are not the necessary results of certain conditions. So probability-raising is a view which fits with an indeterministic universe where the cause is neither necessary (since the effect might happen anyway) nor sufficient (since something may prevent the effect from occurring), but the cause is conditions that raise the probability of the effect.[59] This means that in a broad sense everyone who does not think of causation as effects necessarily following their causes holds a probability-raising view of causation. But Schaffer uses the term in a narrower sense to denote those who think that probability raising is what makes causes into causes.

The second view, process-linkage, understands causation as a physical connection between cause and effect. Schaffer mentions many examples, but I refer only to those that are important to my later discussion: J. Aronson understands causation as the transference of a physical quantity.[60] David Fair holds a similar view, specifying that causation is the transfer of energy or momentum.[61] Among process-linkage views, Phil Dowe distinguishes between transference theories (causation is understood in terms of something transferred from cause

---

category under probability views. Another view is that causation in itself and agent-causation as a specific type of causation are both irreducible and unexplainable concepts. E. J. Lowe's book on metaphysics is an example in which counterfactual theories of causation are treated as a separate category; here is also a good critique against the counterfactual understanding of causation. Lowe himself argues that causality and agent-causality are irreducible concepts, whereas I think that they can be explained in the way I do in this book. See Lowe, *A Survey of Metaphysics*, chapters eight to eleven.

59 Schaffer, "Causes as Probability-Raisers of Processes," 76.
60 Jerrold R. Aronson, "On the Grammar of Cause," *Synthese* 22, no. 3-4 (1971): 421–23.
61 David Fair, "Causation and the Flow of Energy," *Erkenntnis* 14, no. 3 (1979): 220.

to effect) on the one hand and process theories (focused on something persisting through the causal process) on the other hand.⁶² He wants to unite these two views in his own understanding of causality in terms of conserved quantities.⁶³ Similar views can be found in Bigelow, Ellis, and Pargetter, who understand causation in terms of forces,⁶⁴ and Adrian Heathcote, who understands causation in terms of the fundamental interaction described by quantum field theory.⁶⁵ Finally, Heathcote and David Armstrong have together defended a view of (token) causation as identical to instantiations of a law of nature. They understand laws of nature as entities existing in the world which regulate the relations between properties. Because causation is governed by laws, the same causes give the same effects.⁶⁶

Schaffer argues that neither of these two main understandings of causation (probability raising and process-linkage) are sufficient in themselves, no matter how they are refined. Against probability-raising views, Schaffer offers the example of Pam, who throws a brick at a window, while Bob (who is a more reliable vandal) holds his throw to see what happens with Pam's brick. If she does not break the window, he will. In this case, Pam's throw lowers the probability that the window will break as Bob is a more reliable vandal. But her throw is still the cause of why the window breaks, even if her throw lowers the probability of the window breaking. Schaffer argues that the example shows that proba-

---

62 Phil Dowe, *Physical Causation*, Cambridge Studies in Probability, Induction, and Decision Theory (Cambridge: Cambridge University Press, 2000), chapters three and four. Wesley Salmon's theory of causation is given as an example of persistence through the causal process (Wesley C. Salmon, *Scientific Explanation and the Causal Structure of the World* (Princeton, NJ: Princeton University Press, 1984)).
63 More specifically, in a causal process objects possess a conserved quantity, whereas in causal interaction, conserved quantities are exchanged, for example, energy and momentum: Dowe, *Physical Causation*, 90.
64 John Bigelow, Brian Ellis, and Robert Pargetter, "Forces," *Philosophy of Science* 55, no. 4 (1988); John Bigelow and Robert Pargetter, "Metaphysics of Causation," *Erkenntnis* 33 (1990).
65 Adrian Heathcote, "A Theory of Causality: Causality=Interaction (as Defined by a Suitable Quantum Field Theory)," ibid. 31(1989): 102–05.
66 Adrian Heathcote and D. M. Armstrong, "Causes and Laws," *NOÛS* 25, no. 1 (1991). Schaffer places Armstrong among those who hold probability-raising views (Schaffer, "The Metaphysics of Causation," section 2), but Armstrong himself seems to be the most positive to the process-linkage theories of Heathcote and Dowe (see Armstrong, in L. A. Paul, Edward J. Hall, and John David Collins, *Causation and Counterfactuals*, Representation and Mind (Cambridge, MA: MIT Press, 2004), 455–56). Schaffer's categorization can be defended since some laws are probabilistic. But I have placed Armstrong under process-linkage since he favors process-linkage theories but wants to go a level deeper and explain the process-linkage with reference to laws. What this means will be clearer in the later evaluation.

bility-raising is not a *necessary* condition for causation. Nor is probability-raising a *sufficient* condition for causation. Imagine Fred throwing a brick against a window and missing, while Pam throws and hits. As long as both have a chance of hitting or missing, Fred's throw raises the probability of the window breaking, but his miss is not the cause of the window breaking.[67]

Against process-linkage views, Schaffer argues that there can be causes without process-linkage. Imagine Pam standing in front of a window, this time with a catapult. There is a rock in the catapult and the catapult is ready to launch. Imagine further that Pam releases the lever, so that the catapult throws the rock through the window. No relevant physical quantity such as energy or momentum has been transferred from Pam to the catapult or the rock, nor does any persisting entity connect them, so she is not process-linked to the breaking window, but we still want to say that Pam is the cause of the window breaking.[68]

Further, there seem to be events that can be process-linked to an effect without being causes, so how do we determine what the cause is? Imagine that Pam throws a rock through a window and that Tom simultaneously throws some purple paint on the same rock in mid-air before it hits the window. Thus, he is process-linked to the breaking of the window and there is an energy transfer between him, the rock and the window, but of course it is Pam's throw alone that causes the window to break.[69]

A third objection to process-linkage is that sometimes we say that an absence or omission was a cause. For example, the cause of the plant dying was that I did not water it. However, others think that omissions can only be part of

---

[67] Schaffer does not discuss a distinction suggested by Dowe and Hitchcock between net and component effects. The net effect is the probability you obtain when you add Pam and Bob or Pam and Fred, but you may also consider the probability of the effect of the action of just one of them. If you only consider Pam throwing the rock and breaking the window, her throw raises the probability of the glass breaking and so she can be selected as the cause. This does not work in the case of Fred, however, since he is not the cause even if he raises the probability of the glass breaking (Hitchcock, "Probabilistic Causation," section 2.10). As we shall soon see, this solution by Dowe and Hitchcock is very similar to that which Schaffer himself suggests, but there are still other problems for probability-raising views. Hitchcock gives the example of a golfer making a bad slice at the ball, but the ball hits a tree so he has a hole-in-one. Although the slice being bad as opposed to good lowers the probability of a hole-in-one, it is still the cause of the hole-in-one (ibid.). However, this example raises the question of the grainedness of events, for is the ball hitting the tree and then the hole *one* process? Or does a new process start when the ball hits the tree? (Dowe, *Physical Causation*, 150). As mentioned earlier, I postpone the question of grainedness.
[68] Schaffer, "The Metaphysics of Causation," section 2.1.1.
[69] Ibid.

an explanation[70] but not a cause, so here one needs to decide how wide the concept of a cause should be. Schaffer argues that omissions or absences should be understood as causes for four reasons: intuitively, absences are causes; absences, like causes, have predictive and explanatory roles; absences, like causes, have a legal and moral role; and absences mediate causation by disconnection.[71]

So which approach is the best—probability-raising or process-linkage? Schaffer argues that neither of them is good alone; rather, the solution that solves most of the problems is a combination of the two approaches, namely, causation as the probability-raising of a process. This means that among the processes linked to an effect one should assess whether the cause raises the probability of the whole process that leads to the effect.[72] This solves the problem found with Pam throwing the brick while Bob waits, as Pam's throw raises the probability of the process that leads to the window breaking (while Bob's waiting does not). It also solves the problem of not watering the plant, as my not watering the plant raises the probability of the process leading to the plant dying. Finally, it solves the problem with Tom throwing paint on the rock, because Tom throwing paint on the rock does not raise the probability of the window breaking. However, Schaffer admits that there are still problems and exceptions which his view does not solve. It is possible to construct complex events where what we would normally think of as the cause is not process-linked to the effect and lowers the probability of the effect, and so Schaffer concludes that the causal relation remains mysterious.[73]

---

[70] See, for example, Helen Beebee, in Paul, Hall, and Collins, *Causation and Counterfactuals*, 304–06. There are many kinds of explanation, such as deductive-nomological explanations, functional explanations or intentional explanations. One can argue that causation is important in all these kinds of explanation, but I do not have room for this discussion here. I define explanation broadly as explication of which connections there are between states of affairs. An explanation is a theory which helps us understand, while causation is an event in the world. I shall return to the question of how to understand absences when I evaluate Schaffer's theory.
[71] I give examples of all these cases below.
[72] "Causes as Probability-Raisers of Processes," 85.
[73] Ibid., 92 and "The Metaphysics of Causation," section 2.1.2., where Schaffer gives the following example against his own theory: Pam throws a brick at an aquarium so that it breaks and spills water, while Bob (the more reliable vandal) holds his throw to see what happens. We want to say that Pam is the cause of why the carpet gets wet, but her throw lowers the probability of the effect and she is not process-linked to the spilling water, only to the breaking glass.

2.1.4 How are causes selected from other conditions?

When we seek the cause of an effect, there are many events that can be related somehow to the effect. But how do we select the cause or causes among these? This is not the question of how we select causally relevant events from causally irrelevant events—the topic of the previous section—rather, it is a question of how, as we often do, we select one cause among many causally relevant events. There is wide agreement that the selection of causes is not objective.[74] On the other hand, most people will select the same causes in very many events. If you ask people why a house burnt down, they will refer to the short circuit or the pyromaniac as causes but not the presence of oxygen, even if the presence of oxygen was also necessary for the house to burn.[75] So how do people select causes from mere (background) conditions and can the selection of causes be understood as objective or is it merely subjective?

C. J. Ducasse suggested long ago (1926) that a distinction should be made between *conditions*, which are *necessary* for the effect to happen, and *causes*, which are *sufficient* for the effect to happen. However, this clearly does not work to explain the difference between causes and non-causes, for both oxygen and ignition are necessary for the house to burn but neither is sufficient alone for the house to burn; yet both can be selected as causes. Hart and Honoré suggest that when we select causes we select the abnormal conditions as opposed to normal conditions and agents as opposed to non-agents. For this reason we select the (abnormal) ignition of the house rather than the (normal) presence of oxygen, but if it had been a laboratory setting that was supposed to be oxygen free, the unexpected presence of oxygen could have been considered the cause of the fire rather than the ignition.[76]

Schaffer argues that the question of contrastivity solves the problem of selection of causes. His point is that we select contrasts subjectively depending on what we want to understand but when the contrasts are selected, the cause is objective. So those in the laboratory expected there to be no oxygen and wonder why there was a fire as opposed to no fire. When "no oxygen" is the selected contrast, we can agree that the presence of oxygen as opposed to no oxygen is the cause of the fire. On the other hand, when we want to understand why the house burnt down, we expect there to be oxygen present but we do not expect

---

[74] Schaffer cites Lewis and Mackie as examples, see "The Metaphysics of Causation," section 2.3.
[75] Schaffer has this example from Hart and Honoré, see ibid.
[76] Ibid.

any ignition and so "no ignition" is the contrast, thus we select the ignition as the cause.

I think it is clear that sometimes the contrast on the effect-side determines what the cause is. Consider the following example: John is on his way to a party. He comes to a crossroads where he has planned to meet Neil, who knows the way. But Neil is late, and John wants to get to the party where he will get food because he is hungry. He is fairly sure that he should go to the right as he has a relatively good memory of being given directions and recollects being told that he should go right at this crossroads. However, it could also be left as the sign pointing left shows the name of the street where Sarah lives and John knows that she lives close to the party. So, although not absolutely sure, he is fairly certain that he should go right and so he decides to takes the chance since it is quite likely that it is the right way.

In this example, we can ask the cause of why John went right without setting up a contrast on the E-side. But we can also choose two different contrasts on the E-side: (1) Why did John go right as opposed to going left? (2) Why did John go right as opposed to waiting for Neil, who knew the way? In question 1, the cause is that he had a memory of being given the direction to go right. In question 2, the cause is that he was hungry and wanted to get to the party.

2.2 Part 2: Evaluation of Schaffer's Understanding of Causality

We are free to define the concept of a cause in different ways, so by what criteria do we argue which definition of "cause" is the best? Although the *word* "cause" has many different meanings, my goal is to define a precise *concept* of a cause which allows us to refer precisely to causation as something happening in the world. That does not necessarily mean that cause or causation is something that exists as an ontological addition to the world, for maybe causation can be ontologically reduced[77] to something else. The point is that I am not interested in explicating the everyday use of the word "cause"; what I want is a concept that allows me to give a coherent description of the world. In this search, intuitions and everyday use are interesting and the point of departure but cannot have the final say, as intuitions and everyday use may be incoherent with each other and other data.

---

77 "Ontological reduction" is further defined in the following paragraphs.

What, then, are good criteria for defining a concept? On the one hand, the concept needs to be precise in order to refer only to what it is meant to refer to. On the other hand, it is useful if the concept is as general as possible while still referring to that which it is meant to reference. These two criteria may work in opposite directions, so that increased precision means decreased generality and vice versa. The ideal is to be as general as possible while still coherently referring to nothing more and nothing less than that which the concept is meant to reference. If the concept identifies an entity existing in the world, it is easier to evaluate the precision of the definition than if the concept can be ontologically reduced to something else. Some concepts can be ontologically reduced in the sense that what they refer to is nothing but something that other terms also refer to more precisely. For example, heat may be reduced to molecular motion. Heat is not ontologically more than molecular motion, so if there is already molecular motion in the world, heat does not represent an ontological addition to that. However, a concept (such as heat) may still be of practical use, so ontological reduction need not imply eliminativism—that the concept should be eliminated—as in the case of phlogiston, which does not refer to anything.[78]

To be more precise on ontological reduction: There are ontological structures in the world that can be expressed using different concepts in different theoretical frameworks. When the different concepts refer to the same ontological structure, one of the concepts may be ontologically reduced to the other, such as heat being reduced to molecular motion. However, in this case, both heat and molecular motion refer to something that exists in the world. It is then reduced in the sense that heat exists but is claimed to be nothing more than molecular motion. In another case, there may be two different theoretical frameworks that explain something in the world where only one of the frameworks refers to an ontological structure that exists in the world. If a certain behavior is described by one framework as an epileptic seizure and by another as a demon attack, then (if it is an epileptic seizure) the demon attack can be reduced in the sense that it can be eliminated because only one of the explanations refers to an existing state of affairs in the world.[79]

In cases where a concept is ontologically reducible, it is difficult to decide how to balance precision against usefulness. In such cases, it is important also to ask what the goal of the concept is in order to decide how general or specific it should be. As I shall argue later, different interests speak in favor of different

---

78 Humphrey, in Beebee, Hitchcock, and Menzies, *The Oxford Handbook of Causation*, 346.
79 For more on how ontological structures can be expressed in different theoretical frameworks, see Puntel and White, *Structure and Being*.

definitions of the concept of a cause and one important difference is whether one is most interested in understanding as deeply and precisely as possible why states of affairs are as they are, or change or move as they do,[80] or whether one is most interested in the most useful clarifications of how states of affairs are connected in the world. This will become clearer when I return to the question of reducibility and the goal of the concept of causality later.

2.2.1 To what category do causes and effects belong?

As mentioned, the common understanding of causal relata suggests that they are events, although they may also be understood differently. And of course, those who understand them as events define "event" differently. According to Douglas Ehring, there are two main definitions of "event" among philosophers who work with causation. The first definition is associated with Donald Davidson, who defines events as concrete occurrences in space–time. The second definition is associated with Jaegwon Kim, who defines an event as the exemplification of a property or relation by an object or objects at a point in time.[81] The first definition may well be interpreted as including some change or motion happening over time because of the word "occurrences," but such an interpretation is not logically necessary. In the other definition, it is clear that an object undergoing no change over time also counts as an event.[82] The definitions do not focus on something changing as opposed to being static; rather, they focus on something taking place in (space-)time, presumably as opposed to some

---

80 It is common to ask for causes for why states of affairs are as they are; for example, one may ask: Why are humans left-right symmetrical, but not up-down symmetrical or backwards-forwards symmetrical? We also ask for causes of why states of affairs change or move as they do; for example: Why did the ball explode or why did the ball disappear? I write both "change" and "move," even if at a basic ontological level all motion is change and all change is motion (I define "ontological level" later). But at higher ontological levels, it is common to use the term "move" if the focus is on something with a stable internal structure changing place in relation to something else, whereas we use "change" if the focus is on something changing its internal structure. So, for example, a rabbit running past a tree is motion, whereas a rabbit changing skin color is change. I use change or move in accordance with this normal use, even if I think that change and motion are ontologically reducible to each other.
81 Douglas Ehring, "Causal Relata," *Synthese* 73 (1987): 319–20.
82 Kim writes that events include states in Jaegwon Kim, *Philosophy of Mind*, 2nd ed. (Boulder, CO: Westview Press, 2006), 7.

abstract and transcendent fact about the world which is not located in space and time (although a fact may also be defined as part of the world).[83]

Schaffer himself defines events as "coarse-grained worldbound individuals."[84] Here again we see that the interest is in defining events as something occurring in the world as opposed to transcendent facts, and not as opposed to some static state of affairs since a static state of affairs would fall within Schaffer's definition. He also mentions that they are coarse-grained as opposed to fine-grained, a topic which I postpone until I have then presented the arguments and distinctions I need to explain my view.

It seems to me most common to think of "events" as including change while, for example, "state of affairs" is a wider term including both events and static states of affairs. For example "the post office at 50 King's Road" is a static state of affairs, whereas "John going to the post office" is a dynamic state of affairs. In order to include both static states and changes, I would intuitively prefer to speak of causes as states of affairs as opposed to events to clarify that I think that causes may also be static states of affairs.[85] For example, a static and unchanging law of nature can be the cause of other states of affairs in the world.[86] Furthermore, we sometimes seek causes not only for changes but also for why something is the way it is. So it seems clear that both causes and effects need not be events in the sense of something changing over time but may be static states of affairs. On the other hand, since "event" is the term commonly used in the causality discourse and does not necessarily include only changes over time, I could also use the term "event." Furthermore, I agree with the general point that causes should be understood as being entities in the world (this means that I understand, for example, a horse being somewhere in the world as a state of affairs).[87] Since I have now clarified that both "states of affairs" and

---

[83] See, for example, Puntel and White, *Structure and Being*, 232–36.
[84] Schaffer, "Contrastive Causation in the Law" Accessed 25 Oct 2010).
[85] Peter Menzies argues that it would be good to use a term other than "event" to express what sorts of entities causes are, since he wants to include objects as causes (Menzies, in Beebee, Hitchcock, and Menzies, *The Oxford Handbook of Causation*, 346). "States of affairs" would serve this function well.
[86] Later I argue, with D. M. Armstrong, that laws of nature are to be understood not merely as descriptions of regularities in the world, but as entities in the world which make such descriptions true.
[87] Note that by the requirement of causes and effects being entities in the world, I exclude logical and mathematical facts as causes, since I understand these as abstract facts with no other existence than that of logical possibilities. Abstract facts are causally impotent; here I agree with Armstrong's understanding (see D. M. Armstrong, *Truth and Truthmakers*, Cam-

"events" can be understood as both static and changing structures in the world, I will use the two terms interchangeably with this meaning.[88]

2.2.2 How many relata are there in the causal relation?

I agree with Jonathan Schaffer that the causal relation should be understood as contrastive on both sides—or at least that it *may* be so understood. Does Schaffer think that there must be exactly two relata on both sides, giving the sum of four, or is the point of the number four just to say that there is a contrast on each side? One could think of examples where we seek the cause of the effect A as opposed to B or C. For example, why did John suddenly stop as opposed to going right or left as we expected? Schaffer refers to Hitchcock, who points out the fact that in ordinary language when we ask for causes we sometimes set up one contrast, sometimes several contrasts and sometimes no contrasts.[89] Should we take this to indicate that causation is contrastive only sometimes and with a variable number of contrasts?

In order to decide the best answer to this question, we need to discuss the role of contrasts. Are they a part of what it is to be a cause, or are they a part of subjective selection—something to be clarified before the cause can be selected? As seen above, Schaffer argues that contrasts are something we select subjectively before we decide the cause. I agree with this. The way I understand the role of contrasts is that it has to do with the selection of causes. But how should this selection be understood more precisely? Must we select a contrast on one or both sides of the causal relation, so that there is one objective cause, or are there alternative understandings here? The answer depends on how we understand the selection process and for that reason I will postpone the question until the later discussion of selection.

---

bridge Studies in Philosophy (New York: Cambridge University Press, 2004), 100–102). Although I could include abstract facts in a wider sense of "states of affairs," they are excluded from the narrow sense of "states of affairs" here presented, to which causes and effects belong. Note, however, that abstract facts may be efficient ways of describing causes. For example, I can say that the number seven caused me to win the lottery, but what I mean is that the ball with the number seven on it being drawn caused me to win the lottery. I will say more about such efficient descriptions of causes later in this article.

88 I see no need to distinguish between processes and events, which are both dynamic states of affairs in my conception. Further, I do not include negative events (such as "Mary not going to the shop") as events. I will say much more about absences as causes later.

89 Schaffer, "The Metaphysics of Causation," section 1.

2.2.3 How are causes and effects connected?

What makes a state of affairs a cause? As set out above, Schaffer argued that probability-raising alone is not enough. Again, I agree. It seems that a physical connection is required as Fred, who aims at the window but does not break it, is not a cause of the window breaking, even if he raised the probability that the window would break. On the other hand, Schaffer also argued that process-linkage alone was not enough. One argument he gave against process-linkage was that sometimes absences are causes—for example, not watering the plant causes its death. But should absences be considered as causes or should they not? I find this to be an important question that clarifies some important choices one must make in deciding what the concept of causation should be. I will show this in what follows and for this reason I need to spend some time on the question of whether or not absences are causes.

Schaffer argues that absences clearly are causes. He gives four reasons: (a) intuitively, absences are causes, since not watering the plant seems to be the cause of the plant dying; (b) absences have predictive and explanatory roles, just as causes do, so if you do not water a plant, you can predict that it will die and explain why; (c) absences—like causes—have a legal and moral role so we hold people responsible for what they have not done; (d) absences mediate causation by disconnection. For example, decapitation causes death by preventing oxygenated blood from reaching the brain.[90]

Phil Dowe argues against absences as causes. He says that even though we might say something like "The father's lack of attention to his child running into the street caused the child to be hit by the car," we intuit that there is a difference between such causation and other causation, for we do not think that the father's inattentiveness made the child run into the street. Dowe thinks of causation in terms of a conserved quantity and no quantity can be conserved between non-occurring events. On the other hand, there is a great deal in common between absences and events and very often absences are involved in our descriptions of events—sometimes we do not even know whether we refer to an absence or not. Dowe gives the example that drunk driving causes accidents, but arguably alcohol prevents the brain from functioning normally so that an absence of normal functioning then causes the accident. So, there is a difference between citing absences as causes and citing states of affairs that exist in the world as causes and yet they have a lot in common. According to Dowe, absenc-

---

90 Shaffer, "Contrastive Causation," 329–31.

es are counterfactual statements about the world that can be true. As such, they play many of the same roles as causes—such as explaining and the other functions mentioned by Schaffer. But there is a difference, so Dowe suggests that we distinguish between *causation* (excluding absences) and *causation** (including absences).[91]

Schaffer comments upon suggestions such as Dowe's by saying that there are many paradigm examples of causation involving absences; for example, death being caused by the absence of oxygen, or pushing a button that makes a bomb explode (but where the mechanism triggers the bomb by means of disconnection). Although he agrees that there is a difference between what he calls the intrinsic relation between events and citing absences as causes, he argues that it is a hopeless procedure to establish a concept of causation which leaves out many paradigm examples of causation.[92] Dowe, on the other hand, commenting on the suggestion that it would be simpler to include absences in the concept of causation, says that there is an important difference which must not be overlooked.[93]

Schaffer and Dowe seem to agree that there is a difference, but they disagree whether the concept of causation should include absences or not. This is a decision which must be made, but I shall postpone it until I have discussed the connection between cause and effect further, since I will then have more arguments to hand to help me make the decision.[94]

Even if the absence argument against process-linkage is not decisive, there are other arguments against process-linkage to be considered. I do think that Schaffer had other valid arguments, such as the previous example of Pam and the catapult. Other arguments against process-linkage can also help us to understand causality better. James Woodward argues that causes are sometimes found at a higher (more complex) level than the more basic level of energy exchange in the world because sometimes the higher levels allow us to understand in greater depth what happens than do the lower levels. For example, if there is freezing weather and the price of oranges rises, we think of the freeze as the cause of the increased prices. If we started looking for the transfer of physi-

---

[91] Dowe, *Physical Causation*, chapter six.
[92] Jonathan Schaffer, "Causation by Disconnection," *Philosophy of Science* 67, no. 2 (2000): 291–93.
[93] Dowe, *Physical Causation*, 141–42.
[94] I apologize to the reader that I often have to postpone some topics. This is because the different elements of my theory of causation are so interconnected that I have to go back and forth and postpone some parts in order to explain all the parts fully and understandably.

cal quantities or process links between the weather and all the oranges and all the customers and so on, it would only be a confusing muddle. Woodward gives a similar example from physics, where it is much clearer to explain gas pressure by using thermodynamic laws than to consider all the interactions between all the molecules in the gas.[95]

I also have an argument against process-linkage of my own. I shall soon argue that laws of nature can explain effects in the world without there being a physical link or transfer from the law to the entity being explained. Bell's theorem and experiments like those conducted by Alain Aspect seem to suggest strongly that there can be causality-at-a-distance, where nothing physical can be transferred because the supposed effect happens faster than the speed of light.[96] But when laws of nature are considered as causes, it is impossible to decide whether or not they raise the probability of an effect as opposed to some other hypothetical situation with different laws. It seems we should include laws of nature as causes since the only causes we can give for many general features of the world are laws of nature.[97] The list of arguments now given shows that Schaffer's combined solution of causes as probability-raisers of processes does not work any more than do probability-raising or process-linkage individually. But I have a suggestion that will resolve the problem.

I find Woodward's distinction between levels of description to be eminently helpful in clarifying the question of causality and it helps us understand the problems with Schaffer's view. Many who write about causality speak of differ-

---

[95] Although many think that the behavior of a gas can be explained by the trajectories of the individual molecules, some argue that the whole system can have effects on the individual molecules that cannot be explained by their individual motion alone (R. Bishop refers to Ilya Prigogine and the Brussels-Austin group for such a view, see Bishop, in Kane, *The Oxford Handbook of Free Will* (1st ed.), 120–21). If the behavior of the gas can be ontologically reduced to the behavior of its individual molecules, Woodward still has a point, and if Prigogine et al. are right, the argument made by Woodward is even stronger.

[96] A philosopher who argues this at length is Bernard d'Espagnat. The reader can find information concerning Bell's theorem and Aspect-like experiments in his book, for I do not have space to present them here (Bernard d'Espagnat, *On Physics and Philosophy* (Princeton: Princeton University Press, 2006), chapter 3).

[97] For example: Why do particles obey the Pauli Exclusion Principle? In many questions you can keep asking why, until the final answer one can give is that a law of nature makes it so. Ladyman and Ross quotes M.L. G. Redhead saying that laws of nature cannot be causes since they are not events (Ladyman et al., *Every Thing Must Go*, 264; M. L. G. Redhead, "Explanation," in *Explanation and Its Limits*, ed. Dudley Knowles, *Royal Institute of Philosophy Lectures* (Cambridge: Cambridge University Press, 1990). But as argued above, causes should include both static and dynamic states of affairs.

ent levels; sometimes they seem to mean ontological levels and sometimes they seem to mean levels of description.[98] I suggest that we distinguish these clearly from each other. On the one hand, we have ontological levels; by "ontological levels" I mean different levels of complexity in the structures of the states of affairs in the world, from the micro level of particle physics to the macro level of large objects in the world. On the other hand, there are also various levels of description and understanding which allow us to describe many states of affairs as one state of affairs containing many states of affairs.[99] For example, "stretching my arm" includes "several muscles performing some work," which includes "many molecules transporting different substances," which includes "many elementary particles interacting." Instead of "levels of description," I prefer to call them "theoretical frameworks" as there can be several theoretical frameworks that describe the same ontological level. Think, for example, of how differently processes happening in a human being can be described in physics, chemistry, biology, psychology, philosophy, sociology, and theology. With the help of the concepts of "ontological levels" and "theoretical frameworks," I think we can now understand better both what causation is and many of the problems that arise in discussing it. To present my own solution, I must start with a presentation of how motion in the world is understood in physics.

Physics tells us that there are some fundamental forces that lead to motion. Some of their interaction happens only at the micro level, but some interaction also happens over large distances. Much motion can be understood as a direct consequence of the activity of these fundamental forces, for example, due to gravity or electricity. However, at high ontological levels there is much motion that we do not explain in terms of fundamental forces, but rather as due to various kinds of pushing and pulling and resistance or constraint. A stretched rubber band, muscle activity, a swinging door, and so on, can be used to explain why something is pushed or pulled or moved in another way.

Could all this motion at higher ontological levels be ontologically reduced to interaction between fundamental forces and particles/fields as described by

---

[98] See, for example, John Carroll, in Beebee, Hitchcock, and Menzies, *The Oxford Handbook of Causation*, 280.

[99] For a discussion of individuation among states of affairs, see Puntel and White, *Structure and Being*, 263–64. Essentially, states of affairs are ontological structures, and every structure that can be distinguished from another is an individual state of affairs. But one individual state of affairs may also be a configuration of other individual states of affairs, and some such individuals are only loosely internally connected (for example, a heap of leaves consisting of individual leaves), while others are densely internally connected (for example, a human being consisting of individual arms and legs, and so on).

physics? Many philosophers and physicists think so. Bigelow and Pargetter argue that basic causes should be understood as the action of forces and that what we commonly understand as causes supervene on basic causes.[100] Adrian Heathcote understands causation as the interaction of fundamental forces as these are described by quantum field theory, meaning that all basic interaction is the exchange of virtual particles.[101]

But are forces the whole of the matter, or could we go one level deeper in our understanding? To find out, we can start by asking: Why do particles or fields exert or mediate forces? How are they able to push and pull things around? Physicists usually explain this with reference to laws of nature, which are the most general descriptions of how states of affairs interact. How then should these laws of nature be interpreted ontologically?

One can be a realist about laws, meaning that laws are distinctly existing entities that in some sense direct the behavior of entities that fall under them. Or one can be an anti-realist about laws, and anti-realists will typically be either Humean or non-Humean.[102] The Humean answer is that event A is regularly followed by event B not because of a law of nature, for the law simply describes the fact that A is regularly followed by B.[103]

David Armstrong has thoroughly critiqued the Humean regularity view of the laws of nature.[104] A core point for Armstrong is that if laws of nature are understood merely as descriptions of regularities in nature, something must

---

[100] Bigelow and Pargetter, "Metaphysics of Causation," 106–12.
[101] Very briefly: Physics today counts four fundamental forces, namely, electromagnetism, the weak and strong nuclear forces, and gravity (electromagnetism and the weak force can be united into a theory of the electroweak force). These forces are considered to be mediated by elementary particles called bosons: electromagnetism is mediated by photons, the weak force by W and Z bosons, and the strong force by gluons. Some hypothesize that gravity is mediated by gravitons, but the standard view on gravity in physics is still Einstein's theory of general relativity, where gravity is a geometric effect of space-time curving around mass (Roger Penrose, *The Road to Reality: A Complete Guide to the Laws of the Universe* (London: Jonathan Cape, 2004), chapters 17 and 25). If I use the term "force" it refers to all kinds of pushing and pulling, so when I want to refer to just (some of) the four fundamental forces, I use the term "fundamental force(s)."
[102] Angelo Cei and Steven French, "Getting Away from Governance: A Structuralist Approach to Laws and Symmetries," *Methode - Analytic Perspectives* 3, no. 4 (2014): 2–3.
[103] Armstrong, *Truth and Truthmakers*, 127.
[104] *What Is a Law of Nature?*, Cambridge Studies in Philosophy (Cambridge: Cambridge University Press, 1983), chapters 2–5. I follow Armstrong in writing "Humean" instead of "Hume," since it is debated what Hume himself meant. "Humean" then refers to the common understanding of Hume's view (*Truth and Truthmakers*, 125).

make those descriptions true. Why do we find these seemingly exceptionless regularities in nature? If laws of nature are understood not just as descriptions of regularities, but as ontological entities which make[105] those regularities the way they are, then there is an explanation for the regularities.[106] John Carroll argues that it would be an incredible coincidence if the world just happened to be so consistent in its lawful behaviour.[107]

But there is also an anti-Humean kind of non-realism about laws of nature, where this regularity is explained, and the most famous such view is dispositionalism. Stephen Mumford wants to exclude laws of nature as an extra addition to his ontology, and argues in favor of a dispositional understanding of laws, since that avoids laws of nature being a mysterious entity influencing objects from outside, which does not add anything more than the dispositions the objects already have anyway.[108] With Rani Lill Anjum, he defends causal primitivism and argues that causes too should be understood in light of dispositions.[109]

However, there are laws which are not so easily explained by referring to the dispositions of objects, notably symmetry laws and conservation laws.[110] These are good candidates for being laws of nature,[111] and are used by Cei and French to argue against dispositionalism about laws.[112] Alexander Bird has defended dispositionalism and argued that symmetry laws are pseudo-laws that will disappear from physics, while Cei and French argue that they are so central that they contradict dispositionalism.[113] Bigelow et al., has argued that conser-

---

105 I use the term "make" to describe what it is that the laws of nature do in order for states of affairs to behave according to the laws of nature. But I do not know what the real connection between laws of nature and states of affairs is; namely, that which makes it the case that states of affairs behave according to the laws of nature.
106 Armstrong, *Truth and Truthmakers*, 126–31.
107 John W. Carroll, "Nailed to Hume's Cross," in *Contemporary Debates in Metaphysics*, ed. Theodore Sider, John Hawthorne, and Dean W. Zimmerman, Contemporary Debates in Philosophy (Malden, MA: Blackwell Pub., 2008), 76.
108 Stephen Mumford, "Laws and Lawlessness," *Synthese* 144, no. 3 (2005): 408–09.
109 Stephen Mumford and Rani Lill Anjum, *Getting Causes from Powers* (Oxford: Oxford University Press, 2011), 7.
110 A. Chalmers, "Making Sense of Laws of Physics," in *Causation and Laws of Nature*, ed. H. Sankey (Dordrecht: Kluwer, 1999).
111 Carroll, "Nailed to Hume's Cross," 77.
112 Cei and French, "Getting Away from Governance: A Structuralist Approach to Laws and Symmetries."
113 Ibid., 32, referring to Alexander Bird, *Nature's Metaphysics: Laws and Properties* (Oxford: Oxford University Press, 2007), 214.

vation laws and symmetry laws may be a disposition that the world as a whole has. Cei and French reply that "being a world" is an extremely coarse property, and an extremely coarse explanation. It is like explaining all of Socrates' features in terms of "being Socrates".[114]

Cei and French defend instead a structuralist approach to laws, where the laws are more fundamental than objects, and the objects depend on the laws.[115] I am sympathetic to their ontic structural realist approach and their understanding of laws of nature. They find laws to be understood in terms of features by fundamental underlying structures of the world.[116] This is very similar to how James Ladyman thinks of laws as fundamental structures giving the world its modal structure by determining what is possible, impossible and necessary.[117]

Tim Maudlin is another realist about laws. He sees them as fundamental parts of our ontology which help explain things like the difference between what seems coincidentally true and (physically) necessarily true.[118] John Carroll makes a similar argument when he says that there are some generalisations that are true *because of something in nature* (for example, there are no gold spheres larger than a mile in diameter because of the amount of gold in nature and how it is spread) and some generalisations that are true *because of nature*.[119]

He thinks of nature as something like an omnipresent and eternal field.[120] This seems to fit well with the underlying structures that Cei, French and Ladyman think of as laws. There are structures at the fundamental level of nature which determine what is physically possible, impossible or necessary at higher ontological levels in nature, and these structures we formulate as laws of nature.

The debate about laws of nature and their ontological status is big, so this is not meant as an exhaustive discussion, but rather a presentation of my view,

---

114 Cei and French, "Getting Away from Governance: A Structuralist Approach to Laws and Symmetries," 33, referring to J. Bigelow, B. D. Ellis, and C. Lierse, "The World as One of a Kind: Natural Necessity and Laws of Nature," *The British Journal for the Philosophy of Science* 43, no. 3 (1992).
115 Cei and French, "Getting Away from Governance: A Structuralist Approach to Laws and Symmetries," 11–13.
116 Ibid., 12.
117 Ladyman et al., *Every Thing Must Go*, 288.
118 Tim Maudlin, *The Metaphysics within Physics* (Oxford: Oxford University Press, 2009). For a similar view, see Marc Lange, *Natural Laws in Scientific Practice* (New York: Oxford University Press, 2000).
119 Carroll, "Nailed to Hume's Cross," 74.
120 Ibid.

and I will not go deeper into the issue here. I think my approach will work whatever the truthmakers of laws of nature are, so by "laws of nature" I refer to such truthmakers.[121] Suffice it here to say that generally we seek formulations of the laws of nature that give the simplest and most comprehensive understanding of the world, no matter how they should be interpreted ontologically, and my general theory of causation remains the same whatever should turn out to be the truthmakers of the regularities.[122]

As we have seen, Armstrong and Heathcote understand causation as the instantiation of a law. I believe this to be the best approach to causation since reference to laws of nature is the deepest explanation of why things are as they are, or change or move as they do.[123] Schaffer also supports that the best understanding of the physical connection between causes and effects is like the one given by Armstrong, but he thinks that this is just one part of what causation is, since he also wants to include absences as causes.[124] Laws of nature let us understand motion in the world better than forces alone since there are laws of nature making things move in ways other than by means of the four fundamental forces. For example, there is the Pauli Exclusion Principle, which seems to make things move in certain ways without the means of the known fundamental forces. Symmetry laws and conservation laws (in the sense of their truthmakers) are also important reasons why states of affairs are as they are, or move or change as they do.[125]

Laws of nature, then, make certain kinds of motion happen—to a large degree at the micro level—but what about higher ontological levels? Are there laws of nature determining how rubber bands and muscles move? No, there are no specific laws for rubber bands and muscles, but it is logically possible that all

---

121 As Carroll argues, anyone with a metaphysics will include some entities without truthmakers (ibid., 72), and laws of nature do a great systematizing job.
122 This is known as the Mill-Ramsey-Lewis approach (Armstrong, in Paul, Hall, and Collins, *Causation and Counterfactuals*, 446), and I believe that this methodology for discovering or formulating laws of nature is shared by many, regardless of their ontological commitments.
123 I do not share Armstrong's understanding of laws of nature as a relationship between universals. I just agree that laws of nature are the deepest natural explanation of causation.
124 Schaffer, "Causation by Disconnection," 293.
125 Whereas Armstrong thinks of conservation laws as a "not implausible" example of laws which are not causal (Armstrong, *Truth and Truthmakers*, 125), Heathcote argues that the laws of conservation of energy are very important in order to understand motion in the world. He thinks that particle changes lead to other particle changes because of the laws of conservation, so that one could say causality is the exchange of quanta of a field because of the conservation laws (Heathcote, "A Theory of Causality," 104).

motion at higher levels can be understood in the light of the interaction of several laws of nature in that situation. Bigelow and Pargetter believe that this is the case.[126] Armstrong and Heathcote find it very likely that all macroscopic phenomena are aggregations of microphenomena.[127] Indeed, there seem to be many examples to support this. For example, a billiard ball causing another billiard ball to move can be analyzed in terms of electron clouds at their surfaces repelling each other because of the Pauli Exclusion Principle and the momentum of the particles.[128] If Armstrong and Heathcote are right, then the elasticity of the rubber band or the activity of muscles can all be ontologically reduced to interaction between particles.

However, it is also likely that there are some laws of nature that only come into play at higher ontological levels because the properties they regulate only emerge at higher ontological levels.[129] Terrence Deacon writes in great detail about emerging phenomena at different levels, from basic thermodynamic emergence such as liquidity, to morphodynamic emergence such as crystallization, and to teleodynamic emergence as in evolution. Crystallization and evolution are examples where particles and forces alone do not explain why certain shapes come into being; rather, it is particles and forces in interplay with the possibilities of the environment—receiving feedback from the environment—that leads to the forms that arise.[130] Emergent phenomena should make us cautious about reducing phenomena too much, but they do not count against an understanding of causation as the interaction of laws and complex states of affairs. So-called downward causation (emerging wholes influencing parts) fits the picture drawn above as it is a matter of the interplay between laws of nature and aggregations which may place constraints on other states of affairs. I also understand formal causation as constraints of wholes on parts. We just need to remember that there may be laws or boundary conditions that only come into play at higher ontological levels. Furthermore, some of the regularities we see are due to laws of nature expressing necessities or impossibilities, but certain regularities will simply be regularities that have stabilized within the field of the

---

126 John Bigelow and Robert Pargetter, "Metaphysics of Causation," 33 (1990): 106–12.
127 Heathcote and Armstrong, "Causes and Laws," 70–71.
128 I have this example from the Wikipedia article 'Force', http://en.wikipedia.org/wiki/Force (accessed January 5, 2011).
129 Paul Davies gives a list of examples in Philip Clayton and P. C. W. Davies, *The Re-Emergence of Emergence: The Emergentist Hypothesis from Science to Religion* (New York: Oxford University Press, 2006), 36–37.
130 Deacon, in ibid., 124–49.

possible without being necessary, or stabilities that can be explained statistically, as in Boltzmann's interpretation of the second law of thermodynamics.[131]

Summing up so far, we have laws of nature which make things move as they do, either in interaction with particles at the micro level or as a combined result of several laws of nature acting at the same time on complex states of affairs at higher ontological levels. But where does causality come into play in this picture? I believe that it happens in the way set out below.

Similar states of affairs are often followed by similar states of affairs, which make us assume that this is not just a coincidence. It seems that the first state of affairs in some way produces, creates, leads to, or at least influences the other state of affairs. Since the same state of affairs often leads to the same state of affairs, we assume that all states of affairs are created or produced or are the result of other states of affairs. "Causation" is the word for this assumed influence between cause and effect, as well as all the other words used when we say that a cause "produced," "created," "influenced," or "led to" the effect. All these words—"causation" included—tend to be used without clear meaning, trying to express that which goes on between cause and effect; namely, that which makes it the case that after *this* state of affairs *that* state of affairs follows.

Many people think that something happens between cause and effect. Some think it is a link of some kind, for instance, the transfer of energy. Some think that the cause does something that raises the probability of the effect. Often, however, there is nothing happening between cause and effect at the level we are investigating; rather, something is happening at a more basic level of laws interacting with complex states of affairs. The billiard ball causes another billiard ball to move because of the interaction between electron clouds at their surfaces due to the Pauli Exclusion Principle and the momentum of the particles. The stretched rubber band causing something because it is stretched and then released can also be ontologically reduced to fundamental forces between the constituents of the rubber band. Muscle activity can be ontologically reduced to motor neurons triggering muscles, and the neural activity is again due to ions and their charges and the laws guiding electrical charges.[132]

---

131 Ludwig Boltzmann and Brian McGuinness, *Theoretical Physics and Philosophical Problems: Selected Writings*, Vienna Circle Collection (Dordrecht: Reidel, 1974), 13–33. Ladyman and Ross strongly reject the idea that all macroscopic states of affairs are mereological sums of microscopic states of affairs. Ladyman et al., *Every Thing Must Go*, 55, 253. My position is in line with Ladyman and Ross since I include the work of laws of nature at different ontological levels.

132 Of course, this does not answer how neurons and muscles came to be the way they are, which was by means of evolution.

The schema of causes producing effects is then to be understood as a theoretical framework that we try to use at all ontological levels and as part of other theoretical frameworks. In different theoretical frameworks, some states of affairs are identified as causes of other states of affairs and are confirmed as such if there is a regular relation between them.[133] For example, in biology a mutation causes a new skill in an animal, in psychology shame causes a man to blush, in the social sciences a woman being educated causes her to have fewer children, in economics increased demand causes increased prices, and so on. However, all these causes only have effects in virtue of being complex states of affairs in interaction with the combined result of different laws at work. When we want to understand why things are as they are, or move and change as they do, the deepest answer is to be found in the interaction between laws and states of affairs in the world, for the laws make states of affairs change or move as they do.

It is often much more efficient and useful to pick out causes and effects at high ontological levels in different theoretical frameworks because we can then generalize and simplify. As long as one state of affairs is regularly followed by another, this is useful knowledge; by calling the first cause and the second effect, we hypothesize that at a deeper level there is a lawful connection between them. That does not mean that there must be a law governing the high ontological level, for there may be laws governing lower levels pulling in different directions, but still the interaction is such that there is a general regularity.

For the sake of understanding, we take all sorts of shortcuts to establish some general rules. In theoretical frameworks describing high ontological levels, concepts often have imprecise boundaries. For example, what exact number of hairs distinguishes between "bald" and "not bald"? At what exact point in the process of building *Queen Mary*, the ship, did it become *Queen Mary* the ship?[134] Many concepts have fuzzy edges, but even imprecise concepts describing high ontological levels may be much more explanatory than precise concepts in theoretical frameworks describing low ontological levels. We understand the causes of World War Two better in terms of imprecise concepts such as racism, imperialism and so on, than with terminology from physics describing how many atoms moved around in Europe *circa* 1940. This means that many

---

[133] But it will not be finally verified as the cause, since the regular relation may just be a correlation with another cause.

[134] The boat example is from Nicholas Rescher, *Process Metaphysics: An Introduction to Process Philosophy*, Suny Series in Philosophy (Albany: State University of New York Press, 1996), 66.

descriptions of high ontological levels, even when quite imprecise compared with the terminology of physics, are still efficient in terms of generating understanding and so we often describe causes this way.

Other shortcuts are to cite one cause which is elliptical for a series of causes, or to describe several processes as one. For example, "Pam caused the window to break" can be short for "Bob loaded a catapult with a rock and Pam released the lever, which made the catapult project the rock through the window"; in this instance, a lot of information is omitted because the speaker expects that the enquirer only wants to know the person responsible. What, then, is the connection between cause and effect? What is causation, or what does it mean that the effect "causes," "produces," "creates" or "influences" the effect? That depends on how we choose to define the concept of a cause, as already hinted at in the discussion of absences, and it is now time to make such a decision.

It is only the combination of laws and states of affairs that make motion in the world happen and happen in the way it does. By discovering laws and regularities, we understand how we can predict and manipulate things and motion in the future. This is one of the reasons why we seek causes: in order to understand what creates motion, in order to predict and create motion ourselves. However, learning about absences also makes us understand what is connected and what is not and this is also useful for prediction and manipulation. For example, it is useful to learn how to kill an unwanted plant, and if we expected a certain plant to be watered and live, it is clarifying to learn that the person we expected to water the plant did not do so. We often have expectations about what happens and how things are connected and so we are informed when we learn about absent connections—like the fact that no one watered the plant. Furthermore, as mentioned by Dowe, when we enquire about a cause, we often do not know whether it is an absence or an obtaining state of affairs we are seeking. Absences and disconnections are intertwined in our descriptions of many normal processes; thus, in daily speech we do not distinguish between causation by absence and causation by interaction between laws and states of affairs.

Nonetheless, there are important differences. Laws of nature and states of affairs exist in the world, and many descriptions of causes supervene on these. Absences are not ontological constituents of the world and they are no ontological addition to the world. Rather, absences should be understood as statements about the world.[135] Sometimes, they simply point out that something is absent in the world at a particular time. Such a statement can be a true statement, made true by the totality of the world or the relevant area.[136] For example, if I say that there is no unicorn in my office, that statement is true in virtue of all the contents of my office not including a unicorn. However, there are other counterfactual statements that are counterfactual conditionals of the form "If (counterfactually) A had (or had not) happened, then B would have happened." For example, "If the father had paid attention, then the child would not have been hit by the car." Some argue that such counterfactual statements can be true and their truth is commonly understood as depending on what would have happened in the closest possible world.[137] I believe that many such statements cannot be true because of problems with determining what the closest possible world is and what happens there (especially if the world is undetermined, as I believe it is).[138] One may certainly give good inductive reasons for believing that if I do not water the plant, then it will die. But it is *not true* that if I had not watered the plant last week it would have died, for it is impossible to know for sure what would have happened to that plant if I had not watered it.

Summing up, absences understood as causes have many things in common with understanding states of affairs in the world as causes. However, there are important differences. One is that only states of affairs exist in the world, so actual motion in the world takes place only because of states of affairs. On the other hand, absences often effectively inform us about connections or a lack of connections in comparison with our expectations. Also, statements about states of affairs can be true, whereas counterfactual statements about what could have happened open up another kind of discourse that is vaguer.

Should absences then be included in the concept of causation? Should they be separated from basic causation because of the differences (as Dowe argues), or included because of their intertwinement and because of all the paradigmatic examples of absences (as Schaffer argues)? It depends on what you want from the concept of causality. Is the main goal of the concept of causality to understand why states of affairs are as they are, or change or move as they do? This speaks in favor of leaving absences out, since basic motion is due to existing

---

135 Armstrong (referring to Dowe), in Paul, Hall, and Collins, *Causation and Counterfactuals*, 448.
136 Armstrong, *Truth and Truthmakers*, chapter five.
137 David Lewis, "Counterfactual Dependence and Time's Arrow," *Nous* 13 (1979).
138 Good arguments against such counterfactual claims having truth value can be found in Lowe, *A Survey of Metaphysics*.

states of affairs only. Or is the main goal of the concept of causality to clarify connections and/or a lack of connections in the world? In that case, absences are very useful tools.

Causes are predominantly sought in theoretical frameworks describing high ontological levels. States of affairs are then selected as causes when they are regularly followed by an effect and understood as more than a mere correlation; at these levels, absences are often followed regularly by some event (for example, death follows the absence of oxygen). Noting such an absence can often be useful for understanding situations and can do most of what we require from the concept of causation.

If you seek the deepest understanding of motion in the world, aiming for the highest precision and truth, absences should be omitted. If you seek the quickest, most useful and efficient understanding of how things are connected and not connected, absences should be included. In everyday speech, absences are unavoidable as part of the concept of causation, and there is no point in trying to revise this as everyday speech is imprecise and focuses on usefulness. However, in scholarly discussion, precision is crucial. By omitting absences, I can define the connection between cause and effect as an elliptical shortcut description of the laws of nature in various ways, making complex states of affairs behave in the way they do. If absences are causes, then the connection cannot be understood in the same way. If an absence is a cause, then its connection to the effect is hypothesized on the basis of how laws and states of affairs generally interact. For example, not watering the plant is said to cause death because watering enables the plant to continue living.

In this book, I aim for a narrow definition of cause, where absences are excluded from the concept. My goal is to understand precisely what causes our will and our actions, and this narrow concept of causation will best serve that goal.[139] This does not exclude efficient and less precise descriptions of cause, but my goal is that the shortcuts I make may be understood as shortcut versions of a fuller description which can be ontologically reduced to the interaction between laws and states of affairs. In such shortcuts, absences may be a part, but this should again be understood as an efficient way of describing the actual states of affairs involved. For example, in the case of Pam and the catapult, saying that Pam caused the rock to be thrown includes an absence because the

---

[139] It is my focus on what makes things move in the world, as opposed to clarifying connections, that makes me leave out manipulation theories like that of Judea Pearl (Judea Pearl, *Causality: Models, Reasoning, and Inference* (New York: Cambridge University Press, 2000)). Schaffer places Pearl's theory under probability-raising theories of causation.

rock is released by means of disconnection; this is an efficient way of saying that Pam caused the blocking device to be moved and the catapult caused the stone to be thrown. We give such shortcut descriptions because we anticipate that if someone asked what caused the rock to be thrown and we answer "the catapult," they will continue by asking who released the lever on the catapult. Citing an absence in this case is simply a quick way of describing two states of affairs in the world: Pam moving the blocking device by releasing the lever and the catapult propelling the rock. This is quite different from saying that not killing Hitler in 1942 caused the war to last until 1945, which is speculation about what counterfactually would have happened in a possible world.

What, then, should be understood by terms such as "causing," "producing" or "creating" an effect, "influencing" or "contributing to" an effect, "causally relevant," and "most important cause"? Concerning "causing" and all the other related words used to describe the relation between cause and effect, such as "produce," "create," "influence," "contribute," and "lead to," I repeat that, in most cases, there is nothing emanating from the selected cause that influences the effect or creates motion in any way just in virtue of the cause being the state of affairs that it is. It is the laws of nature that make motion happen. Saying that a cause caused an effect is most often an efficient way of describing some regularity where there is a chain of events and this can be ontologically reduced to a combination of laws of nature acting on complex states of affairs. For example, if I say that the helium gas in a balloon caused the balloon to ascend, there is actually nothing in helium that propels the balloon upwards. Rather, it is a shortcut description for saying that gravity pulls the heavier air molecules around the balloon downwards, and because of the Pauli Exclusion Principle, the air molecules then push the balloon upwards.

What about that which the laws *do* that make states of affairs behave as they do? Is that genuine causation? I do not know what the laws of nature do that makes states of affairs behave as they do, and I would not be surprised if the different laws of nature function in different ways. This is an area requiring further research, but this is the deepest level I know for explaining motion. As I do not know how the laws of nature work, or if they work in the same way, there is little gain in calling what they do real causation, even though what they do is also causation. Rather, "causation" is an efficient way of saying that B follows (is caused by) A in virtue of laws of nature interacting with (among others) A. I shall soon say more about how cause A is selected.[140]

---

140 Ladyman and Ross raises the objection that fundamental physics might come to show us that the laws of nature are time symmetrical, and then the relation between cause coming first

"Causally relevant" are all those states of affairs that are involved in the interaction of laws of nature and states of affairs which made the selected effect happen. This "involvement" includes both states of affairs being pushed or pulled by forces, but also states of affairs resisting forces (by means of other forces). So where do we set the limits for what it means to be involved? If the limits are too wide, we end up including everything from the Big Bang and after as causally relevant for everything. I will argue in the next section that causal relevance can be limited by means of contrasts, and that we can search for the most precise state of affairs within the contrasts which lawfully leads to the effect.

I shall raise the question later of whether something can be the "most important cause," and as that is also a question of selection, it is now time to turn to the question of selection. In many cases, there seem to be many causally relevant states of affairs. Take, for example, a car crash where the road, the tyres, the cars, the drivers, the passengers, what the drivers had been doing previously, the weather, and many other states of affairs seem causally relevant to what happened. Does that mean that all these states of affairs are causes? To understand this we need to turn to the question of selection.

2.2.4 How are causes selected from other conditions?

I have considered C. J. Ducasse's suggestion, distinguishing between conditions and causes as necessary and sufficient, and we have seen that this is not a viable route to follow.[141] Hart and Honoré have suggested that if there are abnormal

---

and effect afterwards may break down (Ladyman et al. *Every Thing must Go*, 277). But even if the laws of nature turn out to be time symmetrical, that will not destroy the causal relation. The reason is that time symmetry has to do with all processes being reversible (ice cubes may melt or freeze in coffee or hair may grow in or out), but time would nevertheless flow from past to future, and laws of nature would be the cause of motion even if they make hair grow in or out. The topic of time is huge, so I do not have space to warrant my claims here, but Ladyman and Ross have not warranted the claim that time symmetric laws of nature will destroy the causal relation either.

141 Even if I rejected the distinction between sufficient and necessary conditions as a distinction between causes and mere conditions, I think the notion of "sufficient cause" is useful after contrasts have been set. The reason is that sometimes we find a state of affairs which seems causally relevant for the effect we want to understand, but it does not seem to be enough to explain the effect. For example, if a light blow on a window makes it break, there would not seem to be enough force involved to cause the effect. The cause we have found is then not sufficient to explain the effect and we must seek other causes (for example, maybe there was

states of affairs or personal agents, we select these as causes. Other philosophers have made other suggestions.[142] E. J. Lowe suggests that the only viable metaphysical distinction is between *contributing* causes and *complete* causes, where the complete cause is the sum of all the contributing causes.[143] Similarly, Bernard d'Espagnat suggests that all we can speak of is contributing causes, which he prefers to call "conditions which influence." Among those influencing conditions, we select the most abnormal or unexpected one as the cause according to d'Espagnat. He does not speak of the complete cause, his point being that there are infinitely many conditions that influence any state of affairs.[144]

So what is the best way of understanding the selection of causes? Note that I am not asking what distinguishes causes from causally irrelevant states of affairs, but how people select one cause among the many causally relevant states of affairs, since it seems that most people usually identify the same cause for an event.

Armstrong and Heathcote argue that we find causes by experiment because experiments indicate that a connection between events follows laws of nature. If you vary the conditions but find one state of affairs which constantly gives the same effect, it seems that this is a process that can be reduced to interaction between laws and the selected state of affairs. For example, iron expands when heated, regardless of whether lumps of iron are of different shapes, mixed with other materials, heated at various temperatures, and so on; thus, we say that heat causes iron to expand. By such experiments, we can try to establish as precisely as possible the state of affairs with which the laws of nature interact,

---

an existing crack in the window). In another example: We may ask why a man died and receive the answer that a woman hit him in the face. The cited cause does not seem sufficient, but then we also learn that the blow made him fall and hit his head on the pavement, and then we think that we have the sufficient cause (the blow in the face plus the fall plus the head hitting the hard pavement). Note that this use of "sufficient cause" presupposes that a contrast is set. Let us say that a cited cause that the house burnt down was that a pyromaniac lit a match and put it to the house. The cause does not seem sufficient since the house wall was made mainly out of concrete and it was raining heavily. We then learn that the pyromaniac also added petrol, and now we think that we have the sufficient cause. But we do not care about the presence of oxygen, even though that was also necessary. The question of sufficiency is decided based on what we want to understand, as I argue later in this section.

142 For example, John Stuart Mill suggested that we should distinguish between standing conditions (like the presence of oxygen) and causes that are changes (like lighting a match) (Mill, according to Lipton, in Beebee, Hitchcock, and Menzies, *The Oxford Handbook of Causation*, 623).
143 Lowe, *A Survey of Metaphysics*, 167.
144 D'Espagnat, *On Physics and Philosophy*, 313–14 and 30–32.

for example, that the laws of nature in this case interact with the molecular dynamics of an object and not its volume or shape.

Sometimes many states of affairs seem to be connected nomically to an effect and yet we still select the same cause among these. For example, both ignition and oxygen are connected nomically to a burning object and yet almost everyone selects ignition as the cause of the object burning—but why? This depends on a combination of interest and background expectation. If you are a scientist who just wants to learn as much as possible about the world, then you will probably select both ignition and the presence of oxygen as causes of the fire since both are connected nomically to the fire. If you are like most people, who expect oxygen to be present, but not the object being ignited, you select the ignition as the cause of the fire since your general interest lies in learning how to predict and manipulate. If you are a scientist in a laboratory generating ignitions in a setting in which you expect no oxygen to be present, you will probably select the presence of oxygen as the cause of the object burning.

We set contrasts depending on what we already expect and what interests we have. Even if very many states of affairs are involved in every event, we can simplify by describing states of affairs in broad terms that include many other states of affairs. For example, speaking of Atle today may refer in a wide sense to everything that has made me the way I am today, which then includes numerous events. In addition, we often disregard very many states of affairs as uninteresting because we expect their presence not to be relevant to the contrast we want to understand. Most often we will disregard the burning object being dry, surrounded by oxygen, held together by the strong force of its atoms and so on, and only be interested in the ignition as the cause of it burning as opposed to not burning.

If we do not know of any cause for a concrete effect, we seek any cause we can find. If we know of several causally relevant states of affairs, we select among them based on expectations and interests. Setting up contrasts allows us to specify more precisely what we are after, to find the relevant nomic connection. But what if we have several candidates for causes which all seem necessary for the effect? Is it then possible to say which cause is the most important? This question is important for a later discussion of the role of agents and indeterminism in causing choices.

It is extremely difficult to develop a general criterion for finding the most important cause because importance is relative. In many cases, we may think of a typical cause of why something is the way it is, but of course it is crucial that the subatomic elements are held together or that God keeps it in existence, and so on. Sometimes we know about strong forces involved, but we are looking for one specific and unexpected small extra force or resistance. The reason why we often agree about the cause is that people have much the same interests and expectations and take the same things for granted when they look for causes. Thus, I believe that the best one can do in order to limit the number of causes is to try to specify as clearly as possible the causal contrasts in order to clarify what one wants to understand. The contrasts serve to exclude many causally relevant states of affairs that do not concern us.

In the case of Pam and the catapult, if someone asks for the cause of the window breaking, we answer "Pam." We could answer the rock, the catapult, the spring and all the other states of affairs that were involved in the breaking of the window. But we anticipate that if we answer "the rock" or "the catapult" and so on, the inquirer will keep on asking until we say that Pam released the lever. This is because we assume that the person asking is interested either in finding a person to hold responsible or establishing if it was an accident, i.e., what happened, so that a repetition can be prevented later. However, if a person expected the window to be made of bullet-proof glass and asks why the window broke, the cause he might be searching for is that there was a mix-up in the delivery process so that a normal window was fitted instead of a bullet-proof window. As the examples show, the strongest force, the highest probability and so on are not what determine how people select the cause; rather, it is a matter of what the inquirer wants to understand against the background of expectations and contrasts.[145]

Timothy O'Connor raises an objection against contrastive causation as follows: In an indeterministic world, contrastive explanation will also fail (plausibly) wherever P and Q are mutually exclusive and each had a non-zero chance of occurring. But it does not follow that there can be no explanation of P, or that whatever non-contrastive explanation there may be of P will be somehow deficient—of a lesser variety of explanation than contrastive explanation. We explain—really explain—an indeterministic outcome P by citing and describing the causal factor or factors that brought it about. (The point is a familiar one in scientific explanations of indeterministic phenomena unrelated to free action. If there is a plurality of possible outcomes of the interaction of a pair of particles, the particular outcome that obtains has an explanation in terms of propensities of the two particles that actually were manifested, bringing about that particular result. Once one understands the indeterministic nature of those propensi-

---

[145] The same reasoning as that made here solves the problem case that Schaffer said he could not solve, as mentioned in footnote 73.

ties and others that were not, but might have been manifested on that occasion, one realizes that there is nothing more to explain about that situation).[146]

Although this is put as an argument against contrastive causation, it is no counterargument against the way in which I think of contrastive causation. In cases of indeterministic laws governing the action of particles, there is a cause for why things happen, but in many cases there is no cause for why A happened as opposed to B, which could also have happened.

With this understanding of causality, I can now answer a critique Daniel Dennett has raised against the Consequence Argument. I spend some time on this because distinctions made in this discussion will be important later. Dennett says that incompatibilists who think of determinism as a cause have missed the point of causal inquiry.[147] This critique is one of many reasons for me to spend quite some time on causality. Dennett argues against the incompatibilist claim that determinism makes what happens inevitable. On the contrary, evolution has given us "evitability," the ability to avoid things; for example, eyes to see things about to hit us and which we can avoid by ducking. This is the interesting sense of "avoiding" or "inevitability" according to Dennett.[148] Dennett considers the objection that there may be a sense of "inevitability" in a deterministic world to which he does not respond. He says that he will search for this elusive sense later and then that if there is another sense of "inevitability," it is not something we should care about.[149]

The distinction Dennett should have discussed here is that between type and token in relation to what it is physically possible for a person to do. All of Dennett's arguments only apply to *type* physical possibility. Evolution has given us the general ability to duck and so on, but if determinism is true, what happens in a token situation is inevitable, even if the type event is evitable for many people in many situations. Libertarians want *token* physically possible alternatives, but Dennett only gives them *type* physically possible alternatives.

Dennett probably thinks that type physically possible alternatives are all that free will requires and that one can be the cause of one's action in the relevant sense even in a determined universe. To show this, Dennett presents the case of two computers with different chess-playing programs, rigged to play against each other. They will play a series of games and if restarted, they will play the same games all over again. The scenario is like a small deterministic

---

146 O'Connor, in Kane, *The Oxford Handbook of Free Will* (2nd ed.), 322.
147 Dennett, in ibid., 235.
148 Daniel C. Dennett, *Freedom Evolves* (New York: Viking, 2003), 42–60.
149 Ibid., 61, 94.

universe. Let us further say that computer A wins most of the games. If we ask why A wins so often, Dennett finds it wrong to answer that it is because of the determinism involved. If we ask why computer B lost a particular game, the cause is that it made a blunder in its thirteenth move, and not that it was determined. Could computer B have made a different move? Dennett answers that we must check similar games to see if B then makes a different move or not.[150]

The chess-playing computers illustrate my point that we select causes depending on interests and contrasts and different theoretical frameworks. If my interest is in causality in a chess game framework, I want causes that explain the relations between the chess moves. Then I can say that computer B lost the game because it risked its queen in move thirteen, or that it risked its queen because it was hoping to checkmate computer A by doing so. It is illuminating how Dennett answers the question of whether B could have made another move (he says we must check similar games), for it shows that he is thinking about type physical possibility. If we ask whether B could have made another move in the token situation, the answer is no. Then, of course, the question is whether free will requires token alternative possibilities. In any case, the Consequence Argument shows that a person does not have token alternative possibilities, even if she may have type physical alternative possibilities.[151]

Although I do not have space to discuss it here, I would like to suggest briefly that the understanding of causation I have presented here also solves many other problems connected to causality and that this supports the plausibility of the theory. Concerning how fragile or how fine- or coarse-grained causes should be understood to be, the answer is that it depends on what we want to understand (the selected contrasts) and the ontological level and theoretical framework. The level of fragility or grainedness is not the same for all causes but de-

---

150 Ibid., 77–82.
151 It seems to me that Dennett's position here is similar to the position Kadri Vihvelin defends in her book *Causes, Laws, and Free Will: Why Determinism Doesn't Matter*. She distinguishes between narrow ability (that which we are able to do with our body) and wide ability (the abilities we have which depends on our surroundings) (Kadri Vihvelin, *Causes, Laws, and Free Will* (New York: Oxford University Press, 2013), 6–10). She then argues that even if the world is determined, we have the narrow ability to open doors etc, and sometimes external conditions allow us to use our narrow abilities (ibid., 169–70). Determinism does not prevent free will in that we sometimes get to do things that we have a narrow ability to do (ibid., 193–96). I find that the type-token distinction is better than the narrow-wide-ability distinction since it varies so much what we are able to do with our body. In any case, it seems that she defends a weaker sense of freedom, similar to the one Dennett defends, but leaves out the agent as ultimate cause, which a stronger sense of freedom requires.

pends on what we want to understand. If I want to understand why Mary turned as opposed to not turning, the cause was that John said hello to her. If I want to understand why Mary turned so quickly, as opposed to turning at a regular pace, the cause was that John said hello loudly.[152]

Concerning the question of transitivity,[153] the answer is that some causes are transitive and others are not. At high levels of description giving efficient descriptions of causes, there can be many examples of non-transitive causes. At the level of forces acting directly on states of affairs, there is more transitivity, since one thing being pushed or pulled can lead to another thing being pushed or pulled. Billiard ball A pushes billiard ball B, which pushes billiard ball C, and the causes are transitive. However, as we have seen, there are many causes that do not involve the transfer of energy or momentum and then there need not be transitivity. The hardness of the wall causes the ball to bounce back and the ball causes the flower vase to break, but the wall does not cause the flower vase to break, thus there is no transitivity. We speak of causation to describe regularities at high levels in different theoretical frameworks, but often the regularity depends on the interaction of laws and complex states of affairs at lower ontological levels, and often the descriptions are efficient shortcut descriptions. Naturally, there will therefore be many examples of causation without transitivity.

To conclude, the theory of causality presented here is able to solve many problems and integrate the answers into a coherent framework, thereby supporting this understanding of causality.

---

[152] I have the example from Schaffer, "The Metaphysics of Causation," section 1.2.
[153] The question of transitivity is: If A causes B and B causes C, does A then cause C?

3 The Self

Free will means that it is up to us what choice we make, but what does "us" refer to here? An agent, a person, a self—but what is meant by these terms? I shall argue that a proper understanding of the self is crucial in a theory of free will, and that a detailed understanding of the self is required in order to understand the process of deliberation and choosing. Important ingredients in the deliberation process are consciousness, feelings and memory, desires and thoughts. As was the case with causality, the question of the self is a very complex question which can only be dealt with briefly here. The best way to treat the topic briefly is to select the work of someone who has worked thoroughly with the topics that are most relevant and useful for the overall goal of this book, that of seeking an event-causal theory of free will somewhere between compatibilism and libertarianism. Luckily there is a recent publication which offers a detailed understanding of the self, Antonio Damasio's book *Self Comes to Mind*,[154] and it will be the basis of this chapter. Another reason that Damasio is selected is that I presuppose an event-causal theory of the mind, and Damasio fits well into such an approach. I write more about this presupposition in the subchapter on thinking. I do not discuss Damasio's conception against many other conceptions of the self, rather this book explores whether Damasio's concept of the self can offer a good way of thinking about free will. I present it in quite some detail instead of just referring to the book, since I modify and specify many parts of it, and explain the relevance to the topic of free will.

Antonio Damasio is a professor of neuroscience. He has worked particularly with emotions, but also with many other topics like self and consciousness and he is informed about some of the philosophical discussions about the topics he writes about. His book *Self Comes to Mind* is not so much about how conscious experiences are possible at all, but more about the concrete brain activity that gives rise to the different conscious experiences, and their function. His contribution on the self is what is most important in this chapter, since he gives a detailed understanding firmly rooted in empirical findings. There are different parts of what is normally called the self, which is confirmed by the fact that one can lose some parts and keep others. In order to understand better what it

---

154 Antonio R. Damasio, *Self Comes to Mind: Constructing the Conscious Brain* (New York: Pantheon Books, 2010). I also cite other books by Damasio when these supplement points that are important for my theory.

means to be the cause of a choice, we need to understand more precisely what the self is and how it is involved in causing a choice.

There are two very different theoretical frameworks that can be used to describe the self. One framework uses language from a first-person perspective and describes what the agent is phenomenally conscious of.[155] Examples would be "I see," "I think," "I feel" and so on. The other framework uses language from a third-person perspective without the language of conscious experiences. Examples would be "electromagnetic waves hit the eye," "the neurons fire," "hormones are released" and so on. There is a tight link between these two theoretical frameworks, as there are many good arguments suggesting that brain activity causes the phenomenally conscious first-person perspective experiences. On the other hand, although it seems to be the case that brain activity causes phenomenal consciousness, it is still an unsolved mystery of science how this happens, so the precise relation between these frameworks is not clear. For this reason, one needs to be aware which theoretical framework is being applied.[156] In this chapter I give detailed definitions of concepts like "the self," "the mind," "emotion," "memory," "thinking" and "desire," and link these to biological processes in the brain and body to show how closely related these two frameworks are.

All the main parts of Damasio's book are relevant for the discussion in this book, so I will present that book in this chapter, with some discussion as we proceed. Damasio's book is built up like this: In part one there is a general biological background enabling the reader to understand the life of organisms in general, with a special focus on how all organisms strive for homeostasis – maintaining a stable life-preserving state. This may sound irrelevant, but the principle of homeostasis throws light on many different questions related to free will, so it is a good place to start.

In part two, Damasio is concerned with the brain and the mind. His theory is that the brain creates patterns that can become conscious, and these patterns represent either states of the body or states of affairs in the world exterior to the

---

155 Phenomenal consciousness is the qualitative experience of what something is like, as opposed to being conscious in the sense of just being awake and not asleep or in a coma. Much more will be said about consciousness later in this chapter.
156 Bennett and Hacker argue that many neuroscientists mix these frameworks in problematic ways (M. R. Bennett, *Neuroscience and Philosophy: Brain, Mind, and Language* (New York: Columbia University Press, 2007)). Note that there are many interesting problem cases like subconscious perception which make a clear-cut distinction between these frameworks difficult. I will discuss this further in this chapter.

body.[157] In addition, there are dispositions in the brain for acting in certain ways in reaction to the patterns representing the body or the world. These representations serve to guide the actions of the organism with the help of feelings connected with the representations, which serve to value some representations as more important for survival than others. Such representations and the feelings attached to them are stored in the memory, and become activated when generally relevant for an organism to help the organism make life-preserving choices in the future.

In part three, Damasio writes about consciousness and the self. He distinguishes between three types of self; the proto-self, the core self and the autobiographical self. These three stand in a chronological and hierarchical order, since each self depends on the previous one for its existence. Damasio ends with a discussion of qualia (to be explained later) and the function of consciousness. After my presentation of Damasio's book, I will also say a bit more about thinking and desire, since these are important for understanding the self and choices, and Damasio does not say much about them.

Although I follow the three-part structure of Damasio's book, I have chosen to focus on elements that are especially important for understanding the deliberation process. I start with the biological background which helps us understand some of the basic building blocks in the deliberation process. I move on to the relation between brain and mind to show that the brain causes our conscious experiences and that the different parts of our mental life may also operate non-consciously. This gives strong support to the event-causal theory of mind against alternatives like agent-causal approaches. The next two topics are emotion and memory. These topics are important for understanding deliberation because, when we are about to make an important choice, we can remember earlier relevant events which evoke feelings that influence the choice we are about to make.

After this I describe how different kinds of consciousness are the basis for different kinds of selves. Damasio distinguishes three types, and the autobio-

---

[157] I use the term "neural pattern" to describe a dynamic structure of neuronal firing in the brain, whereas I use "neural structure" to describe static structures in the brain. This is not a strict dichotomy, but more of a continuum on a scale, but the distinction is nevertheless helpful. Some of the neural structures are innate, like the parts and areas of the brain that almost all humans share. Other neural structures change all the time, like the neural structures that are the substrate of our stored memories. I use the term "neural pattern" when these structures are activated by means of neural firing. In addition, when I speak of "representations of the body or the world," this is short for "representations of the body or any part of the body, and representations of the world exterior to the body or any part of the world exterior to the body."

graphical self is particularly important for the topic of free will since I shall argue that we have free will when the autobiographical self is the cause of the desire that leads to action. Since consciousness may seem superfluous in Damasio's understanding of the mind, I then discuss the role of consciousness for free will. Towards the end I first discuss the topic of thinking to show how thinking can be a causal process producing alternatives for us to consider when making choices. I end with the topic of desires to show how our desires cause actions and how our autobiographical self through memories and emotions can cause the desires that cause our actions, which is what it means to have free will. This may seem like much, but as mentioned above, the different parts serve different functions, and presenting Damasio's theory broadly shows its overall coherence and empirical support. I find this important to support my claim that it is not warranted when agent-causalists claim that there are irreducible parts of human agency that event-causal approaches cannot explain. The many examples of non-conscious deliberation and action especially serve this function.

3.1 Biological Background

A single cell resembles a larger organism in many respects, but is of course a lot less complex.[158] It has a cytoskeleton with a comparable function to that of a human skeleton; it has a nucleus which can be likened to the human brain; it has cytoplasm resembling human body tissue and organs; it has a membrane

---

[158] A cell is a living organism and the origin of life was previously poorly understood. There are now good theories, however, that explain every stage from the basic chemicals to the living cell. Small particles below the level of DNA can emerge to form larger structures and replicators, as suggested in Richard Dawkins, *The Selfish Gene*, 30th anniversary ed. (Oxford: Oxford University Press, 1976; reprint, 2006), 13–20), and illustrated well by Terence Deacon, in *Clayton and Davies, The Re-Emergence of Emergence: The Emergentist Hypothesis from Science to Religion*, 137–43. Scientists have been able to replicate RNA from the same ingredients and conditions assumed to have been present on earth 3.5 billion years ago (Tracey A. Lincoln and Gerald F. Joyce, "Self-Sustained Replication of an Rna Enzyme," *Science* 323, no. 5918 (2009)). They have also shown that such RNA could have merged with fat bubbles that were also present, the main ingredients of the replicator and cell membrane needed to make a living cell (Itay Budin and Jack W. Szostak, "Physical Effects Underlying the Transition from Primitive to Modern Cell Membranes," *PNAS* 108, no. 13 (2011)). I mention this in support of the general approach to free will adopted here, i.e., all parts of our mental life have developed through evolution.

comparable with human skin; and some cells even have cilia to help them swim, which are parallel to human limbs.[159]

What constitutes a cell's life? Essentially, it is about getting nutrition in and waste products out, so that the nutrition can be turned into energy which allows the cell to continue getting more nutrition in and more waste products out.[160] This process is what it is for a cell to be alive. But it is difficult work, and there are lots of dangers in the world which can prevent the cell from being able to continue its business. Early in the history of the evolution of life, cells joined forces and specialized to the mutual benefit of all parties. Instead of one cell doing all the work required to survive, different cells could specialize in parts of the job, each doing their part more efficiently. There are examples of such specialization and cooperation at all levels, from a few cells to the whole human body. It is the same logic as Adam Smith used to describe division of labor, and it has produced human bodies with specialized cells and organs. Each part in the body does its bit, and all enjoy the benefit of nutrition via the blood system.[161]

One type of cell, neurons, specialized in a particular way. What is special about neurons (and a few other kinds of cells) is that they can change other cells by sending an electrochemical signal (called "firing").[162] This capability to change other cells gives neurons the opportunity to create changes in the whole organism, for example by making muscles stretch or contract. This ability makes neurons especially apt for helping the organism to survive in a harsh environment, since it is easier to survive if you are an animal, which can move, instead of a plant, which cannot.[163]

Neurons became extremely important because of their ability to create representations and dispositions in the brain. Damasio asks us to imagine an organism being hit, and that some neurons react to this blow by firing. Imagine further that other neurons react to the first neurons firing by making the organism move. The first set of neurons firing in response to the blow could be said to represent the blow, and the second set of neurons firing could be said to actualize a disposition to move—at least we could say this if the first set of neurons

---

159 Damasio, *Self Comes to Mind*, 33.
160 Ibid., 41.
161 Ibid., 33–34.
162 This is the classical description of neuronal interaction, but such interaction might also happen in other ways, such as through coherent oscillation (Pascal Fries, "A Mechanism for Cognitive Dynamics: Neuronal Communication through Neuronal Coherence," *Trends in Cognitive Sciences* 9, no. 10 (2005)).
163 Damasio, *Self Comes to Mind*, 37–38, 50.

fired every time the organism was hit, and the second set of neurons made the organism move when they fired.

A representation then just means a neural pattern consistently related to something which it then represents, like a neural pattern in the brain which is active every time an organism sees something red, whereas a disposition is an "If presence of A, then act by doing B" mechanism, which is triggered by a specific stimulus and gives a particular response.[164]

Concerning representation, I would like to add something to Damasio's definition. I suggest calling his definition a protorepresentation, since it lacks intentionality and the capability to misrepresent. When it comes to representations in the human mind, they have intentionality and the capability to misrepresent, but then something more is needed than merely a consistent relation, namely that the representation must be related to other entities represented in the brain in a certain way. For it to be a representation there should be some structural similarity between how the entity in the world relates to other entities in the world and how the represented entity relates to other represented entities. So, for example, for a neural pattern in the brain to represent a horse, it must not only be activated by seeing something horselike but it must also relate to representations like barn and cowboy, etc. in the brain similarly to how horses relate to barns and cowboys in the world. I add this to avoid common criticism of representationalism, like the disjunction problem or the problem of misrepresentation; unfortunately, there is not room to go into these questions here.

Every now and then in evolutionary history, mutations engender life-preserving dispositions. For example, some neurons started to react to chemical, photo or tactile stimuli, and make a small organism eject something poisonous or move towards light or away from danger and so on. There are known small organisms with all these dispositions. In evolution, brains started with simple mechanisms which evolved into more advanced dispositions. When dispositions started reacting to representations in the brain, organisms started making more and more advanced responses to their environment, and this has now resulted in large networks of dispositions and representation-making capabilities which give us a rich mental life.[165]

---

164 Ibid., 134. Damasio does not define "representation" in his 2010 book, but seems to use the definition he gave in his 1999 book, that "representation" is "a pattern which is consistently related to something" (*The Feeling of What Happens: Body and Emotion in the Making of Consciousness* (New York: Harcourt Brace, 1999), 320).
165 *Self Comes to Mind*, 135.

Human bodies are very complex organisms, and there are many parameters that need to be within a certain range in order for the body to survive; for example, temperature or pH-value. When the different parameters are within these life-maintaining ranges, the body is in functional balance or homeostasis. In order to stay alive it is important for the body to be in homeostasis. If a neural structure representing a part of the body received a stimulus which indicated that that body was moving away from homeostasis, and the neural structure responded with a stimulus to restore the body to homeostasis, it is very likely that such neural structures would be selected by evolution. For example, a neural structure receiving a stimulus from the stomach indicating hunger or a stimulus from the blood indicating low blood sugar, which then caused the organism to eat, would be very likely to be selected by evolution.[166]

3.2 Brain and Mind

Clearly, it would also be extremely useful with regard to homeostasis and survival if neural patterns could represent states of affairs in the world. If a pattern representing good food triggers a response that makes you eat it, it helps homeostasis. If a pattern representing a lion triggers a response that makes you run, you are more likely to survive. If a pattern representing a naked woman makes a man want to have sex, he is more likely to propagate his genes. And so on.

Damasio argues that neural patterns *do* represent the body *and* the world. He argues that the brain creates representations all the time, and reacts to them with its different dispositions, but only a few of these representations become conscious to us. I shall now present his argument and add others to support him. I start with the point that the brain creates representations and then proceed with the point that there is a lot of thinking, feeling, remembering, and desiring that happens non-consciously. But some think that terms like these (thinking, feeling, etc.) should be reserved for conscious thinking, feeling, etc., and so I shall end with a discussion of that. I use a lot of examples since I believe that all the data on non-conscious thinking are data that show why an event-causal approach to the mind is superior to agent-causality and other approaches in giving a simpler account of the data.

The first point is that Damasio argues that neural patterns represent the body and the world. Various senses have evolved to provide different stimuli to

---

[166] Ibid., 41–42.

the neurons which could then be represented in the brain.[167] Not all believe that patterns in the brain represent entities in the world that we can experience, but there is much very convincing neurological evidence that patterns in the brain represent entities in the world in a conscious way for us.

Damasio describes two telling experiments. In one the researchers scan a monkey brain. They cannot see what the monkey is watching but can tell from their scans alone whether the monkey is watching a circle, a cross or one of the other options in the experiment.[168] In the other experiment, carried out by Damasio and colleagues, they found a pattern in the brain which consistently correlated with the conscious experience of a certain sound. What is very interesting about this experiment is that the same pattern was active even when the person was just imagining hearing the sound in his mind, even if no sound was actually made in the world outside his mind.[169]

These examples are two of many similar examples. Every time you have a conscious experience of seeing red, the same area of your brain is active. If that area is destroyed, you will not experience red anymore, and if that area is stimulated, you will experience seeing red even if there are no red objects in front of you.[170] If it is destroyed you will even have problems imagining something red.[171] Another fascinating finding in neuroscience is similar to the ones just mentioned and strongly suggests that the brain creates consciousness. Damage to an area of the brain called the fusiform gyrus of the temporal lobe causes face

---

[167] The evolution of the senses is also well understood. Cells sensitive to light evolved into cells in a cavity which could then register the direction of the light. A lens sharpened the signal, and cells reacting to different wave lengths made further discrimination possible. Eyes have evolved independently many times in evolution. The nose started as cells sensitive to chemical stimuli and pheromones, and, since it is sensible not to eat everything that comes into the mouth, taste developed in a similar way to smelling. Hearing started as reactions to vibrations in the jaw, which evolved into the middle ear, and of course nerve cells in the skin are sensitive to touch. For details, see Rhawn Joseph, *Neuropsychiatry, Neuropsychology, and Clinical Neuroscience: Emotion, Evolution, Cognition, Language, Memory, Brain Damage, and Abnormal Behavior*, 2nd ed.(Baltimore: Williams & Wilkins, 1996), 7–16. Again, I mention these facts to support the general evolutionary approach to our mental life.
[168] Damasio, *Self Comes to Mind*, 69. The physical pattern of the neurons firing even resembled the structure of what the monkey was watching; see pictures in *Descartes' Error: Emotion, Reason, and the Human Brain* (London: Penguin, 1994; reprint, 2005), 104.
[169] *Self Comes to Mind*, 134.
[170] Nouchine Hadjikhani et al., "Retinotopy and Color Sensitivity in Human Visual Cortical Area V8," *Nature Neuroscience* 1, no. 3 (1998); Brian Wandell, "Colour Vision: Cortical Circuitry for Appearance," *Current Biology* 18, no. 6 (2008).
[171] Damasio, *Descartes' Error*, 101.

blindness, and stimulation of this same area causes people to see faces spontaneously.[172]

The correlations are very exact, which indicates that the neural pattern is not just one bit of many necessary conditions but is where the representation takes place: as mentioned above, researchers could distinguish between a circle and a cross represented in the monkey brain. Correlation does not necessarily imply causation, as two things can be correlated without one being the cause of the other, like the correlation between night and day. But correlation can also indicate causation. Do we have any reason to believe that it is the neural pattern which causes the conscious experience? Yes, because the neural patterns in the brain that correlate with conscious experiences always occur several hundred milliseconds before they become conscious.[173] Since causes do not come after their effects, this strongly indicates that the physical substrate gives rise to the conscious experience and not that the conscious experience creates a neural pattern in the brain.

Many problems are thus solved if there is a neural pattern underlying conscious experiences. Hallucinations are explained: they occur since a neural pattern is activated even if what it represents is not present. For example, you can think that you see a red tomato even if no such tomato is present because you have a neural pattern representing a red tomato in your brain, making it conscious to you. Phantom pains are also explained, since neural patterns representing (now lost) parts of your body can become conscious to you even if you have lost the actual limb. Certain phantom pain phenomena are very well explained by this model. For instance, there was a person who lost his arm, and kept feeling it. Then he lost the feeling in his arm, but retained the feeling of his hand, now just feeling that the hand was sticking out from his shoulder. Finally, he lost that feeling as well. This is explained by the fact that the area representing our hand in the brain is much larger than the area representing the arm, and so the neuron connections representing the arm faded away before the neurons representing the hand.[174]

The process of how the brain can represent the world is well understood, especially vision. Humans have feature-detecting neurons, which fire in response to a certain feature being seen in the world. These neurons fire for at least thirty different types of features, like angle, size, movement, contour, col-

---

172 Michael Shermer, "Aunt Millie's Mind," *Scientific American* 307, no. 1 (2012).
173 Damasio, *Self Comes to Mind*, 122.
174 Rhawn Joseph, "Brain Mind Lecture 4 Parietal Lobes Body Image Phantom Limbs" (Sic), (2006), 18:13-19:34.

or, distance from observer, etc.[175] Wolf Singer has shown that identicals fire in response to certain objects fire synchronously, the object is consciously experienced. If two completely different visual inputs are given to each eye, only one of them becomes conscious to the observer at a time, and it switches back and forth which image is conscious to the observer. When the first object is consciously seen, then the neurons detecting the features of that object fire in synchrony. When the other object is consciously seen, then the neurons detecting the features of that object fire in synchrony.[176]

The brain puts together information from the feature-detecting neurons to make a unified picture. We know this because sometimes some types of neurons do not function, and then the brain creates a unified picture of the rest of the information. One case is color blindness. In another example, a person (known as D.F.) was almost blind, but she did receive information from the neurons detecting color and texture. Everything she saw was blurry, but she could see a banana and guess that it was a banana because of its distinctive color and texture, but could not say what position the banana was in or what shape it had.[177]

Note that when there is a lack of visual input it does not create black holes in the visual field, but rather the rest is turned into a unified picture since the brain creates a unified impression based on the input it gets. Some people with brain damage in one hemisphere do not lose half of the visual field, but rather create a whole visual field from the input sent to the one hemisphere. The point is that the input is spread out to create a unified impression. If the brain is given contradictory sensory input it will merge it together in a kind of compromise.[178] Various tests have been performed whereby people are given one visual input but feel something else. For example, they sit on a chair rotating 120 degrees while being shown a film indicating that they rotate less; or a big object is placed before their eyes while they feel a similar, but smaller, object with their

---

175 Michel Imbert, "Sehen ohne zu Wissen." *Spektrum der Wissenschaft (Spezial: Bewusstsein)* 2004, 39.
176 Wolf Singer, "Ein Spiel von Spiegeln," ibid., 25.
177 This phenomenon is further complicated by the fact that we seem to have two distinct visual systems in the brain, where one allows conscious seeing and the other is concentrated on adjusting body movement. Therefore, although D.F. was unable to see a letter-box, she had no problem sticking a letter into the slot. The converse is Balint Holmes syndrome, where a patient can see the letter box clearly but would be unable to stick the letter in. See Peter Carruthers, *The Architecture of the Mind: Massive Modularity and the Flexibility of Thought* (Oxford: Oxford University Press, 2006), 88–89.
178 Michael S. Gazzaniga, "The Interpreter (Gifford Lecture 3)," in The Gifford Lectures(2009). at 50:08–51:55; 1:00:40–1:01.40.

hand. Their brains then merge the information together in a compromise. When they do not receive a disturbing visual input, they guess quite well how much they have rotated or how big the object is. But when they have disturbing visual input, the brain mixes the information together to form one impression so that they estimate the size differently.[179]

None of these examples show that the physical side of reality is ontologically more basic than the non-physical conscious side of reality, which idealists hold to be ontologically basic. For example, it could be that a non-physical conscious mind requires a very complex physical structure to interact with before it can become active. But consciousness does not seem to be an independent or soul-like entity as envisioned by most substance dualists or idealists. Rather, it seems very dependent on the brain, at least slightly indicating an ontological priority to the physical. Many experiences are better explained as made by the brain for the sake of survival than as an accurate depiction of the world by the mind. Things do not have colors independent of light setting and someone watching them. But adding colors to objects makes them easier to see and distinguish, so it makes evolutionary sense that the brain should add colors. The spectrum of light that we can see is the spectrum that most of the radiation from the sun and stars come in,[180] and so again it makes sense that evolution used this spectrum of light as a basis to make conscious experiences of color.

Sometimes the process goes wrong. For example, there are reports that some people see colors when they hear sounds.[181] The neurologist V. S. Ramachandran and the philosopher W. Hirstein suspect that such stories may be more metaphorical than real color experiences, and they cite an even better example. A person lost his sight so that he became totally blind. But after a while he could start to see clearly the objects he was feeling in his hand—not just imagining them in his inner eye, but having an experience which was like seeing the ruler he was holding in his hand. This happened with all kinds of objects.[182] Another fascinating experiment shows something similar with blind and blindfolded people: cameras sent output stimuli on either their back or their tongue, and these stimuli followed patterns consistent with what the cam-

---

179 Isabelle Viaud-Delmon and Roland Jouvent, "Zwischen virtuell und real," *Spektrum der Wissenschaft (Spezial: Bewusstsein)* 2004, 73.
180 Russell D. Fernald, "The Evolution of Eyes," *Karger Gazette*, no. 64 (2001). More specifically, it is what the first animals in the sea would have been most exposed to in the water.
181 Jeffrey Gray, "Mit den Ohren sehen, " *Spektrum der Wissenschaft (Spezial: Bewusstsein)* 2004.
182 Ramachandran and Hirstein, in Shaun Gallagher and J. Shear, *Models of the Self* (Thorverton, UK: Imprint Academic, 1999), 96–97.

era was filming. After amazingly little training, both blindfolded and blind people reported that they started seeing images, and they were able to recognize faces, describe objects, read, manipulate objects and much more. Several times when the camera suddenly zoomed in on something, the blind(folded) people ducked because they felt that something was being thrown at them.[183]

There are also many things we see that are not a correct picture of what we see, and it is useful for us to see things like this. Many optical illusions are based on the fact that the brain distorts what we see to make it fit what it should look like.[184] One example is the moon, which looks a lot bigger if it is close to buildings or mountains than when up in the sky, but there is nothing physical that makes it look bigger. The illusion happens because we know that the moon is much bigger than houses and so the brain makes it look relatively bigger.[185] The illusions are generally useful clues for survival, but not correct depictions of the world. If our conscious minds were ontologically unique non-physical entities with capacities for grasping the world, one would not expect these distortions caused by what is accessible to the brain and its survival value.

To sum up this first point, it seems clear that the brain creates patterns that can become conscious, and that it is the physical side of it that determines how the conscious experience comes to be. The next question is whether or not there can be mind without phenomenal consciousness, that is, non-conscious thinking, remembering, feeling, desiring, etc.[186]

Damasio argues that the brain constantly makes many neural patterns that represent states of affairs in the world or in the body, and these neural patterns can be consciously experienced as images, but he also says that most of them are never experienced consciously. But even if they are not conscious, neural patterns and dispositions seem able to perform their work as a causal chain and do the same work as a conscious person does (sense, think, remember, feel, desire)—often even better. Numerous experiments support this, and I do think

---

183 Eliana Sampaio, Stéphane Maris, and Paul Bach-Y-Rita, "Brain Plasticity: "Visual" Acuity of Blind Persons Via the Tongue," *Brain Research*, no. 908 (2001); Benjamin W. White et al., "Seeing with the Skin," *Perception and Psychophysics* 7, no. 1 (1970).
184 Michael Gazzaniga shows some very convincing examples in Michael S. Gazzaniga, "What We Are (Gifford Lecture 1)," in The Gifford Lectures (2009), 29:30–30:17.
185 At least that seems to me to be the best theory (Lloyd Kaufman and Irvin Rock, "The Moon Illusion," *Scientific American* 207, no. 1 (1962)). See also the similar evolutionary explanation of the Müller-Lyer illusion, in Robert J. Sternberg and Jeffery Scott Mio, *Cognitive Psychology*, 4th ed. (Belmont, CA: Wadsworth, 2006), 117.
186 When I use the term "non-conscious" I do not mean "not awake" but "not phenomenally conscious." I give a fuller description of what this means in the subchapter on consciousness.

that much philosophical confusion could be avoided if more philosophers accepted that there can be conscious and non-conscious thinking.[187] Let us take an example from daily life. Many people have found that they can sometimes drive a car "on automatic pilot" while thinking about something other than driving. But even if they are not conscious of seeing signs, red lights and so on, their driving indicates that the signs and lights have been registered as such and acted upon.[188] A more astounding example is people who are blindsighted or deafhearing. They have no conscious experience of ever seeing or hearing anything, and yet they can move well through a labyrinth, catch what is thrown to them, move towards where a sound comes from and so on.[189]

Priming is another good example. People can be shown words or pictures on a screen so quickly that they have no conscious idea what the picture or the word was, but testing afterwards shows that they must have registered and understood the words or pictures.[190] Damasio uses the example of a cocktail party: you are listening to your conversation, but the brain registers other conversations as well. Suddenly you hear your name or something else in another conversation which is marked as important so that you become conscious of it, and you start listening to that other conversation.[191]

These examples are mostly concerned with non-conscious *sensing*, although some interpretation is also involved. Below I look at emotions and the self, thinking and desiring, and give examples of non-conscious feeling, thinking and desiring. One more example, non-conscious thinking, should be cited here. Damasio and colleagues performed an experiment where people were asked to draw cards from various decks: some decks were good, i.e. leading to a reward, and some were bad, i.e. leading to a punishment. There was also a system determining which decks were good and which were bad, so that if you

---

187 For example, Mark Rowlands argues against thinking as consisting of images in the mind since one can say that the glasses are in the drawer without thinking about the glasses in the drawer, but rather be thinking about the game on TV (Mark Rowlands, *Externalism: Putting Mind and World Back Together Again* (Chesham, Bucks: Acumen, 2003), 78–79). In this case I think it is obvious that the person is thinking at least non-consciously about the glasses in the drawer, and cannot see any other plausible explanation of how he is able to answer the question of where the glasses are.
188 D. M. Armstrong, *The Nature of Mind, and Other Essays* (Ithaca, NY: Cornell University Press, 1981), 59.
189 Carruthers, *The Architecture of the Mind*, 87–88.
190 This is a well-established fact, and the reason why many commercials use subliminal stimulation.
191 Damasio, *Self Comes to Mind*, 173.

cracked the code you could just draw good cards. The subjects played the game while their skin conductance was measured. The interesting thing was that it seemed that the code was cracked non-consciously several minutes before the players understood it consciously and before they started drawing only winning cards; after a while they would get one type of skin response just before drawing from every bad deck, and another type of skin response just before drawing from every good deck. This was so consistent that somehow some part of the brain must have cracked the code, but the person could not consciously tell this and would keep drawing bad cards.[192]

Is it right to use words like "see" and "think" in contexts other than conscious seeing or thinking? This raises the question of first-person and third-person descriptions of events. Damasio formerly distinguished on the one hand between "neural patterns" or "maps" as third-person descriptions of what happens in the brain, and on the other hand "images" as first-person experiences of those neural patterns or maps.[193] In his latest book, however, he uses these terms interchangeably since he believes that they are equivalent.[194] The term "equivalent" is more ambiguous than "identical," since "identical" usually means having all the same properties, whereas "equivalent" might just mean having the same function, and Damasio probably chooses "equivalent" on purpose. Although some kind of identity theory about mind and body might be right, the most common view is that images in the mind and patterns in the brain are not identical.[195] They seem to have many different properties, so the prima facie view should be that they are not identical. Even if they are identical, it is in any case helpful to distinguish between the first- and the third-person perspective. For this reason, I shall specify whether I mean conscious images or not when I write about images.

What about "seeing" and "thinking" and words like that which usually presuppose a first-person perspective? There has been much philosophical critique of neurologists who use first-person language to describe what happens in the brain. Many neurologists speak of the brain as a person and say that the brain does things we normally just say that people do, like "seeing," "remembering," "interpreting," and "mapping."[196] It is important to be clear about the distinc-

---

192 Ibid., 276.
193 *The Feeling of What Happens*, 317–18.
194 *Self Comes to Mind*, 64–65.
195 Kim, *Philosophy of Mind*, 112–113.
196 A list of examples can be seen in Bennett, *Neuroscience and Philosophy: Brain, Mind, and Language*, 154–56.

tion between first-person and third-person perspectives when one is writing about the brain and mind. But it can also be very difficult. The reason is that humans can do so many things non-consciously in the same way as when they do them consciously. We can see, hear, smell and so on without ever being conscious about what we see, hear and smell, and yet we act as if we have seen, heard or smelled it.

Many examples were given above, like blindsight or driving without paying attention. A telling example is split-brain patients where the connection between the two hemispheres of the brain has been cut so that there is no interaction. If you flash the word "spoon" to the left eye only, so that the visual impression is sent only to the right hemisphere, and then ask the person "What did you see?" she will answer "nothing," since the left hemisphere is where most people have their language modules, and obviously nothing was registered in the right hemisphere. But if the person is allowed to put her left hand (which is controlled by the left hemisphere) in a box, she will feel around and pick up the spoon, indicating that the right hemisphere did see the word spoon and understood it.[197] In examples like this it is very tempting so say that one hemisphere saw the word and the other did not, and that the left hemisphere said that it did not see it, whereas the right hemisphere cannot speak. But usually we just use words like "see" and "speak" about people, not about cerebral hemispheres.

John Searle criticizes Damasio for saying that these non-conscious representations are part of the mind. "What is the fact that makes them mental?" Searle asks, and suggests instead that they could be understood as a non-mental step on the way to consciousness.[198] I would answer that the fact that makes them mental is that they are causally related to the objects in the world that they represent and internally related to other representations in a structurally similar way to how objects in the world relate to each other. Several reasons have been suggested for viewing these non-conscious representations as parts of the mind, largely because they perform mental functions. When a brain process can go on non-consciously and have all the same effects as a conscious process that makes it reasonable to think of it as part of the mind.

People may act as if they were consciously sensing and thinking and yet they do not. The reason they can is that the brain creates neural patterns that

---

197 A film of this experiment can be seen in Michael S. Gazzaniga, "The Distributed Networks of Mind (Gifford Lecture 2)," in The Gifford Lectures (2009), 25:30–28:00.
198 John R. Searle, "The Mystery of Consciousness Continues," *The New York Review of Books* (2011), http://www.nybooks.com/articles/archives/2011/jun/09/mystery-consciousness-continues/?pagination=false.

represent what happens in the world, and this triggers dispositions that the brain works according to. This happens all the time to everyone, and we are conscious only of a few of the things that go on in the brain. It is possible to describe it in uncontroversial third-person language, but it is much more efficient to say simply that a person "sees" the object instead of saying that the object "activates a representation of the object."[199] For instance, in the card game test described above I said that the brain cracked the code before the players did, since the skin conductance always matched the good and bad decks even if the players drew the wrong cards. The expression "crack a code" is usually used about people, but in this case it seems a very appropriate and efficient description of what has happened.

It is also difficult to distinguish clearly between first-person and third-person language since there are so many words that have been used as metaphors so frequently that they acquire a literal meaning. For example, it is common practice to write that "an argument shows," but one could complain that only people can show something, depending on how the word is defined. Above I wrote that "the brain creates neural patterns," and again one could complain that only people can create something in one definition of "create." The term can also be used, however, to mean something like "to cause."

So, on the one hand it is difficult to separate first-person and third-person language, and of course I want also to show how similar conscious and non-conscious brain processes are, since I think that what we usually call sensing, thinking, etc., implying a conscious first-person perspective, may well happen non-consciously and be correctly described in a third-person perspective. It is my aim to show the close connection between a phenomenological description from a first-person perspective and a neurological description from a third-person perspective. On the other hand, I do want to keep the distinction since I believe that consciousness and the subjective perspective make a difference, and we shall come to a discussion of what difference consciousness makes. My solution to the problem of first-person and third-person language is to use terms like thinking, feeling and so on in third-person perspective description but specify whether I refer to conscious or non-conscious activity in the brain. Hence I shall distinguish between non-conscious thinking and conscious thinking, non-conscious feeling and conscious feeling, and so on. I would say to those who

---

199 A neural pattern being "activated" means that the neurons that actualize the pattern are firing, and then the representation they constitute "occurs" in the mind. Activation need not mean that it is conscious however, as I argue with different examples of conscious and non-conscious mental events.

think that these terms are meaningless when used about non-conscious events that the examples show that the descriptions make sense after all.

Some brain activity can never become conscious (is *not* consciously experienc*eable*), some activity can become conscious (*is* consciously experience*able*, and this is called non-conscious), and some activity becomes conscious (*is* consciously experienc*ed*), and we know quite a lot about where the different things happen. It is quite specific, so that certain areas of the brain can create conscious experiences, and activity in other parts of the brain never becomes conscious. Common to the areas that create conscious experiences is that they are complex clusters with massive interconnectivity organized around a gate of input from the world outside or the body, and this fits well with the view that the brain at a certain level of complexity creates conscious experiences out of its input.[200]

3.3 Emotion

So far we have seen that the brain has dispositions and can create patterns which may serve vital functions even if they do not become conscious. Damasio mentions a small worm called *C. elegans* which has only 302 neurons. It generally approaches food alone, but if it smells danger it allies with other worms so that they can approach the food together.[201] Another example is the baby bird's reaction to a large shadow flying over it, which makes it huddle and sit still.[202] There are numerous examples of very small organisms behaving in life-preserving interaction with their environment, where there is no reason to argue that there must be conscious thinking or conscious feelings involved, since everything that happens can be explained as simple dispositions resulting from causal stimulus and response.

The automatic response to stimuli has evolved into the advanced responses that we call emotions. For example, the disposition to spit out something poisonous evolved into the general emotion of disgust which makes us avoid a lot of unhealthy things.[203] But how did this development happen? Homeostasis is again an important part of the answer. In advanced organisms the brain contains a representation of the body in homeostasis which can be compared with a

---

[200] Damasio, *Self Comes to Mind*, 86–87.
[201] Ibid., 57.
[202] *The Feeling of What Happens*, 69.
[203] *Self Comes to Mind*, 117.

representation of the body as it is now. Those brains which could detect a difference and make something happen to restore the body to homeostasis would be selected by evolution.[204]

In even more advanced organisms, the brain could detect the degree of departure from homeostasis and the degree of need for correction. An example would be registering whether there was little need for food or great need for food, and then creating the response, i.e. our being a little hungry or very hungry, which would make us eat a little or a lot. In order to make the organism act to achieve homeostasis, incentives or disincentives like pleasure and pain are required. I have used words like "hungry," "pain" and "pleasure," and it seems that these states require consciousness in order to make sense. For how can anyone be motivated to achieve pleasure if the pleasure is not consciously experienced? Actually, emotions and incentives need not necessarily be consciously experienced in order to function as they do. All that is required are some "If presence of A, then act by doing B" dispositions in the brain, and this can explain the actions performed by the organism.[205]

Another advance made by organisms was the evolved ability to detect likely threats (animal with sharp teeth approaching) or likely delivery of goods (partner preparing to have sex). It is important for the organism to have rules on when to move and some motivation that actually makes the organism move. This is achieved by the brain sending out molecules through the blood vessels and signals through the nerves to warn the organism and prepare the right response. This is an important part of what emotions are about, and fear is a good example: something is registered as threatening, and the brain sends out molecules that prepare the body for fight or flight. In this way, emotions allow for more differentiated and optimized responses to stimuli than automatic action-responses.[206]

Damasio distinguishes between emotions and feelings. An emotion is a series of events happening in the body. A neural pattern representing something in the body or the world outside activates trigger regions of the brain, which sends out various chemical molecules in the blood and different signals through the nerves. This prepares the body for certain actions and usually also triggers certain kinds of thoughts. As Damasio says, running from a gunman, you do not

---

[204] Ibid., 48–49.
[205] Ibid., 52. For examples, see how Peter Carruthers explains very many workings of our mind by employing such "If A, then B" dispositions, in Carruthers, *The Architecture of the Mind*.
[206] Damasio, *Self Comes to Mind*, 54.

think about what to make for dinner tonight.[207] An *emotion* is therefore a series of events which places the body in a certain state. A *feeling* on the other hand is a term Damasio uses to denote a neural pattern in the brain representing the body's being in that state of emotion. It is a neural pattern representing the body's being, for example, in a state of fear or happiness or anger. This neural pattern may become conscious or not, which means that we need to distinguish between emotions (a series of events in the body), non-conscious feelings (a neural pattern in the brain) and conscious feelings (a consciously experienced feeling/neural pattern).[208]

Only conscious feelings are experienced consciously from a first-person perspective. It may seem strange to speak about non-conscious feelings, but again there are good reasons to distinguish between them. Non-conscious feelings can become activated and change our body state before we become consciously aware of what we are feeling. I have already mentioned how the body can react emotionally to pictures shown so fast that they are not consciously registered. Another example is when we suddenly realize that we are anxious, tense, uncomfortable, pleased or relaxed, and it is obvious that that state of feeling must have begun before we noticed it.[209] Yet another example is the case of David, who was unable to consciously remember any events that had happened and just lived in the moment. When exposed to several people, some of whom were nice to him and others not so nice, he could not remember any of them later. He was then shown pictures of the same people and he did not recognize any of them or consciously feel anything identicalfor any of them; they all appeared to be strangers. If asked which of them he would ask for a favor, however, he picked the ones who had been nice to him.[210] This seems to suggest that he had a non-conscious memory of people and also a non-conscious memory of a good feeling connected with them, which then made him select as he did.

The distinction made here is that between emotions as body states and feelings as neural representations of that body state, which may become conscious or not. There are some universally recognized emotions, namely happiness, sadness, anger, fear, surprise and disgust.[211] Several of these emotions have

---

207 Ibid., 144.
208 Ibid., 109–10, 14.
209 *The Feeling of What Happens*, 36.
210 They made sure there were some pretty women among those who were mean to him so David would not select people for their looks.
211 Ibid., 50.

their own distinct physical patterns in the body, meaning that a scientist with the right apparatus can to some degree know what you feel without your telling her.[212] Again, there are many aspects of emotions and feelings which support the idea that they have evolved as survival-enhancing mechanisms rather than something ontologically unique in another dimension of mind. The basic emotions have distinct physical patterns, and areas of the brain can be stimulated electrically to make people feel extreme anger or fear.[213] The fact that we have the basic emotions we do, with their clear survival value, also suggests their origin in evolution. Even the fact that feelings show in the face can be explained with evolutionary reasons.[214] These facts all fit well with an evolutionary account of our mental life.

A survey of feelings becomes much more complex as feelings combine with different thoughts, as then we can speak of many different feelings, although what is happening in the body may be very similar.[215] Damasio himself distinguishes between universal emotions, social emotions, background emotions, moods, drives and motivational states. These distinctions are not so important here, although we shall return to drives and motivations when we look at desire.[216] Pain and pleasure are important for our topic, however, so where do they fit into this picture? Many feelings have incentive and disincentive functions. Some are negative and can be experienced as punishment; they are meant to make the organism withdraw from something negative. Others are positive and can be experienced as rewards; these are meant to make the organism approach something positive. Pain is clearly negative, but it is almost as basic as an au-

---

212 Ibid., 61.
213 Electrical stimulation of the hypothalamus can cause extreme rage, and electrical stimulation of the amygdala can cause both fear and rage (Joseph, *Neuropsychiatry, Neuropsychology, and Clinical Neuroscience*, 173–74, 82–83).
214 Steven Pinker, *How the Mind Works* (New York: Norton, 1997), 414–15.
215 Damasio speaks of secondary emotions, which are combinations of cognitive states and basic emotions, and these can evoke numerous feelings with subtle variations, like the differences between euphoria and ecstasy based on happiness, or melancholy or wistfulness based on sadness, or panic and shyness based on fear, and so on (Damasio, *Descartes' Error*, 134, 49–50). Feelings like jealousy, envy, *schadenfreude*, etc., may feel quite similar. In an experiment, people were given a drug which puts the body in a certain state. When different groups were in the same room with an actor behaving a certain way, the people interpreted their own feelings in the same way as the actor behaved (S. Schachter and J. E. Singer, "Cognitive, Social, and Physiological Determinants of Emotional State," *Psychological Review* 69, no. 5 (1962)).
216 Damasio, *Self Comes to Mind*, 111, 22–26.

tomatic response to a stimulus.[217] It has the function of making the organism withdraw from that which creates the pain. Pleasure is a common name for different good feelings, and motivates the organism for doing things that are good for survival and a good life but also for sexual reproduction.[218]

So far I have said that feelings arise when the organism senses something in the outside world or its own body, and I shall argue that this is often an important influence when people make choices. An emotional influence of the body which is important for understanding free will is the fact that we can remember earlier emotional experiences we have had. When we are about to make an important choice we can remember earlier relevant events which evoke feelings that influence the choice we are about to make. Feelings are stored in memory and influence choices, and this is a good reason to take a closer look at memory.

3.4 Memory

Damasio starts his chapter on memory with a telling example from Scott Fitzgerald's *Tender is the Night*. After witnessing a woman shoot her lover at the train station, the character Dick Diver asks: "Will any of us ever see a train pulling out without hearing a few shots?" The remark illustrates several important points about memory. The brain can reproduce events in our mind regardless of our choosing. Memories are stored together with the feelings that we reacted to the situation with, and the more emotional memories are better remembered and more easily recalled. This is generally an advantage for humans, since it often makes us recall important earlier events when we are in similar situations and can take advantage of what we learned the last time. But it can be a disadvantage for particular individuals, for example, people with post-traumatic stress disorder who constantly recall horrible events. It is not the event alone

---

[217] The area which is hurt sends signals to the brain through special nerve cells called C-fibers and A-δ-fibers. The destroyed cells in the area release chemicals and these also send a signal to the brain. The input from these different fibers and nerve cells creates representations in the brain of the body being in pain in a certain area, and as these patterns become conscious we have a conscious experience of being in pain (*The Feeling of What Happens*, 71–73). The same C-fibers also mediate itching, but they cannot be used for both itching and pain, so if you are itching in an area which is then hurt the itch will disappear and only the pain will be experienced (Uwe Gieler and Bertram Walter, "Scratch This!," *Scientific American MIND* 19, no. 3 (2008): 54–56).
[218] Damasio, *Self Comes to Mind*, 52–53.

that is stored in the memory, but our relation and reaction to the event and our feeling at the time.[219]

Several different functions of feelings have been mentioned, but feelings have another function as well, which has to do with memory and choice. Damasio has put forward a hypothesis known as the somatic marker hypothesis. The main point is that neural patterns representing events in the world are connected to feelings which give the different neural patterns different levels of importance. This explains what we become conscious of both in sensing and in remembering, for at any one time there are numerous neural patterns that could have become conscious: the ones that are more important because of their connected feeling are selected by the brain, which has a disposition for selecting the ones with the strongest feelings attached to them.[220] If I throw something towards your face, it will catch your attention even if you are busy with something else, because clearly organisms need to become consciously aware of things about to hit their face. Other factors complicate this picture, but the connected feelings are an important part of explaining which images we become conscious of.[221]

Furthermore, the somatic marker hypothesis explains how people make efficient choices despite the so-called "frame problem" which means that in any situation there are numerous things that could be considered before one makes a choice, which would delay the choice for a long time. But when feelings are connected to the different images, the brain sorts them according to importance and generally makes the choice much easier. Damasio supports this hypothesis with findings from patients whose brain injuries left all knowledge and logical capabilities intact but whose feelings of emotions were lost. They then also lost their ability to make rational decisions.[222]

All of this is important for the understanding of deliberation and free will, since when we are deciding what to do in important situations memories and feelings will often be activated (without us choosing that that should happen) and influence what we think and feel about the different alternatives for action, thereby influencing or changing our initial desires. Which alternatives pop into

---

[219] *The Feeling of What Happens*, 130–32.
[220] Which feelings are the strongest also has an evolutionary base: those who experience food and sex as strongly positive and being hurt as strongly negative pass on their genes more often.
[221] Damasio, *Self Comes to Mind*, 174–75.
[222] *The Feeling of What Happens*, 40–42. For example, Damasio gave such a person a choice of two dates for their next meeting, and he wavered between the two dates for almost half an hour before Damasio stopped him and decided the date for him (*Descartes' Error*, 193).

mind may seem undetermined, but may nevertheless be a regular causal process with no indeterminism in it. Much more will be said about this in the next chapter.

There are different kinds of memories which must be stored somewhat differently since it is possible to lose all memories of one kind but not those of another. Short-term and long-term memory is a distinction most people know of. It is also usual to distinguish between procedural memory (remembering how to play the guitar or ride a bicycle) and fact memory (remembering facts or events). There are some who cannot consciously remember what a thing is or does, but are still able to use it correctly because of their procedural memory. A more interesting distinction for our topic is that between general facts and episodic memories. One patient, E.D., could remember many facts about Kilimanjaro without remembering having been on the top of it.[223] Damasio mentions a person who looked at pictures and correctly identified them as portraying a wedding, but he did not remember that it was his own wedding.[224] Most important for the question of free will are fact memories and memories of past events. The reason is that fact memories activate images of alternative actions that can be chosen, which again activate autobiographical memories and feelings connected to each alternative possibility for action.[225] I shall argue later that these memories influence the initial desires we feel and thereby the choice that is made.

3.5 Consciousness

The evolutionary understanding of humans and their minds is that they are organisms made out of cells. They receive input like light waves and sound waves through their sense organs, and these give rise to neural patterns in the brain. In addition there are consciously experienced images, like the sight of a red tomato, the sound of a trumpet, or the feeling of hunger, and there are thoughts, such as the thought that Hitler died in 1945. But what are these images and thoughts? Where are they? Who is seeing them or thinking them? If you close your eyes and imagine a car, you are not actually seeing a car with your eyes and there is no car in your brain, so where is this conscious experience of a

---

[223] Hans J. Markowitsch, "Neuropsychologie des menschlichen Gedächtnisses," *Spektrum der Wissenschaft (Digest: Rätsel Gehirn)*, no. 4 (2004): 52.
[224] Damasio, *Self Comes to Mind*, 138–40.
[225] *Descartes' Error*, 196.

car? A trumpet can make the air vibrate, which again makes little hairs in your ears vibrate and this gives rise to a consciously heard sound. If some of those hairs are damaged, they can start moving on their own and the brain interprets it as an incoming sound, resulting in tinnitus and constant sound.[226] But out there in the world there are only air and hair vibrating, and there is no sound in the brain, so where is this consciously heard sound? And where is the thought that Hitler died in 1945? We might find the neurons that give rise to the thought that Hitler died in 1945, but they are not the conscious thought. Let us assume that the neurons giving rise to the thought that Hitler died in 1945 occupy two millimeters of space in the brain: would anyone say that this thought about Hitler is two millimeters long? And *who* is seeing the car, hearing the sound, and thinking the thought if there is just an organism consisting of a lot of cells? None of the single cells or neurons can see or hear or think, so what is this self that can see, hear and think?

Damasio refers to these problems as the two problems of consciousness, although he also points out that they are tightly interconnected: what are the conscious images, and what is the self that experiences the images? The conscious images are often referred to as qualia, but the term is defined in many different ways. Damasio defines it as sensory qualities to be found, for example, in colors and tones,[227] but I will define it more widely to include all mental states with a subjective character, including thoughts.[228] I use this wide definition since the key problems seem to be the same: they are subjective experiences requiring a self, they are private and possible to introspect, and they are difficult to locate in space. I also define it this way since I agree with the neuroscientist V. S. Ramachandran that qualia associated with perception (seeing a blue car) and qualia associated with thoughts (imagining a blue car) are closely

---

226 Gary G. Matthews, *Introduction to Neuroscience*, 11th Hour (Malden, MA: Blackwell Science, 2000), 101. The tinnitus example also strongly supports the idea that the brain creates conscious experiences.

227 I refer here to Damasio's 1999 book, since the definitions he gives of the problem of consciousness and of qualia are much clearer there than the definitions in his 2010 book; see *Self Comes to Mind*, 157–79, 253–62.

228 There are various opinions on how widely the term should be defined. Jaegwon Kim gives a narrower definition than the one I suggest, whereas John Searle has the wider definition I suggest here (John R. Searle, *Consciousness and Language* (New York: Cambridge University Press, 2002), 40, and Kim, *Philosophy of Mind*, 15).

linked to each other with more of a quantitative difference (degree of vividness) than a qualitative difference—a view that Damasio seems to share.[229]

A famous definition of qualia is that there is something it is like for a subject to experience them.[230] Presumably it is not like anything for a hat to be a hat or for a hat to hear a trumpet sound,[231] but there is something it is like for me to be me, or for me to hear a trumpet sound, and the trumpet sound is different from a flute sound because they are different qualia. Qualia defined like this are the same as phenomenal consciousness, the qualitative experiences we are aware of, like sense impressions, thoughts, feelings, and desires. This is also how Damasio uses the term *consciousness*, and it is how it is used in this book.

There are three entities that need to be distinguished in Damasio's theory of the mind; wakefulness, mind and self. As mentioned, Damasio thinks that the mind can work without being conscious. For him, "the mind" is the neural patterns, but these require cooperation with a self in order to become conscious. There can be no consciousness without a self, although a quite minimal self might be enough.[232]

This means that in Damasio's definition of the mind there can be a functioning mind without a self, although there cannot be consciousness without at least a minimal self. As noted above, Damasio claims that there is abundant evidence showing that a mind (not just brain activity, but understanding) can work non-consciously. Another example is that of patients in a coma whose brains were scanned; they were told to think of tennis if they meant to answer yes, and to think of the way home if they meant to answer no. The brain scans showed a clear difference between their thoughts about tennis and their thoughts about the way home. The patients were asked yes or no questions, and the scanner revealed whether they were thinking about tennis (yes) or the way

---

229 Damasio distinguishes between perceptual and recalled images, and says that a recalled image is less vivid than a perceptual image, but it is the same patterns in the brain that are active when an object is perceived and recalled (Damasio, *Descartes' Error*, 96–97, 101, 08). This fits with my own experience: If I visualize something with my eyes closed at daytime, I get a poor and blurry image very different from seeing something live, but just before I go to sleep, I visualize things much more life-like, and of course dreams can be as vivid as experiences at daytime.
230 Thomas Nagel, "What Is It Like to Be a Bat?," *The Philosophical Review* 83, no. 4 (1974): 436.
231 Even if panpsychism should be true, consciousness at the lowest levels would not be anything like consciousness at our level.
232 Damasio, *Self Comes to Mind*, 159–61.

home (no). By so doing they could answer detailed questions correctly, like: Is your father's name Alexander? Yes. Is your father's name Thomas? No.[233]

Another example is patients with certain epileptic seizures called epileptic automatism. Such patients can for a period of time have an empty look in their eyes and not respond to language but walk around aimlessly and perform actions with minimal purposes, e.g. picking up an empty cup and trying to drink from it or walking through a door. Picking up a cup to drink means that the cup must have been recognized as a cup, but there is otherwise no sign of consciousness or self-presence. So, there can be wakefulness and a functioning mind, as there probably is in many of the smallest animals, but only when a self is added is there the subjectivity that makes consciousness possible.[234]

There are two kinds of consciousness which it is useful to distinguish when we talk about the self. The distinction may not be a sharp one but rather denote differences on a continuous scale. These differences concern the *scope* of consciousness. Damasio calls the minimal scope consciousness "core consciousness," which is consciousness about being a self here and now. Big scope consciousness, on the other hand, Damasio refers to as "extended consciousness"; he also calls it autobiographical consciousness. This kind of consciousness is able to be conscious about several things at once, and it is called autobiographical since, with this kind of consciousness, we can be consciously aware of our own past and future.[235] The distinction between these two kinds of consciousness is legitimized by the fact that people can lose their extended consciousness but retain their core consciousness.[236]

3.6 The Self

These two kinds of consciousness are tightly connected to stages of the development of the self. As seen above, Damasio thinks that the brain creates consciousness by adding a self process to wakefulness and mind. But how did the self develop? I spend some time on this since it helps us understand who the agent is who has free will. Damasio argues that the self was built in three different stages. I will present these stages in more detail after a quick overview first

---

233 Martin M. Monti et al., "Willful Modulation of Brain Activity in Disorders of Consciousness," *New England Journal of Medicine*, no. 362 (2010).
234 Damasio, *Self Comes to Mind*, 161–66.
235 Ibid., 168–69.
236 *The Feeling of What Happens*, 17.

to make it easier to follow. The first stage is the proto-self, which is a neural pattern representing the whole organism. This proto-self produces a primordial feeling, which is the feeling of my own body existing, but without any further connection to the world. In addition to the proto-self, the brain creates neural patterns representing objects and events in the world, but it also creates neural patterns representing the relationship between the organism and the outside world. From moment to moment there is a series of neural patterns representing how the organism changes in relation to the outside world. This creates changes in the primordial feeling which are consciously felt as an experience of changes in the world. The representations of change create pulses of core consciousness that together constitute the core self, which is the second stage. The core self is this series of consciously experienced changes that arise because of the neural patterns representing changes in the body in relation to the world outside. Finally, these conscious experiences can be held together in extended consciousness to create the autobiographical self, which is a neural pattern representing the life story of a person, created by memories and continuously reconstructed.

In more detail: Damasio defines the proto-self as "an integrated collection of separate neural patterns that map, moment by moment, the most stable aspects of the organism's physical structure."[237] The proto-self is constituted by three different kinds of neural patterns (which Damasio calls "maps"). The first kind represents the body—not the whole body, but the most stable parts of the body. Damasio argues that that is important, since it can explain the stability of the self process, and this is also the reason for the last part of the definition of the proto-self. It is this representation of the body which gives rise to the primordial feeling, which is the basis for all other feelings. The second kind of neural pattern which constitutes the proto-self is a general representation of how the main parts of the body relate to each other when the body is not moving, and it is then constantly compared with patterns representing how the body is moving right now. The third kind of neural pattern is representations of the sensory portals of the body (eyes, ears, nose, tongue, skin), and these have the function of locating where the body is relative to the sense impressions. Not only do we see and hear, but we also feel that we see with our eyes and hear with our ears. This creates an experience of having a certain perspective and particular location in the world.[238]

Damasio does not think that the proto-self and primordial feeling are enough to account for the phenomenon of self which we humans experience

---

[237] *Self Comes to Mind*, 190. Emphasis in original.
[238] Ibid., 190–98.

today. Had it only been a proto-self its experience would have consisted only of a primordial feeling of being a self from moment to moment with no connection to anything. What is needed is a clear experience of being a protagonist connected to events in the world, and Damasio thinks that this happens in the following way: When the organism encounters something, this changes the organism and makes the brain construct a new pattern representing the change. The change in the proto-self leads to a change in the primordial feeling, and this change is experienced as a conscious experience of the object. But it is also experienced as something happening to a protagonist, to a self. The narrative of objects encountering a body and giving rise to different feelings in the body also suggests that there is a protagonist to whom things happen, who feels and acts and has a sense of ownership of the experiences. The self is, so to speak, deduced from the narrative and experienced as such a self.[239] Damasio has also described it by saying that our conscious mind is like a movie, and when we ask who is watching the film the answer is that the watcher is a part of the movie.[240]

I find it useful to distinguish between a minimal self or basic subjectivity and the more complete sense of self which the core self is. By "basic subjectivity" I mean the phenomenon that something is like something *for* something or someone, and I shall argue that this is presumably what Damasio means by his "primordial feeling." Something cannot be *like* something unless it is like something *for* something or someone. What is expressed in this "*for* something or someone" is what I mean by basic subjectivity. Even if the core self can be deduced from changes in primordial feeling, it requires a basic subjective element in the primordial feelings in the first place. What I want to do here is to add some support for the idea that the core self can be deduced from changes in primordial feelings.

A sense of self, by which I mean a sense of being a single conscious subject, may not need to imply a physical or non-physical continuous self which has this sense of self. Pete Mandik has argued that a self can be deduced from experiences in the same way that we can see a picture and deduce that there must have been a camera at such and such an angle and distance from what is seen in the picture. The perspective and distance suggest where the camera must have been to take the picture, but the picture may have been computer-generated and given a certain perspective. Mandik's point is that there are a lot of subjectively conscious experiences going on in the brain which may create a

---

239 Ibid., 201–04.
240 "Wie das Gehirn Geist erzeugt," *Spektrum der Wissenschaft (Digest: Rätsel Gehirn)*, no. 4 (2004): 11.

sense or thought that it must have been a self having these experiences, but in fact there is just a series of experiences including the experience that there is a self having the experiences. We understand temperature as hot or cold and we experience things as good or bad relative to ourselves. But there could be something in the nature of the experience that makes us assume a continuous self is having the experiences even if there is no such continuous self. Perhaps there is just a series of experiences, pulses of core consciousness, which give the illusion of a self owning the experiences—and even the sense of a self as the agent of certain events even if they just happen as a causal chain of micro events.[241]

But must it not be *someone* who deduces that there is a self? No, the suggestion is that there are subjective experiences out of which a self arises. Ontological subjectivity is therefore a feature of the world, as argued by John Searle,[242] which can create a self. This does not explain what basic subjectivity is, or how basic subjectivity is possible at all, but it is an explanation of how a full-blown self can arise from experiences that are subjective in a basic sense.

The third stage in the development of the self is the autobiographical self. The autobiographical self consists of our memories, including memories of our thoughts about the future and who we are. Whereas the core self is always present, either in focus as self-awareness or in the background since attention is on something else, the autobiographical self is either dormant or active. It is important to understand that every time memories are recalled, they are modified a little, and the feelings they are connected with may change a little. This means that the autobiographical self is reconstructed all the time.[243]

The autobiographical self can be constructed only because the extended consciousness is able to hold several elements present over time. Different memories can become conscious to a person and grouped together or seen in

---

[241] Pete Mandik, "Mental Representation and the Subjectivity of Consciousness," *Philosophical Psychology* 14, no. 2 (2001).

[242] John R. Searle, "Biological Naturalism," in *The Blackwell Companion to Consciousness*, ed. Max Velmans and Susan Schneider (Malden, MA: Blackwell, 2007), 327.

[243] Damasio, *Self Comes to Mind*, 210–11. Interestingly, this explains how (parts of) psychoanalysis work(s): non-conscious memories from childhood might be activated in the mind or in dreams, but without becoming conscious to the awake person. If there are bad feelings connected with the memories, these may create more negative feelings or problems like anxiety or depression, while the memory itself is still non-conscious. When the memory is recollected in consciousness, new feelings are connected to it in the same way as all recalled memories. But now one may see the incident in a whole new light, or relate to it in a safe context, and connect new feelings with the memory which might stop or reduce the negative influence on the person.

the light of each other, thus giving a coherent picture of who that person is. I have already mentioned Damasio's somatic marker hypothesis, which is important fact for understanding free will. It says that every time an image is recalled, it is automatically marked with a certain value in the way that a certain feeling expresses this value it is connected with, and this valuation is constantly revised. The image of who we are—our autobiographical self—is also marked by such a feeling and constantly revised. Damasio argues that this marking depends partly on preset dispositions acquired through evolution, so that things which are important for survival are considered important. But the marking also depends on values acquired through life, things we have come to see as important for us in the light of our individual experiences and reflections.[244] This will become important in the next chapter, because it means that things we have come to see as important through our experiences and thoughts are stored in our autobiographical self and influence the later choices we make.

It is useful at this point to sum up the terminology concerning the self that will be used in the rest of the book. The core self is the stream-like and narrow-scoped consciousness of what happens here and now together with a feeling of what that is like. It is a series of conscious events—the stream of consciousness consisting of experienced qualia. The core self is a process of conscious experiences, and the physical basis for the core self is patterns representing changes in the interaction between the proto-self and the environment. The autobiographical self is a person's understanding of herself based on memories and their connected feelings. The autobiographical self is a physical neural pattern which can become conscious. This image of oneself also influences how it feels to be that person in any moment of core self-consciousness, and this will be covered in fine detail in the next chapter.

Sensing, thinking, feeling, desiring and remembering happen in our mind consciously and non-consciously, and the different terms will be defined shortly. When something in the mind is conscious it is still very dependent on what happens in the brain, and what happens in the brain is influenced by input from the body and the world outside. The core self is the consciously experienced sense that this sensing, thinking, feeling, desiring and remembering is all happening to one self. Every person is born with a slightly differently working body and a differently working brain. Every person also has unique experiences in life. The inputs from the world and the body, and how that is received by the individual brains and bodies, create different sense impressions, thoughts,

---

244 Ibid., 212–14; *Descartes' Error*, 177–80.

feelings and desires in every individual. These sense impressions, thoughts, feelings and desires are stored as memories. Some memories are stored for a long time, some for a short time, and some are easily recalled, and others not. Because of these memories, in the continued process of input to the mind from the body and the world, there is also input to the mind from the memories stored in the brain, influencing what is felt, thought and desired.

Memories of what has happened—consciously or non-consciously—in the mind (sensing, thinking, feeling, desiring) constantly return to the mind and influence what happens in the mind the next time. A person has experiences and these lead to feelings and thoughts that are stored in the memory. The more memories of thoughts and feelings a person has connected to her experiences, the more and more these memories will influence what the person desires later, since desires also depend on what we feel about different alternatives (as I argue under "Desire" below). The autobiographical self is a collection of memories of thoughts and feelings which influences the desires and choices of every person. Our choices are not only influenced by the autobiographical self, since we are born with many dispositions and other non-chosen influences (e.g., a non-chosen acquired mental disorder) that can also come into play. But the autobiographical self becomes a larger and larger influence on most people's choices during their lives, since a larger and larger collection of thoughts and experiences can be remembered and they influence future choices.

I use the terms "person" and "agent" interchangeably for a living human body with a mind and a core self. What happens in the core self is stored as memories and added to the autobiographical self, which in turn influences what happens in the core self. The term "autobiographical self" can be understood in several different ways. Every person has many experiences and these are stored as memories. A neural pattern is constructed in the brain representing the person who has had these experiences, and this is a coherent pattern of important memories. This pattern changes over time and can become conscious. This neural pattern is what I mean by 'the autobiographical self," and although it can be seen as a process over time, I use it largely to mean the neural pattern as it is today or at the time of discussion. The autobiographical self is not all my memories, but a selection, and although it can become conscious, not all details of this neural pattern can be conscious at the same time. For some people there are probably parts of their autobiographical self that never become conscious, and this means that they may have a conscious understanding of themselves that does not match their autobiographical self as neural pattern at all points. For example, they may have experienced something disgraceful which they nonconsciously deny ever happened as a survival technique. They may think that they handle certain situations well, but in these situations the non-conscious and denied memory may still be non-consciously activated so that they behave strangely in these situations—which they may also fail to realize.

I will end this subchapter by noting some meanings of the terms "self" and "sense of self" on which I do not focus in the rest of the book. I have already mentioned the primordial feeling based on the proto-self, which is the subjective experience of being present, whereas the core self is the experience of being an agent owning the experiences, and this experience is based on representations of changes happening to the proto-self. This experience explains why agents feel that they own their actions even if there is no homunculus inside our body but rather a series of causal processes happening in the mind. The sense of being someone who acts is based on the fact that actions follow intentions.[245]

The term "sense of self" can include many different experiences. There is the sense of presence, which is the primordial feeling. There is the sense of being *one*, which is based on our unified conscious experience, and I shall discuss this further in the next subchapter. There is the sense of being one with your body, which is based on the core self experience of being a protagonist to whom changes happen, and this is the same as the sense of ownership of your own experiences. The sense of where your body is and how it is positioned is based on a constant comparison between a master map of the body in repose and the position of the limbs relative to this.[246] The sense of where you are located in the world is based on the perspective of your conscious images.

What about the sense of identity over time? Since a person can consciously remember what has happened to this body with this core self, the person will have a sense of persisting identity over time, and identify with that same body and its core self of several years ago. The memories are what give the *sense* of persistent identity, but the greater metaphysical debate about what constitutes identity over time from a third-person perspective is beyond the scope of this book.[247] Most important for the question of free will is the autobiographical self,

---

[245] Similar distinctions are made in Shaun Gallagher, "Philosophical Conceptions of the Self: Implications for Cognitive Science," *Trends in Cognitive Sciences* 4, no. 1 (2000).

[246] This sense can be disturbed, and scientists have managed to stimulate an area of the brain which allows them to create out-of-body-experiences for the person so stimulated (Olaf Blanke et al., "Neuropsychology: Stimulating Illusory Own-Body Perceptions," *Nature* 419, no. 19 September (2002)). There are also many simple experiments that one can perform on oneself to disturb this sense; see for example Hirstein and Ramachandran, in Gallagher and Shear, *Models of the Self*, 105–07.

I do think, however, that at this level of detail many paradoxes about continuous personal identity dissolve. Examples of such paradoxes are each half of your body united with another

the neural pattern which represents a person's life right now and is a product of earlier thoughts, feelings and actions influencing future choices.

Whereas the core self is a series of conscious experiences, the proto-self and the autobiographical self are physical neural patterns, and the person is the combination of a physical substrate including the physical mind, representations in the brain, and the conscious experience of the core self. What about the concept of "the self"? (I will not use this term in isolation hereafter, but specify just which self I am referring to.) It is normal to think of the self/agent/person as a continuous entity which is the cause of actions. But the core self is not one entity with a continuous existence; rather it is a continuous series of experiences only interrupted by certain forms of sleep and anesthesia/coma. As I shall argue in chapter four, actions are caused by desires triggering motor neurons, and these desires can be caused by the autobiographical self or other causes. It is the physical substrates which give the experience of continuity, the sense of identity with the body and memories, even if both the memories and the body change gradually. Much of what happens in our conscious mind depends on non-conscious physical activity in the brain and body. So those who wish to speak of the self as continuous or a cause of actions should include a physical aspect of the self. I find it better to leave out the concept of "the self" altogether in favor of more precise terms.

As regards these concepts - agent, person, core self, autobiographical self— what does the term "I" refer to? What do I identify with when referring to my-

---

half, or that each particle in your body was removed and replaced one at a time while you are anesthetized, so that two identical replicas are created, and the question is: which of them is you? "You" is ambiguous, since it can refer to the person, the autobiographical self or the core self. What happens is that the physical structure of the body and the autobiographical self are made into two versions of the original. These two bodies and autobiographical selves now give rise to one core self each, which in their first waking moment have exactly the same memories, but from the next moment on have distinct experiences, thoughts and feelings and start to change their autobiographical selves into two different autobiographical selves. One person has turned into two, just as it sometimes happens that an embryo splits into two and gives rise to twins. Jack in 2011 becomes Jack 1 and Jack 2 in 2012. Jack 1 and Jack 2 were Jack in 2011, but neither of them is Jack 2011 anymore. This is what has happened, so there is no philosophical reason to be imprecise and insist that one of them must be the original Jack, although Jack's wife might have pragmatic reasons for seeing it differently (may I pragmatically suggest to Jack's wife that we make a copy of her as well, and then the two new couples can share house, money and responsibility for their children?). Derek Parfit argues well that what should matter to people when it comes to survival is psychological connectedness and/or continuity for any causal reason (Derek Parfit, *Reasons and Persons* (Oxford: Clarendon Press, 1984), part three). I generally support Parfit's take on the discussion of personal identity.

self? When I want to be the cause of my choices, what is the cause that is *I*? I certainly identify with a body with a conscious mind which can act now. But I also identify with the same body with a conscious mind at earlier stages which made choices that shaped the autobiographical self I have today. When the term "I" is used in daily life, it can refer to several different things – a body, a core self, an autobiographical self - now and over time, but even if the term is ambiguous in daily speech, it should be precise here. When I, the author of this book, use the terms "I" or "my" about myself it refers to a particular body with a mind, a core self, and an autobiographical self from its birth and development in 1977 until today. In other words, when people say "I," in my definition they refer to that which I define as a person, and the autobiographical self that persons usually develop over time.

There are so many philosophical problems that it is difficult to give a coherent definition of what a person is and what the conditions are for (personal) identity over time, but the most important question is what actually exists in the world, and that is bodies with minds and core selves which usually develop autobiographical selves over time. I suggest that the term "I" should be thought of as referring to this whole configuration of structures (a body with a mind and core self and usually an autobiographical self), but in daily speech it is often ambiguous what "I" refers to since it refers to different parts of this configuration. Thus, if I say that I am six feet tall, "I" refers to the body which is so tall, but if I say that I am thinking, "I" refers to the conscious brain activity that occurs in the same body. Or I can say that I was 25 years old ten years ago and refer to the body, the memories of which are stored in my autobiographical self now.

If the concepts of person and personal identity over time cannot consistently integrate the facts, the problem may be in the concepts and the theoretical framework used to explain them. That "I" refers to such a configuration and its parts is not a problem in the configuration ontology of Lorenz Puntel, although it may well be a problem in a substance ontology.

3.7 The Function of Consciousness

Damasio does not have much to say about what consciousness is and how it is possible for the brain to create consciousness. He thinks that at the beginning of the history of consciousness there were some first flickers of subjectivity, some early proto-feelings, a first spark of consciousness—and that these scaled up to become the full-blown subjectivity, feelings and consciousness we know today.[248] Damasio believes that further investigation of this is the way to go in order to find out what is this proto-sensitivity which can be scaled up to consciousness, but he does not claim to have solved the qualia problem.[249]

We have seen much support for the claim that the brain causes consciousness and can function non-consciously and that physical events precede conscious experiences. But if mental events are causal in virtue of physical properties, does that not lead to epiphenomenalism, which is the view that consciousness does not have causal power but only follows physical processes like a shadow? Most philosophers want to avoid epiphenomenalism since experience seems to support the causal efficacy of conscious beliefs and desires and since it seems very unlikely that evolution would have selected conscious processes if they have no effect. This is reason enough to ask for the function of consciousness. It may seem to play no role in Damasio's understanding of the mind, but many will reject a theory where consciousness does not have any function, and so this objection must be discussed.

What does Damasio think about the function of consciousness? He thinks that consciousness has several functions and that it would not have been selected by evolution if it did not. First, he notes that pain as punishment and pleasure as reward are more efficient in guiding an organism's behavior if they feel like something. Note that they do not *have to* feel like something, for there could be a disposition in the organism to avoid situations which activate the physical substrates of pain and to seek situations which activate the physical substrates of pleasure. But if they also feel like something, that increases the efficiency of their guiding function.[250] Second, he notes that it is advantageous if there is a conscious self which is concerned with what happens now and later and has conscious feelings connected with this.[251] When the conscious mind started using language and reasoning it made detailed planning and deliberation possible. A great advantage of this was the ability to imagine possible scenarios and evaluate them. This in turn made choices possible, like choosing a long-term good instead of a short-term good, or making compromises and sacrifices as elements of a greater plan.[252]

---

248 Damasio, *Self Comes to Mind*, 252–53.
249 Ibid., 256–58, 62.
250 Damasio, *Self Comes to Mind*, 259.
251 Ibid., 267–68.
252 Ibid., 268.

There are many examples showing that the brain can do its work better when not conscious, mainly because of its capacity for parallel processing. Damasio mentions the Dijksterhuis experiment whereby people were briefly shown information about houses and cars, but not allowed to think consciously about which were best; they chose the better houses and cars, but those who were allowed to reflect consciously about which houses and cars were best made poorer choices.[253]

There are many other similar experiments where people are not able to solve a problem consciously but when they are allowed to sleep or think of something else, the problem is solved non-consciously. I have already mentioned the card game experiment in which the bodies of the participants showed that some part of their brains had cracked the code before they did so consciously. In another experiment, subjects were given a tedious task. There was a simple way of doing the job, but the subjects were not told about it. After a while, one group of subjects went to sleep, but the others stayed awake doing something else. When they returned, 59% of those who had slept figured out the simple way of doing the job, but only 23% of those who had not slept did so. The experiment indicates that the brain works on solving problems while we sleep, even when we are not conscious there is a problem to solve.[254] Personally, I experience something similar very often. Almost always when I have struggled with a crossword and can go no further, and return to it later without having thought consciously about it in the meantime, many of the correct words immediately pop up in my mind. Obviously, there has been non-conscious activity in my brain working with the crossword.

It is clear that non-conscious thinking can be rational and efficient, and this explains why people can often have good intuitions, that is, their intuition is the product of non-conscious thinking. But non-conscious thinking can also be irrational, especially for the individual. Non-conscious thinking is based on dispositions acquired through evolution based on their general usefulness. In a specific situation or a specific individual, however, the desire that results from non-conscious thinking may be fatal. Damasio gives the example of drug abuse. Some drugs create a body state which sends the same stimuli to the brain as a body in homeostasis. There are strong dispositions in the brain to do more of

---

[253] Ibid., 273–74.
[254] Robert Stickgold and Jeffrey M. Ellenbogen, "Quiet! Sleeping Brain at Work," *Scientific American MIND* 19, no. 4 (2008): 28. An alternative interpretation is that some people were more tired than others, but many different experiments support the conclusion that the brain solves problems while we sleep (ibid.).

what gets the body into homeostasis, leading to a strong desire for more drugs, but taking the drug has damaging long-term effects for the individual.[255]

There are also many examples of how reasoning processes work in general which can be explained by their evolutionary efficiency, although such reasoning sometimes does not apply in particular situations. Answer quickly: would you choose to take a medicine if you knew that of those who took the medicine 200 got better and 75 showed no improvement, whereas in the control group of those who did not take the medicine 50 people got better and 15 did not? The first hunch of many people would be to say yes, because of the many confirmations of improvement, and as a general rule confirmations give inductive support. But a little mathematics shows that your chances of getting better are higher if you do not take the medicine. The philosophy of science has shown that falsifications are often more important than verification, but for most people this must be learned and is not generally intuitive.[256] Damasio warns about the irrational decisions made by our prejudiced non-conscious minds, and suggests that reflection and reassessment, fact checks, and reconsiderations are important.[257]

So, non-conscious mind activity can be both rational and not so rational. But could not rational reflection and reconsideration also happen non-consciously? Is not all thinking a matter of neural patterns being activated in the brain anyway? Why need they be conscious in order to be more rational? Does consciousness necessarily have any function? Damasio said that it is likely to have, since it is selected by evolution. But things have been selected by evolution as by-products without a function, like the red color of blood.

I think that consciousness has several functions. Although it could have been selected as an unnecessary by-product, there are other reasons to believe that it has a function as well. For example, it is the most important neural patterns that become conscious, and this suggests that there is some reason why they should become conscious.

First, I agree with Damasio that something probably feels differently when it is conscious. Against this, one could say that the relevant aspects of feeling and emotion are also physical in Damasio's conception, so why should it matter that they are conscious? Consciousness is able to unite different physical inputs

---

[255] Damasio, *Self Comes to Mind*, 282.
[256] For this example and many more, see Keith E. Stanovich, "Rational and Irrational Thought: The Thinking That IQ-Tests Miss," *Scientific American MIND* 20, no. 6 Nov/Dec (2009).
[257] Damasio, *Self Comes to Mind*, 277.

into one unified experience, and it seems to have this ability in virtue of its being conscious, and not in virtue of something physical. This unity makes experiences interpreted as something happening to *one* person. That helps give the sense of persisting identity which, as Damasio observed, makes us care about what happens to our body in the future.

Organisms without consciousness also act in the interest of their own survival, but their actions are based on dispositions for certain actions acquired through evolution. These can be very useful, but they are selected for their general usefulness. A conscious person, on the other hand, is much better equipped to meet the particular changes facing her than organisms without consciousness. The reason is the combination of the points above. When experiences feel like something, and I think that what happens to my body in the future is something that I will feel, I have a strong motivation for acting to ensure a good future for myself. When feelings feel like something, they are good guides to how I will act to ensure a good future for myself. Since I care about the future, I think about the future, and feelings connected to different alternatives guide me so that I make good choices for the future.

Choices can be made non-consciously. It only feels like making a choice when we are conscious of reasons and/or feelings for acting a certain way, but a deliberation process may happen non-consciously. For example, a stimulus triggers a desire which activates different possible scenarios for fulfilling the desire. One of the scenarios activates a memory with a bad non-conscious feeling connected with it, since the last time the person tried that solution it did not go well. The other scenario activates a memory with a good non-conscious feeling connected with it, since the last time the person tried that solution it did go well. With the aid of a disposition for when the threshold for motor neuron activation is reached, the scenario with the good memory activates the motor neurons which lead to the action carried out. This could happen consciously: if I felt like taking one of the two candies on the table, but I remembered the trouble last time when I took my wife's favorite candy, I then chose the other one. Or the same thing could have happened non-consciously: while watching a movie I take a candy and eat it without thinking consciously about it before the candy is in my mouth, but non-consciously my brain helped me select the candy that does not land me in trouble.

I often make choices non-consciously. I may say to myself consciously that I will not take any more chocolate or potato chips from the bowl while watching a movie, only to find my hand in the bowl or even the snack in my mouth before noticing it consciously. A while ago (in 2013) I started thinking about why I always take out my boarding card from my bag at the airport and hold it in my hand as I walk through security. At Norwegian airports you show the boarding card before entering security and there is no need for it afterwards. But then I remembered that I once left it in my luggage and was yelled at by airport security in the USA in 2006. I assume that non-consciously I remembered the event and thought that I should keep my boarding card ready, so I now pick out the boarding card every time. In my theory that amounts to a non-conscious choice.

So, is there no difference between non-conscious and conscious choices? I believe there is an important difference, which is that conscious choices are more likely to be delayed than non-conscious choices, whereas non-conscious choices are often executed at the first chance they have of not being prohibited. Why is that? First of all, they are delayed because conscious deliberation is a much slower process than non-conscious parallel processing in the brain. When feelings are consciously felt in a deliberation process, they play a more important role since there is a conscious core self present which feels what is at stake and which cares about the future. The disposition for being sure before one acts will play a greater role when the feeling of what is at stake is greater. When choice is delayed, more memories and more thoughts will be activated, so that the autobiographical self gets a greater chance to influence the choice made. Consciousness leads to delayed choices, which leads to more thinking and feeling before the choice is made, and this is an important difference since the autobiographical self then often plays a greater causal role in the choices.

This delay function seems to be a crucial part of the function of consciousness. Deheane and Naccache refers to neuroscientific research which seems to have established some specific mental operations that require consciousness to work. Consciousness seems necessary for durable information maintenance. Non-conscious content of mind changes rapidly, but consciously experienced mental content can remain in focus for a longer period of time. This seems required for finding novel solutions to problems like using new combinations of operations previously learnt. It even seems necessary for typical intentional behavior. Patients with blindsight will not on their own initiative start walking through a labyrinth etc, but when forced, they find the right way.[258]

Consciousness thus seems to have different functions. One function is that there is a difference between a feeling that is consciously felt and a feeling that is not. Another is that conscious mental operations are slower, which seem necessary for certain mental capacities and which involves the autobiographical self in choices to a larger degree.

---

[258] Stanislas Deheane and L. Naccache, "Towards a cognitive neuroscience of consciousness: basic evidence and a workspace framework," *Cognition* 79 (2001), 8–12.

3.8 Thinking

Damasio does not say much about thinking. He seems to make a principal distinction between images and dispositions. Images are neural patterns representing something in the body or the world (or a possible world in the case of imagined or false images, by which I mean images of states of affairs that do not fit into the real world), and these can become conscious. Dispositions on the other hand do not become conscious, but determine how such images are processed in the brain. For example, dispositions allow us to process images in different ways, such as manipulating the images or applying reasoning to them.[259] Although the word "image" suggests something visual, Damasio underscores that images are images of everything, not just sights, but all kinds of sense impressions and feelings, and they can be concrete and abstract, conscious or nonconscious. The images come from sense impressions, from memory, or from a combinations of these, and the process of mind is a continuous flow of images.[260] In addition to images, Damasio thinks that we have dispositions which allow us to store and recall memories, and they are also what make imagination and reasoning possible.[261]

This is all a very brief consideration of thinking. The neuroscientist Lawrence Barsalou has examined it in detail. Barsalou refers with consent to Damasio several times, and his position fits well with Damasio's. Readers who are interested in how Damasio's thinking about thinking could be further developed would find Barsalou's writings of considerable help.[262] Many will, however, disagree with the approach of seeing mind as a causal process and argue that it cannot explain things like intentionality and the normativity of thinking.[263] The same applies to this book, in that many will reject a solution to the problem of free will that sees the mind as a causal process since it cannot explain things like intentionality and the normativity of thinking. That is a good reason to discuss thinking here. On the other hand, the philosophy of thinking consists of extensive debate that cannot possibly be treated within the frame of

---

259 Ibid., 63, 143.
260 Ibid., 71–72.
261 Ibid., 143.
262 Lawrence W. Barsalou, "Perceptual Symbol Systems," *Behavioral and Brain Sciences* 22 (1999).
263 See for example John Henry McDowell, *Mind and World: With a New Introduction*, 1st Harvard University Press paperback ed.(Cambridge, MA: Harvard University Press, 1996), 73–75, and Hilary Bok, *Freedom and Responsibility* (Princeton, NJ: Princeton University Press, 1998), 203 – 04.

this book, since there is not space enough to reach a well-argued conclusion. My best option is therefore to direct the reader to other scholars who defend a causal understanding of the mind, although I do not agree fully with any one of them.

Later, I give the following example of a deliberation process which is fully causal but can also be understood as acting for reasons. I include it here as an indication of the direction of my thought. A person sees a chair and a woman approaching. The visual impression of the chair and the woman activates in him two desires; a desire to sit and a desire to get to know her. The same visual impression also activates fact memories like the fact that he can offer the chair in order to get to know the woman, and that it will be considered rude to sit down in the chair in front of the woman. These fact memories further activate autobiographical memories concerning being rude previously and bad feelings connected with that and being polite to women before and good feelings connected with that. The good feelings remembered are connected with the desire to offer the chair and the bad feelings with the desire to sit. The desire to offer the chair becomes the strongest and activates the motor neurons that make the man offer the chair. In this process, every event was causal, because it was all about neural patterns firing and thereby activating other neural patterns with which they were connected. The process could also be described as a man acting for a reason. He offered the chair and the reason was that he wanted to get to know the woman, since that was his strongest desire. So acting for reasons does not exclude acting for causes.

Alfred Mele defends an event-causal understanding of the mind against many common critiques. He says that a causal theory of the mind was defended by Aristotle, Thomas Aquinas, Hobbes, Spinoza, Locke, Kant and William James, and that even though Wittgenstein and Ryle were against it, it now seems to be the orthodox view.[264] Mele thinks that no non-causal theory of the mind has been able to answer Donald Davidson's challenge in 1963, which was to specify what it means to decide for a reason if the reason is not understood as the cause of the choice. In virtue of what is it true that a person acts upon a particular goal if it is not that the intention is the cause?[265] Mele uses many arguments to defend causalism and attack non-causalism and I refer the interested reader to those discussions.[266]

---

[264] Alfred R. Mele, *Irrationality: An Essay on Akrasia, Self-Deception, and Self-Control* (New York: Oxford University Press, 1987), 31.
[265] *Motivation and Agency* (New York: Oxford University Press, 2003), 39, 58.
[266] See *Springs of Action*, chapter thirteen; and *Motivation and Agency*, 39–50.

Another scholar who has defended how a causal understanding of the mind can explain normative thinking is Peter Carruthers.[267] I present some of his relevant thoughts in the next subchapter on desire. There is still much more that could be debated concerning questions like externalism, meaning and intentionality. There are no single authors I agree with on these questions; suffice it to say that I presuppose a causal understanding of the mind, so my aim is to investigate a new solution to the problem of free will given that presupposition. Of course, there will be some who will not be convinced by such an approach, but they will probably not be convinced by just one book on the topic in any case.

Is it a great weakness that important criticisms can be leveled against presuppositions which I do not have space to defend? In the philosophy of mind there are many great debates, and the question of consciousness and its relation to the physical world is poorly understood, so any approach in the philosophy of mind will be connected with great unsolved questions that cannot be well defended within the limits of one book. Some will argue that a causal approach to the mind is nevertheless so reductionist that any attempt is hopeless. One has to choose between going for the causal understanding and believing that unsolved questions will be solved in the future or believing that consciousness and mental life are something ontologically independent of the physical although one does not know what it is or how it is possible for consciousness to interact with the rest of the world. I believe that the first approach is the more coherent for the time being, and thus best argued, but that cannot be defended well in just one book. That is why I presuppose it here and continue with my main project which is an investigation of a new approach to the problem of free will.

3.9 Desire

Damasio does not have much to say about desires, but he does distinguish between emotions on the one hand and drives and motivations on the other, which he says are simpler constituents of emotion.[268] I interpret Damasio's terms "drives" and "motivations" as having roughly the same meaning as "desires," since he exemplifies them with hunger and thirst, which seem like obvious examples of desires.[269] But just what are desires? Damasio seems to think of

---

267 Carruthers, *The Architecture of the Mind*.
268 Damasio, *Self Comes to Mind*, 109, 11.
269 *The Feeling of What Happens*, 77; *Descartes' Error*, 116.

them as dispositions in the brain that are meant to help the organism achieve homeostasis.[270] That is a third-person perspective description of the physical realizer of desires and their function. I shall focus mostly on the first-person perspective experience of desire and return to the physical side later.

From a first-person perspective, "desire" is a concept that can be defined quite widely to include all sorts of wishes and preferences or even judgments that something is good. On the other hand it can be defined more narrowly to include a feeling often related to pleasure or displeasure. I may judge that something is good (e.g. that I give money to aid projects in Africa), without having a desire that it should happen that I give money to Africa. Since Damasio uses the terms "drives" and "motivational states," he seems to focus on this *felt* desire which is supposed to lead to action. Hunger is a feeling meant to make the hungry act on their desire and eat, and the same goes for thirst or sexual desire. I thus understand desire as including both a thought that something is good and a feeling that makes the person want the desired state of affairs to happen.

Alfred Mele offers several helpful distinctions when it comes to desires. He defines a desire for A as an A-focused attitude which constitutes motivation for A.[271] Here one should distinguish between a desire to perform an action (go for a walk) and a desire for a state of affairs to be true (that my team will win the cup).[272] Most desires are desires for a state of affairs to come true which includes doing something in order for it to come true (I mow the lawn since I desire a nice garden), but not all (I may desire to be someone else). In order to avoid constantly interrupting the text by making reservations about counter-examples, I focus on action desires, which include thoughts about some states of affairs one wants to become true. I also focus on proximal desires, which include the desire to do something now, although there are also distal desires, which are desires to do something later.[273]

Mele further distinguishes between occurring and standing desires: I may always desire that there should be peace on earth but that does not mean that that desire is always activated or felt.[274] Some desires are intrinsic, meaning that one desires something for its own sake (maybe to whistle), whereas other desires are instrumental, which is when you desire to do something to achieve something else (go to the dentist in order to have good teeth). Desires can also

---

270 *Self Comes to Mind*, 55.
271 Mele, *Motivation and Agency*, 170.
272 Ibid., 16.
273 Ibid., 167.
274 Ibid., 30.

be a mix of the intrinsic and instrumental; for example, you enjoy swimming for its own sake but also do it in order to get into better shape.[275]

One might think that there are just two desires—a desire for pleasure and a deterrent desire for pain—and that all other desires are sub-desires. But some of the most common desires seem to have physical realizers located at different places in the brain, and it is good if the vague concept of desire can be related to something empirical. There are different areas of the brain that can be stimulated electrically and the people stimulated will report that they feel a certain desire. Animal tests confirm the same. The lateral hypothalamus is active when we are hungry or thirsty and also when we see food and drink. If it is stimulated electrically, we will feel compelled to eat and drink, whereas when it has been destroyed in animals they stop eating and drinking and must be force-fed if they are not to die. Parts of the amygdala and hypothalamus can be stimulated and people will suddenly feel a strong sexual desire and perform explicit sexual acts even if these are inappropriate in the situation. There are also famous experiments that have discovered what seems to be a pleasure center in the brain. If they are stimulated electrically in humans, the latter will report that they feel great. When animals are allowed to press a button that stimulates them they will continue to do so ceaselessly until they are exhausted.[276]

Although there may well be a general mechanism for doing what feels good and avoiding what feels bad, the real picture is more complex. People can desire all sorts of things, like desiring their football team to win, and it is impossible that there should be an innate area in the brain responsible for all kinds of concrete desires. Of course, very many desires are instrumental desires or sub-desires falling under an intrinsic or more general desire, and can be explained in that way. An intrinsic desire for food can make me desire many different kinds of food, depending on what is available and my other feelings for the food, but these sub-desires can all be explained by the general desire for food. There seem also, however, to be a lot of intrinsic desires that do not fall under the main innate desires (such as those for food, drink and sex). How can these more particular intrinsic desires be explained?

I find it likely that there is a set of dispositions to desire certain things that people in general are born with, such as desires for food, drink, sex, pleasure, survival, safety, predictability, respect, control, rest, and other things, but I am not sure what the exact list should look like. There are also deterrent desires, of

---

275 Ibid., 33–34.
276 These examples strongly suggest that there is a physical side to desire strength and that desire strength can cause action—a topic to which I shall return.

which the desire to avoid pain is probably the best example. Other deterrent desires fall under more basic emotions, like disgust and fear, and can cause aversion to different things. I suspect that all of the various desires one can have for specific states of affairs can be explained as combinations of the desires we are born with in combination with what we otherwise think and feel. The desire for pleasure will often be relevant, but what people think and feel will greatly influence what gives them pleasure. For example, I may desire respect and (foolishly) believe that I can achieve this by writing a book about free will, and then desire to write a book about free will and feel pleasure doing it. But I also desire to find out what is true, maybe as a sub-desire under a desire for control, and that also motivates me to write a book about free will. I also desire to have a job writing books like this, falling under a desire to make money, falling under a desire to eat and drink and have power—and so on. Many different desires, thoughts and feelings create specific desires in us.

Desires shaped by beliefs about how they are best fulfilled can make desires compete. A person may desire to live well and desire to avoid pain, and believe that if she abstains from sex God will let her live forever, but if she does not there is eternal pain waiting, and so these desires and beliefs together make her act on the desires to live and avoid pain and not on the sexual desires. Or a sexual desire can make a person eat less and work out more to impress someone. Thoughts and feelings influence the strength of the different desires. This is important for the question of free will, and before I discuss it further I must discuss what it means that desires have different *strength*.

Desires as consciously experienced seem to have a variable degree of strength: for example, one can be more or less hungry or thirsty, and experience stronger or weaker sexual desire. The strength of desire allows a person to have a preference when they have contradictory desires; the strongest desire is preferred the most. But what is the variable in virtue of which the desire is stronger or weaker? Here I suggest that it is the feeling of pleasure and displeasure which is the main variable, although it comes in different shades, in the same way as different feelings can give different kinds of pleasures or displeasures. The variable is in the amount (how much it occupies the conscious mind) and the felt intensity of the pleasure or displeasure. Pleasure and displeasure are felt in different ways by the one who desires something: she may desire something and feel displeasure since she does not have what she desires, or feel pleasure when she thinks about achieving what she desires, and feel pleasure when she actually achieves what she desires. Note that this description was concerned with different degrees of *consciously felt* strength of desire. I shall complicate the picture later by adding a non-conscious and a physical aspect to the strength of desires to explain why we do not always act on the desire that consciously feels the strongest.

So far I have argued that there are competing desires, and that these are influenced by thoughts and feelings. How does such influence happen? I envision it in the following way: Different desires are triggered by stimuli either from the body or from the world outside. The situation triggers memories, both facts about the situation and possibilities in the situation, and autobiographical memories from similar situations and the feelings that the person had in that situation. Autobiographical memories are especially activated if there is a strong feeling connected with them. The thoughts about possibilities for action in the situation may also activate autobiographical memories from earlier similar situations. Consider again my chair example: a tired man may see an empty chair and desire rest, but he may at the same time see a woman approaching the chair, desire to get to know her, and remember that offering a chair is a way to make positive contact with someone, while swiping the chair in front of them can be considered rude. Maybe he remembers earlier episodes of either offering a chair or swiping a chair, and more generally of getting to know women or being criticized for his behavior. The sight of the woman and the chair can activate thoughts about many possibilities for action and the possibilities that these actions can further lead to, and memories and feelings connected with all of these.

The feelings activated by earlier memories blend in with the feelings that the first desires give rise to. Maybe the man in the example above first had a strong desire for rest and so wanted to sit on the chair, but as he thought about the possibilities of getting to know a woman by offering her the chair and the possibilities of what would happen if he did not offer the chair, chair-offering was connected with good feelings and chair-swiping was connected with bad feelings, and so the felt desire to offer the chair was strengthened and the felt desire to take the chair weakened. My wife is a good example of how recalled feelings blend with desires. In the first stage of her pregnancy, the black coffee she usually drank and the pizza I usually cooked made her sick. When her appetite returned, she still did not desire black coffee or my pizza at all, but she did desire different variants of coffee and different variants of pizza. These different kinds of coffee and pizza tasted quite similar to regular black coffee and the pizza I made, but whereas she would desire some kinds of coffee and pizza very much, she would not at all desire something which tasted almost the same, namely regular black coffee and my pizza. The most likely reason for this is that the memory of that special coffee and that special pizza had a bad feeling of sickness connected with it, which reduced her desire for it strongly.

The process I have here described is in essence the following: a situation triggers alternatives for action that a person desires with different degrees of strength, and activated memories mark the alternatives with feelings which change the strength of the desire for each alternative. Damasio describes this process similarly, although quite briefly. In a given situation different alternatives for action are activated, and Damasio's somatic marker hypothesis holds that the different images are connected with a feeling. This somatic marking influences which alternatives become conscious at all, and it influences how long we consider something and what we end up choosing, since feelings influence the strength of desire. Parts of this process are conscious and parts of it are non-conscious, according to Damasio.[277] Peter Carruthers also understands the process of practical reasoning like this, and he refers to Damasio when he describes it: we envision different alternatives and register our emotional response to the different alternatives.[278] Also Chandra Sripada thinks similarly when he describes different ways that what he calls the deep self can influence choices.[279] This is important for the question of free will, since it means that the experiences a person has had in her life (including thoughts and feelings) and stored in her autobiographical memory will influence the future choices she makes. Consequently her autobiographical self will play a causal role in some of the choices she makes.

What happens between the process where after some deliberation one desire becomes the strongest and the point when a person acts on her strongest desire? How does the strongest desire lead to action? Damasio does not have much to say about that process. He says that the somatic markings provide incentives for a person to act and that we have an innate preference system for what we like and do not like and dispositions to act in order to achieve pleasure and avoid pain.[280]

Peter Carruthers has developed in much more detail what happens between when a person considers her desires and when she acts. Since his theory is good and fits well with what Damasio says elsewhere, I add it here. Carruthers argues that we have different desire modules, which correspond to the different innate desires that I mentioned above.[281] There is also a different module which Carruthers calls the practical reasoning module. This module selects as its input the

---

277 Damasio, *Descartes' Error*, 174, 84–87, 96.
278 Carruthers, *The Architecture of the Mind*, 137–38.
279 Sripada, "Self-Expression: A Deep Self Theory of Moral Responsibility", 13.
280 Damasio, *Descartes' Error*, 174, 79.
281 Carruthers, *The Architecture of the Mind*, 113–14.

desire it registers as the strongest, and then starts to follow a set of heuristic rules. A basic sketch of these rules is as follows: The input is a desire for P. The practical reasoning module scans autobiographical and fact memories[282] to find a memory of the "If I do Q, then P will occur" sort. If it finds such a memory, it will search through a set of action schemata that are stored in memory and check if such an action scheme is doable here and now.[283] If not, then the module will search for memories of the "If I do R, then Q will occur" type in order to make the action scheme doable. If this process goes on for a while without success, the module will turn to the second strongest desire, and start the process over again.[284]

The details may be different in real life, but this is a scenario which describes the reasoning process as a causal process. The description above was serial, but the brain probably processes different desires in parallel and then the practical reasoning module selects according to certain rules; for instance, that it is worth considering a very strong desire for a certain period of time before

---

[282] Carruthers uses the term "belief," but I understand beliefs as fact memories and their implications.

[283] The theory that there are motor schemata guiding our actions has been developed by Richard Schmidt, among others. (Richard A. Schmidt, "A Schema Theory of Discrete Motor Skill Learning," *Psychological Review* 82, no. 4 (1975).; "Motor Schema Theory after 27 Years: Reflections and Implications for a New Theory," Research *Quarterly for Exercise and Sport* 74, no. 4 (2003)). The theory explains why many of our actions are not caused directly by desires. Rather, we desire some overarching goal and then motor schemata actualize the desire. For example, when we write something, we do not make a decision to press every letter; rather there are motor schemata for the different words. There is constant feedback from the world interacting with our desires to find out whether a program should continue or be substituted with another. This happens on small scales and larger scales. An example of a small-scale motor scheme is the fact that when I want to type the word "Damasio" I always write "Damasion," which may well be because I have stored a small motor program for the ending "-sion" on English words. An example on a larger scale is driving familiar routes. When driving from my house I almost always take the same route into a roundabout and further into a tunnel. Sometimes I go another way and have to change lanes before the tunnel, but I have often ended up in the tunnel. That is probably because the normal route is a stored program and then I have to think consciously about changing lanes when it is time to do so – otherwise I end in the tunnel. The existence of such motor programs is my answer to the charge that event-causal theories of the mind cannot explain how we do many actions that are not directly caused by desires (Steward, *A Metaphysics for Freedom*, 164–65).

[284] Whereas Carruthers uses this module to describe the whole deliberation process, I employ it to describe the final part of the process: from something becoming the strongest desire to the desire being executed in action.

choosing to act on a less strong desire instead.[285] The main point is that it is a mechanism which decides the strength of desire and follows a set of heuristic rules to turn the desire into action by selecting an action plan which is sent to the motor neurons for execution.[286]

Although Carruthers thinks that much of our practical reasoning happens like this, he follows Daniel Kahneman in distinguishing between two systems of reasoning, known as system 1 and system 2. System 1 works fast and quite reliably according to the general rules described above. System 2 is a conscious and slow-working reasoning process, but it is more reliable than system 1 and can trump system 1 decisions.[287] System 2's reasoning processes are typically concerned with important and difficult choices, and since I argued that consciousness plays a causal role this allows for consciousness to have a causal role in important choices.

I have so far argued that the strongest desire leads to action via the workings of a practical reasoning module that translates desires into actions. But there are two objections against this that should be considered, and both have been raised by Alfred Mele. He argues that intentions play an important role in reasoning which cannot be reduced to a combination of desires and beliefs. It is not good enough to say that the strongest desire leads to action, for there are many examples where the strongest desire is not the same as a person's intention. For example, the strongest desire of both Alan and Bob may be to insult Carl at a party, and they do, but still it may be correct that only Bob had the intention of insulting Carl at the party. What the concept of intention adds to the reasoning process, according to Mele, is that intentions settle which desire a person wants to act upon. A person has thoughts and can assess different desires in order to identify the best one and intend to act accordingly. What a person judges to be best can be different from his strongest desire. So in Mele's understanding of the deliberation process there are desires and one of the desires is the strongest, but it is a process of assessment producing an intention which settles which desire will lead to action, and that need not be the strongest desire.[288]

Carruthers also discusses how we should understand the relation between what we judge to be best and what we desire the most. How can the judgment of something as best lead to action? Carruthers answers that we probably have an

---

285 Ibid., 131–32.
286 Ibid., 131, 38.
287 Ibid., 254; Daniel Kahneman, *Thinking, Fast and Slow* (New York: Penguin, 2011), 20–22.
288 Mele, *Springs of Action*, chapters eight and nine.

innate desire to do that which we judge to be best. How then is weakness of the will possible? Weakness of the will is not doing that which you judge to be best. It is easy for Carruthers to answer: even if we have a desire to do that which we judge best, we also have other desires, and sometimes these are stronger. So, even if Bob judged it best not to insult Carl at the party, he did it nevertheless, since his desire to insult Carl was stronger than his desire to do what he judged best (not to insult Carl).[289] I shall say much more about weakness of the will in the next chapter.

What about intentions? How can a person intend something which is not her strongest desire? Both Carruthers and Damasio think that desires can be at work non-consciously, and it seems that Mele does so as well.[290] The answer is close at hand: even if a desire is not felt consciously as the strongest, it is still the strongest in virtue of the non-conscious feelings connected with it, and selected by the practical reasoning module as the strongest. The module selects the strongest desire, and this is what settles the reasoning process. One could use the term intention, but as long as there are thoughts, desires and a disposition in the brain for transforming the strongest desires into action there is no need for intention as referring to a separate entity in the brain.[291]

Using non-conscious desires in this way may seem like a non-falsifiable theory, but I shall defend it later when discussing weakness of the will in chapter four, and answer more critiques from Alfred Mele. As mentioned above, however, both Damasio and Mele also believe that non-conscious desires influence our choices. Carruthers defends this belief by arguing that it works that way in animals, and that an account of the human mind must be evolutionary in the sense that it can show how the mind has been gradually built from animals to humans.[292] Much more could be said about desire, of course, but here I have said what I need to say about the self and the mind in order to lay the foundation for my solution to the problem of free will—how it is possible to have free will. This, then, comprises the content of the next chapter.

---

289 Carruthers, *The Architecture of the Mind*, 391–92.
290 Ibid., 400; Damasio, *Descartes' Error*, 185; Mele, *Motivation and Agency*, 30, 164.
291 Mele has many suggestions echoing Carruthers, since Mele thinks that there are mechanisms in the brain which by default select what is assessed as best as the intention of the person and activate motor schemata to execute the intention (*Springs of Action*, 167, 221, 30–37).
292 Carruthers, *The Architecture of the Mind*, 403.

4 Free Will

The time has come to explain what it means to say that humans have free will. We have already seen the basic definition of free will: that it is up to us what we choose among alternatives and that the source of the choice is in us. Different scholars disagree on how to understand the parts of the definition, how the concept of free will should be used, and which definitions refer to a kind of free will that actually exists. For most of them, the goal is to find a coherent definition of free will and to find out how free the human will is. This is also my goal and, having considered the topics of causality and the self, I now have the resources to explain in much greater detail *who* chooses, what it means to choose *among alternatives*, and how the choice makes the agent the *source* or the *cause* of the choice.

I shall start by defining "free will" and argue that we have free will when (but not only when) the autobiographical self is the cause of the desire that makes us choose one alternative as opposed to another. In order to explain why we have free will when the autobiographical self is the cause of the desire that causes the choice, I must explain what I mean by alternative possibilities and then discuss the question of determinism. I can then explain how the autobiographical self becomes what it becomes and why we have free will when the autobiographical self causes the desire that causes the choice. But we have free will and responsibility not only when an independent autobiographical self causes the choices we make. After explaining what I mean by responsibility, I argue that free will is a matter of inner-directedness and exists to different degrees along a continuum. I present and discuss different degrees of free will along this continuum and in the final chapter of the book I discuss various test cases and counterarguments to see how well I can explain typical difficult cases. The conclusion is that all these cases can well be answered, so that the theory of free will presented here integrates data in a coherent way, which makes the theory plausible.

4.1 What Is Free Will?

There are very many variables at play when people act, which means that actions and deliberation processes can be very different. I now mention some of these variables to show the complexity of the issue and to introduce some distinctions that will be useful later (see figure below for an overview). Sometimes a desire leads to action, but other actions happen without a desire causing it, such as if I break a glass by accident.[293] When desires lead to action, sometimes the desire will be conscious, but other times it will be non-conscious, such as if I grab a handful of popcorn on the table while watching a movie without thinking consciously about whether I should take some popcorn or not. Sometimes the desire that leads to action is an innate desire—a desire the person is born with—like the desire for food or sleep. Sometimes the desire can be an acquired desire, such as a desire for rare stamps.[294] Sometimes desires lead directly to action without the occurrence of any additional thoughts or feelings between the desire and the action happening. So, for example, a man might see someone being rude to his girlfriend, desire to hit that person, and then immediately do so. But instead of immediately hitting him, he could think about what to do and plan an attack later.

Between a desire to act and the action, there are many different things that may happen in a person's mind. The desire may activate fact memories, autobiographical memories and new thoughts and feelings. Between desire and action, a person may consider alternative possibilities for action or not, and there may actually be alternative options that are possible for the person to do, or not—independently of what the person thinks. Sometimes the autobiographical self will be activated between the desire occurring and the action happening, sometimes it will not. Sometimes the autobiographical self and the desire fit well together so that the person is happy with having the desire, but at other times the person may dislike having a certain desire. I distinguish between voluntary and involuntary desires, and by voluntary desire I mean a desire where the autobiographical self contains an approving attitude[295] to that desire (and not also a disapproving attitude), making it a desire that the person is happy with having. For example, a woman may voluntarily desire her husband, but involuntarily desire the married man at work, so that she wishes she did not have that desire. Sometimes we experience competing desires; either competition among voluntary desires, among involuntary desires, or between voluntary and involuntary desires. One of these desires will usually win through and lead to action. For example, a person may have an involuntary desire for cake and a voluntary desire for fish, and perhaps end up choosing the cake. Sometimes the

---

293 One could argue that this does not even constitute an action, if the term "action" is taken to require a purpose or intention in action.
294 Some desires are innate, but modified, or innate as a potential, which may be actualized.
295 An approving attitude to a desire is a representation of the fact that you have that desire and a positive feeling connected to that, while a disapproving attitude to a desire is a representation of the fact that you have that desire and a negative feeling connected to that.

autobiographical self is activated and changes the initial desire[296] and sometimes it does not. For example, a person may see a chair and a man approaching it and desire to sit. But then autobiographical memories are activated, about not having offered a seat to someone previously and receiving negative feedback, and about having offered a seat with positive consequences; then the initial desire to sit weakens and the desire to offer the seat to the other person strengthens. Initial desires may also change because of new thoughts and feelings as the brain is capable of making new connections between neurons.

The autobiographical self can be more or less involved between an initial desire and action, depending on the number and emotional strength of memories considered before action. And finally, the autobiographical self may be more or less independent. An autobiographical self becomes increasingly independent through life as it changes initial desires by a process of thinking and feeling about alternatives. Even if the autobiographical self does not decide what to think or feel, such a change in initial desires is nevertheless caused from within the mind, but I shall need to defend this last claim in more detail later. In all these cases I have presupposed a normally functioning capacity for feeling and reasoning. If these capacities are not functioning normally, it will influence freedom and responsibility, as I shall also argue later.

The different scenarios just sketched are depicted in Figures 1a–d.

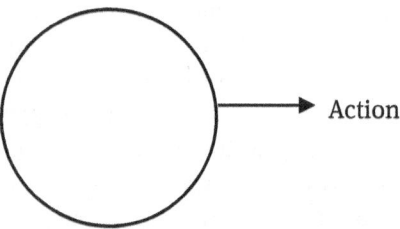

Fig. 1a: Action not caused by desire.

---

296 I use the terms "initial desire" and "changed desire" in a similar way as Harry Frankfurt uses the terms first-order desires and second-order volitions (Frankfurt, "Freedom of the Will and the Concept of a Person," 7, 10). However, he defines first-order desires as related to doing something or that something should happen, while second-order volition is about the first-order desire, while what defines changed desires is not their object, but the fact that they have been changed by the autobiographical self. What is common to Frankfurt and my own view is that the first-order desires have been evaluated, but I explain in greater detail how this evaluation happens.

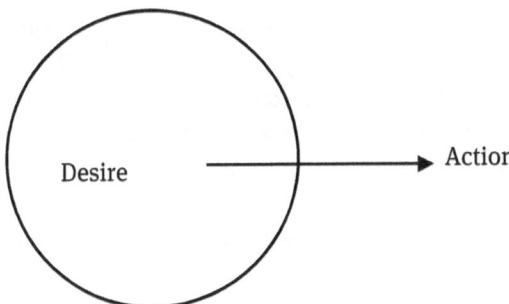

Fig. 1b: Action caused by desire (may happen consciously or non-consciously).

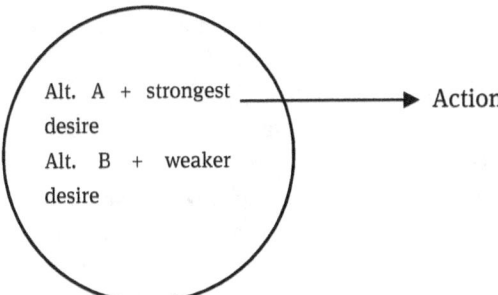

Fig. 1c: Two alternatives for action are considered, the one desired the most leads to action.

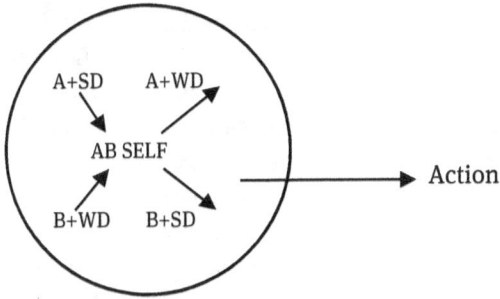

Fig. 1d: Alternative A is connected with a strong desire (SD), B with a weak desire (WD). Both alternatives activate memories in the autobiographical self which changes the strength of desire connected with A and B.

As this introduction shows, processes of deliberation can be very different. I shall later relate these different kinds of processes to the definition of free will and argue that free will comes in degrees and that these different processes exemplify different degrees of free will. This will give a more detailed and precise understanding of the definition of free will. The common definition of free will is that it must be up to us what we choose among alternatives and that the source of the choice must be in us if we are to have free will. I shall now examine the details of this definition.

The first part says that it must be up to us what we choose among alternatives. This means that among alternative possibilities of action, the choice of one alternative must be caused by a desire in us and not by something else. Further, it says that several alternatives must have been possible (we shall return later to what kind of possibilities these alternatives are). The reason for the requirement of alternative possibilities is presumably that for the agent to be the cause there must be several possibilities. If there is just one possibility, the agent is not considered the cause of the choice; the choice is not even considered a choice, for a choice must be between alternatives ("not doing anything" is considered an alternative). If there are no alternatives, there is nothing to choose between and no choice is involved.

However, it is not enough that the agent's desire is the cause of which alternative is chosen (as in the first part of the definition). The source of the choice must also be in the agent, as stated in the second part of the definition, and this means that the agent must be the cause of her own desire. What this part is meant to establish is that we do not have free will if, for example, God has determined that all we desire to do is to play the harp. If God had given us all a desire to do nothing but play the harp, the first part of the definition of free will could still be fulfilled. We could have the choice between playing the harp and the piano, and our desire to play the harp causes us to choose the harp. But this is not enough for there to be free will. The source of the choice must be in us and not in God's decree, meaning that we must also be the cause of our desire to play the harp if we are to have free will when we choose to play the harp. To sum up so far: In the process of deliberation, something causes the strongest desire, and the strongest desire causes the selection of one alternative possibility for action as opposed to another alternative. In order for us to be free, the agent should be the cause of the strongest desire.

So far, I have only explicated the parts of the definition of free will. But who is the agent who causes the action and even causes her own will, and how does this causation happen? I start by answering these questions before turning to the question of how to understand the alternative possibilities. First, I will address the question of who the agent is.

In chapter three I defined a person as a human body with a mind and a core self, while the autobiographical self is a neural pattern in the brain representing the life story of that person, including memories of experiences, thoughts and feelings. In all cases in which a desire leads to action, I suggest that it is right to say that the person is the cause of the choice, since it is a desire in that person that causes which alternative is chosen.[297] At least this is so as long as there are several possible alternatives for action. So, one can say that the person is the cause of the choice in the sense that a desire in the person is the cause of the choice that is made (which motor neurons are triggered). But the person need not be the cause of the desire that causes the action, rather it may be a desire the person was born with and that person may even hate the fact that he or she has this desire.

Can a person also be the cause of her own desires? There are different scenarios in which I suggest that it is right to say that the autobiographical self of the person is the cause of the desire. One such scenario is where the autobiographical self is activated and causes the initial desire to change, as in the case of a person seeing a chair and a man approaching the chair, where the desire to sit changes to a desire to offer the seat to the other person.[298] Another scenario is where the autobiographical self has acquired certain desires which are then triggered by something in the world. For example, a person who has taken up stamp collection as a hobby may see a rare stamp and feel a great desire for this stamp. This desire is then caused by her autobiographical self. A third scenario is different, but related, and has to do with the desires a person is born with, but which are endorsed by her autobiographical self as voluntary desires. An example would be an innate desire for sex which is concretized as a person's desire

---

[297] Possible exceptions, such as a desire caused directly by God or a mad scientist, are discussed later.

[298] Why is that a change in initial desire instead of just one initial desire being followed by a new initial desire? Because there was nothing new happening in the world or the body independent of the autobiographical self. It was the activation of the autobiographical self that changed the initial desire and it would not have changed if the autobiographical self had not been activated—at least, that is my hypothesis. But is not the initial desire, for example, to sit in a chair, the same in strength, but another desire like being polite, stronger? Sometimes it will be the case that the initial desire changes strength only relative to other desires, so that what has changed is what the strongest desire is. But sometimes the initial desire itself changes strength and is, for example, weakened. Perhaps I see a plate of food on the table that I really desire, but then I learn or remember that it is Magda, (in)famous for her poor cooking abilities, who has made the food today and the desire changes so that I no longer desire the plate of food.

for sex with a partner, and the person may endorse this desire as a good part of herself.

Thus, when the definition of free will uses the term "us" and says that it is up to "us" what we choose, "us" may refer to either the person or the autobiographical self. If we say that a person causes the choice (the selection of an alternative), that is an imprecise description which means that either desires the person was born with cause the choice that is made, or the autobiographical self of the person causes the desire that causes the choice that is made, or maybe even new thoughts and feelings that occur in the mind of the person in the moment causes the desire which causes the choice that is made. So, the desires of the person that cause which alternative is chosen are either caused by genes, or by the autobiographical self, or in some cases by new thoughts and feelings in the person's mind. How does this causation of an action by a desire happen?

There are dispositions in the mind that trigger motor neuron action when a certain threshold is reached. How this occurs in detail is probably more complex than neuroscience has thus far discovered. The crude version is that when a desire reaches a certain level of strength and is not blocked by something else, there is a disposition for triggering the motor neurons to actualize the desired action, as argued in the previous chapter with reference to Peter Carruthers. I shall continue the discussion based on this assumption although I imagine that there are empirical facts about when and how motor neurons are triggered which actually make things more complicated than how I describe them here (and things are already quite complicated).[299]

If there is just one desire occurring in the mind and it can be actualized and nothing blocks it (such as a memory saying "this will mean trouble"), then it will generally cause motor neurons to be triggered, which then leads to action.[300] If there are several desires occurring in the mind and they can be actualized and are not blocked by something else, then the strongest desire will be selected by the relevant dispositions in the brain to cause motor neuron action. (I shall later return to what it means to say that the desire is strongest.) If a desire occurs in the mind and the autobiographical self is then activated with

---

[299] Adina Roskies gives an overview of neuroscientific research which gives good support to the general point that a choice amounts to certain neuronal activity reaching a threshold which then leads to action (See Roskies, in Mele, *Surrounding Free Will* (Oxford: Oxford University Press, 2015), 231–54).

[300] Wolf Singer is a well known neurobiologist who understands the process roughly like this. See Singer, in Christian Geyer, *Hirnforschung und Willensfreiheit: Zur Deutung der neuesten Experimente* (Frankfurt am Main: Suhrkamp, 2004), 56–58.

memories and feelings that change the strength of the desire(s), then the strongest desire is still the cause of the selected action, but the autobiographical self can then be the cause of which desire becomes the strongest. A desire may be changed by new thoughts and feelings occurring in the mind, or new thoughts and feelings occurring in the mind can trigger a desire; in both cases, the new thoughts and feelings can be the cause of the desire that leads to action. Human brains have a general capacity for new thoughts by making new neural connections and since we also experience things we have never experienced before, we can also have new feelings. When I say that desires change, this happens as described in Damasio's somatic marker hypothesis—the brain connects thoughts and memories with feelings and sorts them according to the strength of the feeling.

As a first approach to explaining how humans can have free will, I start by noting that there are some cases that most people (at least if they are not philosophers) would think of as examples of free will. Cases in which the autobiographical self causes the desire, which again causes which alternative is chosen, are examples of free will if everything else is normal (that is, if we leave out brainwashing or other special cases). These cases seem clearly to fulfill the definition of free will. There are certainly other cases that many people would also think of as examples of free will and definitely more cases where most people would think that a person is responsible, but I shall start with the least controversial cases and move to the more controversial cases later.

The cases that are considered uncontroversial among lay people are of course controversial among philosophers (what isn't?). A crucial question that must be discussed is: What causes the autobiographical self to become what it becomes? The question is relevant, for we need to find out why we are free if the autobiographical self causes the desire. If everything is determined, the autobiographical self is simply the way it has to be, determined before a person is born, and so there can be no free will. I have described everything that happens in the mind and the autobiographical self as a causal process and so it seems wrong to select the autobiographical self as the cause of a desire. It seems rather to be a chain of events determined at a micro level where the autobiographical self has no active role to play.

In order to explain why we have free will when the autobiographical self is the cause of the desire that causes the choice, I must start with a detailed look at what is meant by alternative possibilities and then discuss the question of determinism. I can then explain how the autobiographical self becomes what it becomes and why we have free will when the autobiographical self causes the desire that causes the choice.

4.2 Alternative Possibilities

In order to address the question of alternative possibilities, we need more terminology. What does it mean to have alternative possibilities? I have already introduced the distinction between token and type physical possibility.[301] A person may *imagine*[302] several alternatives that are *type* physically possible for that person to do (for example, opening the fridge door), but it does not follow that the specific alternative actually is *token* physically possible in that situation (perhaps events in the brain determine that the person will not open the fridge door in that situation).

These distinctions are necessary for me to make the following point: A person does not need to have alternatives for action that are token physically possible for that person to do in order for the autobiographical self to be the cause of the person's desire. For the autobiographical self to be the cause of a desire, it is enough that there are imagined alternative possibilities for action in the mind, regardless of whether these actions are token physically possible for the person to do. Again, at this point I am not interested in whether the person can perform several alternative actions in a particular situation; I am only interested in whether the autobiographical self is the cause of the desire which causes the choice of alternative action. In what follows, the focus is on this kind of process of deliberation, namely cases in which the autobiographical self changes the initial desire.

In order for the autobiographical self to be the cause of a change of desire in a person, there must be several imagined alternatives in the mind, regardless of whether they are token physically possible for the person to perform. Why? How can the autobiographical self be the cause of the desire in such a case? What happens is that when different alternative actions are imagined in the mind, memories from the autobiographical self are activated connected to each alternative, and these memories also activate feelings which are then connected to the different imagined alternatives. This whole process, whereby the autobiographical self changes the desire, happens before any actual alternative for action is carried out by the person. For this reason, whether the alternatives are actually token physically possible to perform at the moment of action is irrele-

---

301 I find the two concepts of token and type physical possibility to be precise and useful, so that I do not need less precise concepts such as "ability," "opportunity," "skill," "know-how," "freedom from constraints," etc.

302 By "imagine an alternative" I mean that a neural structure representing an alternative for action is activated either consciously or non-consciously.

vant since the desire is caused by the autobiographical self before the act is performed.

The process by which the autobiographical self causes changes in the initial desire is itself a causal process. In this process, one desire becomes the strongest, the strongest desire leads to action, and the action which is caused by the strongest desire may very well be the only token physically possible action that the person can perform. Is it then right to say that the autobiographical self is the cause of the choice of action if only one action is token physically possible? Yes, because it is the process happening in the mind where the autobiographical self is involved that makes that one alternative the only token physically possible alternative. It is *because* the self makes that desire the strongest desire that only that action is token physically possible for the person to do. People act on their strongest desires and the only action they can take is the one they desire the strongest.[303] But if their autobiographical self causes the strongest desire, then it is right to say that the autobiographical self causes the desire and so causes the choice that is made. The only thing required for the autobiographical self to become the cause is that different alternatives are imagined in the mind. The fact that we imagine alternatives and act on the strongest desire also explains why we feel free, even if we can only do what we desire the strongest and what we desire the strongest has to become what it does because of causal processes in the mind.[304]

But even if the autobiographical self causes the desire that causes the choice that is made, the problem raised in the Consequence Argument remains: If everything is determined before we are born, then it is not up to us what we choose and the source of the choice is not in us, rather it has been determined before we are born, and the cause is laws of nature and states of affairs happening before we were born. It does not help to say that the autobiographical self is the cause if the autobiographical self is causally determined to be what it is before a person is born. The autobiographical self must also be the cause of how it is, but how can it if the world is determined? The time has now come to discuss determinism and how it can suffice for free will that the autobiographical self causes the desire that causes the choice that is made.

---

[303] This claim will be explained and warranted below.
[304] Sometimes two desires are equally strong, and then there is presumably a disposition in the brain that results in one option being selected after a certain time of deliberation. Carruthers argues that the mind works after certain "stop and do X instead" rules when a kind of deliberation has taken a certain amount of time (Carruthers, *The Architecture of the Mind*, 228–29).

4.3 Determinism

If everything is determined, then we do not have free will in a strong sense of the term.[305] As seen in chapter one, by "determinism" I refer to the belief that everything that happens necessarily must happen exactly as it does because of previous physical causes and the laws of nature, so that there is at any time only one possible future. I agree with the Consequence Argument that we are not free if there is one unique future determined before we were born. If that is the case, then all we do in our lives are things we have to do and then our autobiographical self is the way it is and causes what it does because of events prior to our birth.

The question of whether or not the world is determined is very likely never to be finally solved, since it is highly probable that we can never know for sure whether the world is determined or not. Even if quantum mechanics today seems to support indeterminism at a low level in nature, there can always be a lower level where either everything is governed by laws we do not know, or where everything is random, but still leaves most things intelligible and orderly at our level of life. Does science today nevertheless give us reasons to think that the world probably is determined or not at the macro level of humans? It is often argued that quantum indeterminism usually decoheres at the macro level. But technology is now being produced based on quantum mechanics which seemingly can take this indeterminism to the macro level. I mentioned the example with the scientist who says that she will go to lunch after three clicks on the Geiger counter. It thus seems plausible to believe that there is indeterminism at the macro level of humans. Further, as John Earman shows, classical physics describing the macro level is also indeterministic. For example, in Newtonian physics, atoms can collide in ways that make their continuing trajectories undetermined.[306]

I think that indeterminism with undetermined macro-effects is necessary in order for us to have free will. However, unlike libertarians like Robert Kane, I do not believe that indeterminism has to be located in the brain. If the world is determined, we do not have free will, but since we will never know whether or

---

[305] When I talk about free will in this chapter, I mean it in a strong sense of the term.
[306] John Earman, *A Primer on Determinism*, University of Western Ontario Series in Philosophy of Science (Boston, MA: D. Reidel Pub. Co., 1986), 30–32. Earman also gives other examples from Newtonian and relativity physics. Important examples are briefly summarized in Lawrence Sklar, *Philosophy of Physics*, Dimensions of Philosophy Series (Boulder, CO: Westview Press, 1992), 203.

not it is determined, I shall presuppose that it is not, and I think that this is a warranted presupposition.[307] More precisely, my assumption is that indeterminism is something that occurs in the world in general and that has undetermined effects at the macro level of our human world. But what goes on in human brains may well happen as if the whole world were determined. If all this is true, then there is not one unique future that will happen as a matter of necessity. For example, a thunderstorm may occur because of sensitivity to small undetermined events. This kind of indeterminism does not exclude the scenario that a person in a certain situation may only have the token physically possibility to do one thing. Something like the following may happen without anything else being token physically possible for that person to do in that situation: A sense impression enters the brain and activates neural patterns that are experienced as imagined alternative actions, which again activate feelings connected to the alternative actions, which again lead to the neural pattern with the strongest feelings connected to it, activating motor neurons leading to action.[308]

Over that short period of time, the process may have occurred as if the whole world were determined, so that only one process in the brain was token physically possible there and then. And yet, it is important for free will that the world in general is not determined—but why? Let us say that the person in the example above faces a storm that was undetermined, and sees a young child in the sea about to drown. The person imagines two alternatives: to help the child or not. The process goes on in the person's brain as if determined and leads to action. The reason why it is important that the world in general is not determined is that then people will continually face situations that are not determined by the past. When they face these situations, processes go on in their mind, leading to one desire becoming the strongest, which then leads to action. But even if the process in the mind happens as if the whole world were determined, that is not important. What is important is that if the world is not determined, then it is right to select the autobiographical self as the cause of the strongest desire, which again is the cause of which alternative for action is chosen. Indeterminism in the brain is not required, but indeterminism in the world is required for it to be right to select the autobiographical self as the ultimate cause.

---

307 If I am wrong, I still had to make this presupposition since it was then determined before I was born that I would do so.
308 The neurobiologist Wolf Singer rejects free will and understands the process roughly like this. See Singer, in Geyer, *Hirnforschung und Willensfreiheit*, 56–58.

Why is it right to select the autobiographical self as the ultimate cause of the choice that is made if the world is not determined? In the example just given, the storm was undetermined, which means that it was not determined before the person was born whether she should save the drowning child or not. Since the storm was not determined to happen, it is right to select the autobiographical self as the cause if the following happened: The person saw the child and imagined two alternatives, to jump into the sea to save the child or not. The immediate desire is not to jump into the cold sea, but then memories from the autobiographical self are activated about being a person who does the right thing, thoughts about what people think of those who do not help children in need, and so on—and maybe also fear of death, so that the person has problems choosing. But when the person finally decides to jump into the sea, it will (sometimes) be the autobiographical self that causes saving the child to be the strongest desire, which then causes the person to jump into the water. When we select saving or non-saving as the contrastive effects and ask for the cause of why the person saves the child as opposed to not saving it, the answer is that the cause is the autobiographical self of the person. This means that even if everything in the person's brain happens as if the whole world were determined, if the world is in fact not determined, then sometimes it will be right to select the autobiographical self as the cause of a choice, and sometimes it will be right to select a person as the cause of a choice.

But is not the undetermined event that led to the storm now the cause of the person jumping in, not the person and not her autobiographical self? No, as one can see by considering contrasts. The undetermined event leading to a storm is not the cause of why the person jumps as opposed to not jumping. The undetermined event is the cause of why there is a storm as opposed to no storm. It creates a new setting in which a choice must be made, but it does not cause the choice. In the undetermined setting, the person and her autobiographical self is the cause of why she jumps, and that is why macro level indeterminism is required for free will.

But is not the undetermined storm a sufficient condition for the person jumping into the water, since I have said that everything may happen as determined in the mind of the person? No, and the reason is as follows: In the chapter on causation I used several examples to show that the distinction between sufficient and necessary conditions does not work to explain what a cause is. For example, both oxygen and ignition are necessary for a house to burn, but neither of them alone is sufficient for the house to burn, and yet both can be selected as causes. The reason is that we find causes by setting contrasts depending on what we already expect and what interests we have. In the case of the house burning, we are interested in why the house burnt as opposed to not burning, given that there was oxygen present. In the case of the storm, we are interested in why the person jumped as opposed to not jumping, given that there was a storm. If you say that the house burnt because there was oxygen present, I will keep asking why it burnt because oxygen is not the condition I am interested in. And if you say that the person jumped into the water because there was a storm, I will keep asking why the person jumped in because the storm is not the condition I am interested in. But when you cite a certain autobiographical self as the cause (a person with a heroic character, for example), I am satisfied with the answer. In questions concerning free will, our interest is in why people do A as opposed to B given certain conditions. If the cause is their autobiographical self, they act freely.

Here the challenges raised by Daniel Dennett against libertarianism mentioned at the end of chapter two are again relevant, for it seems that I could say the same in a deterministic world: The autobiographical self caused the desire to become what it became, just as the chess-playing computer caused the other computer to win by making a flawed chess move. You can say both that the computer was the cause of the chess move and that the particular chess move was determined, but it does not seem that indeterminism is required to select the computer as the cause. Thus, one could think that indeterminism is not important in order to select the autobiographical self as the cause. An important difference is that in Dennett's examples you have two causes selected at different levels, the computer and determinism. But in the case in which you save a child from drowning, there are not two causes—the autobiographical self and determinism. There is only one cause: the autobiographical self, for it is not determined that you will save the child. That the autobiographical self is the cause alone without it also being determined is what makes the autobiographical self the ultimate source, so that is what I mean by the expression "ultimate source" or "ultimate cause". This is the way in which the free will requirement of oneself being the ultimate source of a choice is fulfilled: The choice is not determined, but rather the cause of the choice is the autobiographical self.[309]

---

309 Alfred Mele discusses the difference between proximate and ultimate control, which is similar to John Martin Fischer's distinction between guidance and regulative control. Even in a deterministic universe, the driver controls the car in a way other than the passenger, but that may only be proximate and not ultimate control. But what is the difference between proximate and ultimate control? Mele suggests that the difference lies only in ultimate control being proximate control without determinism (Mele, *Free Will and Luck*, 7). That is also what I suggest here, but we differ in that Mele requires internal indeterminism for ultimate control while I find external indeterminism sufficient (*Autonomous Agents*, 213).

It may seem strange to create a divide between the brain and the rest of the world and suggest that there is indeterminism in the world, but not in the brain. But that is not what I am doing. What I am arguing is that it is very uncertain that in the small portion of the world that consists of brains you will find the right kind of indeterminism that will give us free will. It is much more likely that somewhere in the whole world some indeterministic events have effects that make more than one future possible at the macro level of humans. I am not proposing an ontological divide between brains and the world; I am only saying that it is more likely that any kind of undetermined macro level effect exists in the whole world than that a specific effect exists at the right place in the brain. The advantage of my theory is that it only requires external indeterminism for agents to be the causes of their actions, and not a more specific indeterministic process in the brain that we do not know exists at all. This makes the theory more robust.

After this discussion, I also have the resources to refute Alfred Mele's arguments against external indeterminism as a solution to the problem of free will. Mele has four counterarguments.[310] The first argument is that if an indeterministic bomb exploded, for example, on September 15, 1969, it gives another future than if it had not exploded, but it does not give us free will. I argue that it does, because in this scenario it is not determined before our birth what will happen. In this scenario, one can select the self as the cause of an action without determinism also being the cause of the action, and thus the self becomes the ultimate source of the choice. In this scenario, since undetermined events like the bomb are possible, other events will also be undetermined, and so our selves will be the cause of many actions.

Mele tries to push the point further by suggesting that if the bomb did not explode on September 15, 1969, and that were the only indeterministic devices in the world, then we would no longer be free after that date. But Mele finds it preposterous to suggest something like that. I reply that such a world would be extremely close to a deterministic world. If the bomb were set such that it would either explode or not on September 15, 1969, then only one future would have been possible up to that date and after that only one future would be possible. In effect, the world would have been determined up to that date and after that date, and so I agree that we would not have free will in such a scenario. But it is still important that the world is undetermined in general, with several undeter-

---

[310] *Autonomous Agents*, 195–96.

mined events, and the argument does not refute that.[311] The more undetermined the world the world is, the larger role our selves can play.

Mele asks us to consider two worlds, one of which has undetermined bombs and the other determined. Let us then say that none of the bombs go off, so that everything that happens in the two worlds is identical. Could it then be right to say that those living in the determined world are not free, but that those in the undetermined world are free? Here it is open whether the two worlds by accident happen to be identical, or whether everything in the world with the undetermined bombs (except for the bombs) is determined. If everything is determined but the bombs, my reply is like above, that it almost becomes a determined world. But if it accidentally is the same, but many events were undetermined, our selves will play a larger role. So an example with only a few undetermined bombs not going off does not show that a world with indeterminism as a general feature cannot support free will.

Mele's final point is that external indeterminism does not secure free will, as libertarians want the future to be up to them. I agree that free will implies that what happens in the future is up to the agent, but what that means is that the self is the ultimate cause of the action, and the self can be that as long as the world is not determined. The way I see it, none of Mele's counterarguments refutes the solution I here offer to the problem of free will.

So far, I have shown how the autobiographical self can be the cause of a choice, but how does the autobiographical self become the way it is? It does not help free will that the autobiographical self is the cause if the autobiographical self itself is caused by factors external to the person, regardless of whether the world is determined or not, for then it would seem that the agent being the ultimate cause disappears. In the following argument, we shall see that the autobiographical self shapes itself into an increasingly independent self through choices where the autobiographical self changes initial desires. Because the world is undetermined, it is right to say that internal processes in the autobiographical self shape the autobiographical self from within over time.

4.4 Independence of the Self

At the beginning of life children follow their initial desires, and they are told by their caregivers who they are and what is right or wrong or good or bad. The

---

311 New quantum technology suggests that it is actually possible to construct bombs such as this because of technology sensitive to quantum indeterministic events.

children act on their desires or do as they are told and we do not blame them morally for what they do wrong to the same degree as we blame adults for doing the same. But most children are born with a capacity for reasoning and feeling and thinking new thoughts and making new connections in their minds, which gives them a general ability to find out what is true and good and right.

Imagine then a situation which is not determined to happen: a young girl meets a foreign boy. The girl has been told by her parents what should be done: Stay away from those foreigners, for they are evil people! Until now, she has believed the stories she has been told by her parents about foreigners, so her initial desire is to back away. But then there is a process in the mind of the person of thinking and feeling based on her general capacity for thinking and previous experiences. "Maybe the foreigner is a nice guy? One cannot judge all individuals based on their group identity. Other people have turned out not to be as I expected. He does actually seem quite nice," etc. This process of thinking and feeling then leads to the result that the girl ends up thinking differently from what she was told and feeling differently from what she initially felt. Her new thoughts and her desire then make her approach the foreigner instead of backing away.

What caused the desire that caused the alternative that was actually chosen? The concrete situation she was in was not determined to happen. What caused the final desire was the process in the mind of the girl. These thoughts and this action and the whole experience are then added to her autobiographical self. Later, she experiences new processes in which new thoughts and feelings change the initial desires and cause action. Again, the autobiographical self is changed from within the mind of the person. And even in new choices, the old choices and experiences from the autobiographical self change the initial desires, and again the experience is stored in the autobiographical self. So, sometimes a mind-internal process happening independent of the autobiographical self can change the autobiographical self, for example if a new experience gives rise to a new thought or a new feeling. But most often, when the autobiographical self changes, the process will involve the autobiographical self so that there is interplay between the autobiographical self and new thoughts and feelings. This means that as long as the world is not determined, it will often be right to select the autobiographical self as the cause of a change in initial desires *and as the cause of new changes in the autobiographical self*. This is illustrated in Figures 2a and 2b.

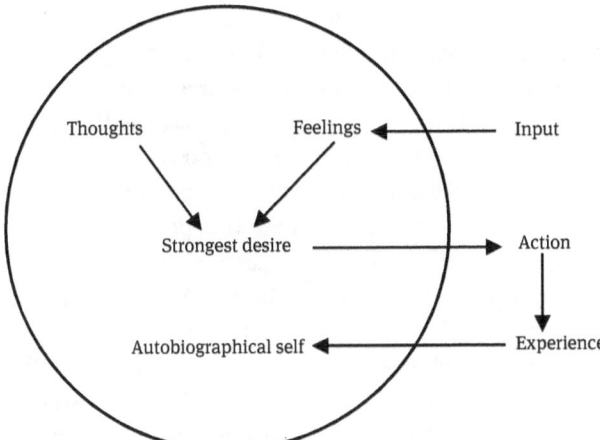

Fig. 2a: Input comes through the senses and thoughts and feelings influence what is desired the strongest. The person acts and the action is stored as a remembered experience in the autobiographical self.

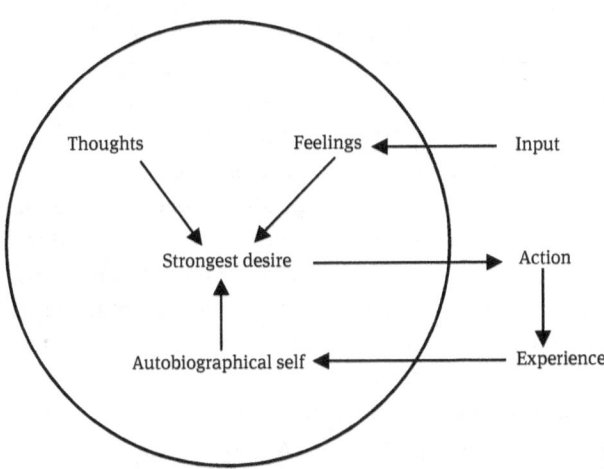

Fig. 2b: Input comes through the senses and thoughts and feelings influence the desire. In addition, the autobiographical self also influences which desire becomes the strongest. The person acts and the action is stored as a remembered experience in the autobiographical self. In this way, the autobiographical self can cause changes to itself over time.

When this interplay happens in the mind, the autobiographical self changes itself in a mind-internal process to become more and more self-formed, or to use another word: independent. In each token situation, the processes in the mind happen causally as if the whole world were determined. But because the world is not determined, it will often be right to select the autobiographical self as the cause of a desire which again causes a certain choice to be made. We shall consider later situations in which the self does not become independent, for this independence is a matter of degrees. But now I shall recapitulate what has so far been said about free will in those cases in which the autobiographical self changes initial desires. Such cases fulfil the definition of free will in the following way: That "it is up to us what we choose among alternatives and that the source of the choice is in us" means that by recalling memories, the autobiographical self of a person changes the initial desires of the person so that the autobiographical self causes the desire which again causes the choice that is made, and this autobiographical self is formed from within through similar earlier choices in which the autobiographical self, in interplay with new thoughts and feelings, was the cause of the change.

There may seem to be a vicious regress here, similar to the one Galen Strawson lays out in his Basic Argument, that we follow causes backwards and backwards to before the agent can make an ultimate choice.[312] But there is no vicious regress here. A person starts life without an independent self, but by use of the general capacity for thinking and feeling in meeting with new and undetermined experiences, that person builds up from within an autobiographical self from experiences experienced as good or bad, and the autobiographical self gets an increasingly larger role, by which the person gets more freedom and more responsibility. It is the indeterminism that breaks off the regress, since like in the example above with the storm, when the previous causes like the storm were not determined to happen, it was right to select the autobiographical self as the cause. In the beginning it is not an independent autobiographical self we select as cause, but over time a more and more self-caused and independent autobiographical self can be selected as cause.

Of course, the choices made by this autobiographical self do depend on the general capacities for thinking and feeling that it starts out with, and which experiences it has will often be a matter of luck, but that is the start package from which an autobiographical self is built, and we cannot demand from free will that there should be an uncaused beginning—that would not give any more

---

[312] Galen Strawson, "The Impossibility of Moral Responsibility," *Philosophical Studies* 75, no. 1/2 (1994): 5–7.

freedom, either. It is logically impossible for anything to cause itself before it starts to exist, so we must start with something given, and from there more freedom and responsibility can be achieved. If this general starting point does not work properly, or gets destroyed by causes outside, we find that this reduces freedom and responsibility, as I shall say more about below.

Why all this focus on the autobiographical self? How is it related to me having free will? When I am concerned that "I" have free will, what does "I" refer to then? What is it that makes it important for us to have free will? What should be the cause of our choices in order for us to have a free will worth wanting? I shall later defend the claim that free will is about inner-directedness. When a choice is made, a desire in a person causes that choice. In that sense it is inner-directed since it was caused by something inside a person. But for "me" or "I" to have control, we also want our desires to be something we have formed from within and have control over. The way in which that happens is that desires cause actions, the memory of the experience of those actions is stored in the autobiographical self, and the experiences stored in the autobiographical self can then later change desires and thus be the cause of future choices. When the autobiographical self causes the choice of a person, then that person is not just inner-directed in the sense that actions are caused by desires in his or her body, but it is also an inner-directed inner-directedness since choices over time have shaped the autobiographical self that caused the choice. So when the autobiographical self causes choices, we are inner-directed to a larger degree since the choice is then inner-directed by something inner-directed; in other words it is an accumulation of inner-directedness. This understanding of free will fits well with experience and intuitions. The most paradigmatic cases of free will are those in which we make choices based on how we have shaped our character over years, whereas more spontaneous actions that are caused by desires in us but contrary to our character feel less free. That makes people say "I was not myself when I did that," and we may hold them less responsible, as I shall show later in an example of spontaneously knocking a person down as opposed to planning it. These experiences support the theory that we are free when the autobiographical self is the cause of our desires. I will develop these points further, but mention it here since readers may otherwise wonder why I am focusing so much on this autobiographical self.

Thus far, I have been concerned only with cases in which the autobiographical self causes the desire but, as mentioned before, there are many different kinds of deliberative process, and it is common to think that people are free and responsible in many cases in which the autobiographical self does not change any initial desires. It is important for my argument to specify that the relationship between freedom and responsibility can be understood in different ways. It is common to think that responsibility requires a certain kind of freedom, so that you are not responsible if you do not have this kind of freedom. But I shall use the term free will in the sense of inner-directedness and explain what this means and how we can have different degrees of free will, while I shall argue that responsibility is best understood as something we can ascribe to people in order to make them behave better. Some will think that we cannot plausibly hold people responsible if free will is what I suggest that it is. For that reason I shall now present my understanding of responsibility, and then turn to the other cases of deliberative processes to decide whether they are examples of free will and choices for which one is responsible.

4.5 Responsibility

The question of responsibility is a major one with many positions I cannot discuss in detail here. This subchapter is meant as a brief description of a coherent understanding of responsibility, but it is not possible to address all the possible objections. The main purpose served here is to discuss a kind of thinking coherent with what is said about free will, and it directs the reader to where more on the same can be found. I start by presenting some theories similar to my own, and then some relevant distinctions and problems, before finally presenting my own view.

Typically, libertarians will focus on responsibility being something which requires free will and control, so that people can fairly be held responsible and deserve their blame or praise. An alternative approach usually just found among compatibilists is to consider the good consequences of holding others responsible even if they do not have the kind of control libertarians imagine. An important question is then the question of basic desert: do people deserve praise or blame just in virtue of what they have done, or does praise and blame have other kinds of justification, like people wanting others to behave better?

P. F. Strawson famously argued that moral responsibility should be understood in light of reactive attitudes: resentment and praise are attitudes by which people react to other people's actions. Even if one could argue that some people will not deserve the blame or praise they are given, Strawson considered this way of interacting as a part of our psychological make-up which we cannot change.³¹³ Derk Pereboom is a free will skeptic who argues in favor of a theory of moral responsibility without basic desert. He finds that we should still punish people by putting them to jail, by then with the same logic as when sick people are put in quarantine—it is done to protect others. Generally, Pereboom finds that treatment of criminals should be much more humane and constructive than what it is today.

Michael McKenna quotes Pereboom, saying that we should stop blaming people and engage more constructively with them, but McKenna finds blame (the way he understands it) to be a constructive engagement with others.³¹⁴ His theory compares moral responsibility with conversation and says that moral responsibility fundamentally is an interpersonal process between a person who is morally responsible and a person who is holding the other morally responsible by interacting with her in certain ways.³¹⁵ The actions that a person is responsible for express the quality of the will of that person, and other persons can respond to these in a similar way as one does in a conversation.³¹⁶ He is here inspired by Strawson in finding the practice of holding others responsible as a practical attitude people have towards others,³¹⁷ and by Gary Watson, who argued that holding others responsible is a way of communicating our moral expectations,³¹⁸ and by George Sher, who argues that we blame people because we want them to behave according to common moral standards.³¹⁹

McKenna does not think that a plausible theory of responsibility requires the element that it must be deserved, but he nevertheless includes it in his theory. He does not include it in the sense that people deserve to be harmed as a revenge for what they have done wrong. Rather, he thinks that there is harm in blame which comes from how blaming reduces the blamed person's possibilities for good interaction with others (and this is why blame only hurts people

---

313 P.F. Strawson, "Freedom and Resentment," in *The Philosophy of Free Will: Essential Readings from the Contemporary Debates*, ed. Paul Russell and Oisín Deery (New York: Oxford University Press, 2013 (1962)), 13.
314 Michael McKenna, *Conversation & Responsibility* (New York: Oxford University Press, 2011), 147–48.
315 Ibid., ix.
316 Ibid.
317 Ibid., 2.
318 Ibid., 3, referring to Gary Watson, "Responsibility and the Limits of Evil: Variations on a Strawsonian Theme," in *Responsibility, Character, and the Emotions: New Essays in Moral Psychology*, ed. Ferdinand David Schoeman (New York: Cambridge University Press, 1987).
319 McKenna, *Conversation & Responsibility*, 168, referring to George Sher, *In Praise of Blame* (New York: Oxford University Press, 2005).

who care about not being blamed).³²⁰ McKenna finds it good that people interact socially, and that when someone acts blameworthy, others communicate their moral demands, expectations or disapproval, which may harm, but that is a part of the social game.³²¹

A similar approach to McKenna, can be found in Manuel Vargas' revisionist approach. He defends the view that blame and praise are justified by the general effect that they have on people in cultivating moral agency.³²² He finds that the common critique against such "moral influence" theories fail when one considers the effect on a general level. So even if individual cases of holding others responsible do not have the intention or effect that a person behaves better, it is a practice which in general make people responsive to moral considerations.³²³

Concerning the charge that moral influence theories do not have room for basic desert, Vargas comments that "deserve" can mean many different things, and that there is no good reason why basic desert should be a special kind of desert especially important to the practice of holding others responsible.³²⁴ Vargas rejects basic desert, but defends desert in a wider sense, similar to Christopher Bennett's social self-governance model of deserving blame. Here the point is that it is crucial to the practice of holding people responsible that people acknowledge that they deserve blame and, due to this, morally reorient themselves.³²⁵ My own understanding of responsibility lies close to the theories of Vargas and McKenna and focuses on the good consequences of holding others responsible. Before presenting it, I shall consider some relevant distinctions and problems which help us understand the problem better.

There is a difference between *causal* responsibility, which is when someone is the cause of something, and *moral* responsibility. One can be causally responsible for something without being morally responsible, e.g., if you do something by accident, and one can be morally responsible also for things you do not do in a certain situation.³²⁶ Another distinction is between responsibility

---

320 McKenna, *Conversation & Responsibility*, 138, 67.
321 Ibid., 141–45.
322 Manuel Vargas, *Building Better Beings: A Theory of Moral Responsibility* (Oxford: Oxford University Press, 2013), 166.
323 Ibid., 172–73. For a more detailed defense, see ibid., 187–95.
324 Ibid., 249–56.
325 Ibid., 262–66, referring to Christopher Bennett, "The Varieties of Retributive Experience," *Philosophical Quarterly* 52, no. 207 (2002).
326 McKenna here holds that moral responsibility presupposes causal responsibility, whereas I disagree.

as *attributability* and responsibility as *accountability*. Responsibility as attributability is an evaluation of an agent as moral agent: she is a saint or a coward. Responsibility as accountability is when a person is treated as someone who should live up to certain expectations and included in the practice of blame and praise. This is the sort of responsibility relevant for the debate on free will.

This distinction between two kinds of responsibility is similar to two other distinctions between two kinds of blame. McKenna distinguishes between private blame and overt blame, where private blame is attitudes experienced by a person who privately blames someone, but not outwardly manifested as in overt blame.[327] Manuel Vargas makes a distinction by the terms Blame 1, which is a judgment-like attitude where one cognitively judges that something is wrong, and Blame 2, which are blaming reactions felt emotionally.[328] He calls Blame 1 blaming in a minimal sense, while Blame 1 and 2 together are blaming in a robust sense.[329] McKenna finds that merely a judgment that someone has not acted right is not enough for holding them responsible; there must be a practical attitude toward the other, in addition.[330] As he argues, Satan can think that you did something morally wrong, but without holding you morally responsible.[331]

This raises the question of the relation between holding responsible and blaming, and between holding responsible and being responsible. I consider blaming as one kind of holding responsible (when one thinks a person has done something wrong), while praising is another kind of holding responsible (when one thinks that a person has done something good). I shall focus on blame in what follows.

An important distinction is between being responsible and being held responsible. McKenna rejects Strawson's position that holding responsible is more fundamental than being responsible.[332] Rather, he finds them to mutually dependent, metaphysically speaking.[333] *Being* morally responsible is to be able to participate in the practice of being held responsible, i.e. being able to grasp and appreciate instances of praise and blame and react accordingly.[334] When it comes to *holding* one morally responsible, McKenna offers the following definition: A holds B morally responsible and blameworthy for act x if (1) A believes

---

327 Ibid., 26.
328 Vargas, *Building Better Beings*, 116–21.
329 Ibid., 117-18.
330 McKenna, *Conversation & Responsibility*, 36–38.
331 Ibid., 106.
332 Ibid., 3.
333 Ibid., 54.
334 Ibid., 49.

that B is blameworthy for x-ing, (2) A endorses the moral basis for judging that x-ing is morally wrong, (3) A desires that B not have x-ed, (4) A's reason for desiring that B not have x-ed is that conditions 1 and 2 are satisfied, and (5) because conditions 1 through 4 are satisfied, A is either disposed to regard and in some cases responds to B negatively, or believes that it would be appropriate to do so.[335]

Condition 1 is a necessary presupposition for blaming; condition 2 excludes the case of Satan who believes that B is blameworthy, but does not endorse the moral basis; condition 3 extends holding responsible to being more than a mere judgment, condition 4 excludes cases where a person desire that B not have x-ed for the right reason (for moral reasons, and not for example in order to win a bet); and condition 5 extends the concept of holding morally responsible to include a practical attitude.

When McKenna focuses on holding responsible and blaming as practical attitudes to be understood in light of conversation, one could ask in what sense it is meaningful to blame people who are absent or even dead, which it seems we often do. McKenna understands these as derivative cases where we act as we would have acted if they were present.[336] But he thinks that within his conversational model it makes less sense to say that one can blame Custer or Caesar since they are so far away that we hardly know how we would interact with them.[337]

Manuel Vargas mostly writes about what justifies the practice of holding responsible, and argues that it is the general effect of cultivating agency. Since blaming is meant to have this general effect on people it is no problem to including blaming dead people, which is something that we today still can learn from. Vargas ends his book by asking whether this means that people really *are* morally responsible. He answers that moral responsibility—"whatever that is"—is what licenses the practice of blame and praise, which again is a social web of interactions cultivating agency. Maybe, he says, there is no such thing as responsibility as commonly thought, only responsibility*, but he finds it most important that the practice of holding others responsible is justified and should continue.[338]

I agree with very much of what McKenna and Vargas say about responsibility, although I find it important that holding others responsible becomes more

---

335 Ibid., 25.
336 Ibid., 176–77.
337 Ibid., 177–78.
338 Vargas, *Building Better Beings*, 310–11.

important and meaningful in an indetermined world, whereas McKenna and Vargas are compatibilists.[339] I will start with some more terminology to be precise about where I differ from them and how I would explain some things differently.

For understanding responsibility, I find it very important to see that when we hold others responsible we compare a person's action with a moral standard concerning what a person in general should have done in such a situation. This means that when you are in a situation, people will hold you responsible *according to a standard* related to that situation, which means that you can also be held responsible for something that you have *not* done. If a child is drowning while you are nearby, people think that the morally right thing to do in such a situation is to jump into the water and try to save the child. If you do not, people will hold you responsible and blame you according to this standard, even if you did not cause the child to drown.[340] If you do not do what people think you should have done, or do what they think you should not have done, it is considered blameworthy, whereas a high score on the moral standard of situations is considered praiseworthy.[341] I think that this makes it clear that one can be morally responsible for something one is not causally responsible for, contrary to what McKenna holds.[342]

Usually, one will compare another person's action with the moral standard that one acknowledges as the right standard to follow, but of course there are also cases like McKenna's Satan-case, where Satan can compare your action with a Christian moral standard or his own preferred standard. One may also philosophically compare an action with standards from different ethical models.

---

339 McKenna, *Conversation & Responsibility*, 13, Vargas, *Building Better Beings*, 53.
340 If one has a broad understanding of causes, including absences as causes, moral responsibility and causal responsibility are not so different, since one could then claim that not saving the child caused it to drown. But let us say the child had inhaled so much water that she could not have been saved, even if the person had jumped in to save the child. Then the person was not in any way the cause of death, but we would still have blamed the person for not jumping in and trying to save her because the person failed to act according to our moral standard. Thus moral responsibility and causal responsibility remain different.
341 The main idea that responsibility is about comparing actions and motives with a standard related to the situation is similar to the view found in Bok, *Freedom and Responsibility*, chapters four and six.
342 McKenna, *Conversation & Responsibility*, 7.

Holding responsible and blaming/praising[343] are concepts that are used in various ways in daily speech. Above, I mentioned different distinctions offered by McKenna and Vargas. I want to be even more precise and list up different components that are ingredients in different kinds of holding responsible or blaming. I sort them according to what is logically the most fundamental part, which means that the later parts presuppose the earlier parts. I will explain the distinctions afterwards:

1) Compare what a person does in a situation with any standard or your acknowledged standard for what should or should not be done in that situation;
2) Judge cognitively and/or feel emotionally that a person in a situation failed to act according to your acknowledged standard;
3) Judge cognitively and/or feel emotionally that a person in a situation should act according to your acknowledged standard;
4) Express with language or body language that a person in a situation failed to act according to your acknowledged standard;
5) Express with language or body language that a person in a situation should act according to your acknowledged standard;
6) Express that a person in a situation failed to act according to your acknowledged standard with no desire that the person[344] should behave according to that standard;
7) Express that a person in a situation failed to act or should act according to your acknowledged standard without a conscious desire that the person should behave according to that standard (this one may fit with either 6 or 8);
8) Express that a person in a situation failed to act or should act according to your acknowledged standard with a conscious desire that the person should behave according to that standard;
9) Consider oneself justified in expressing that a person in a situation should act according to your acknowledged standard.

Concerning number 1, I find it to be essential, and most commonly people will compare other people's actions or lack of action with their own preferred moral standard. Concerning numbers 2 and 3, people may judge cognitively and/or

---

343 In the following I will focus on blame only.
344 I write "person" in singularis, but it may refer to persons in general, since sometimes we consider what we think people in general should do. For example, people should help victims in a car accident.

feel emotionally that a person in a situation failed to act according to your acknowledged standard or should act according to it. When it is only judged cognitively or felt emotionally, it is private and not expressed as in the next points. I distinguish between judging that a person *failed to act* as opposed to *should act*, since sometimes people note that people did not act according to standard, but they do not care about them doing so, and so they do not judge that they should have acted thusly. I may, for example, find that a person did something stupid without caring about what he should have done instead.

Concerning numbers 4 and 5, these are versions of 2 and 3 where what is thought or felt is also expressed. Again I distinguish between expressing that someone *failed to act* in number 4 as opposed to expressing that they *should have acted* a certain way in number 5. Number 5 will be an instance of holding responsible, whereas number 4 may be just an instance of ridiculing or something else where the person expressing her thought/feelings need not care about what the person ridiculed should have done.

The first five points let us see that one may make a judgment with or without holding responsible, and one may hold responsible in the sense of internal judgment or externally expressing the internal judgment. 1 and 2 constitute an internal judgment only. It is not an act of holding responsible in any sense, but it might have a similar function nonetheless, influencing your own behavior in the future. Numbers 1, 2, and 3 constitute holding responsible in the sense of making an internal judgment of responsibility. 1, 2, and 4 constitute expressing an internal judgment only. It is not an act of holding responsible, but might have the same function nonetheless, in influencing future behavior. 1, 2, 3, 4, and 5 constitute holding responsible in the sense of external expression of internal judgment.

These first five components can be combined with different desires and/or intentions, consciously or non-consciously, which I have tried to specify as different options in points 6, 7, and 8. In number 6, one specifically does not want the other person to change or does not care how the considered person behaves. In number 7 there is no conscious desire that the person should act according to standard, so non-consciously there may be either a desire that she does, or does not, or no non-conscious desire at all, which makes number 7 compatible with either 6 or 8. In number 8 there is a conscious desire that the considered person should act according to standard.

It seems to me that 1, 2, 3, 4, 5 and either 7 or 8 are what McKenna would think of as a full-fledged instance of holding responsible. Number 9 is included to understand the cases where a person judges that someone else has failed to act according to standard and she desires that the other person should act according to standard, but she does not feel that she has the right or that it would be proper for her to express it. Maybe it concerns other people's children or maybe you have done the same mistake yourself, etc., and so you do not feel entitled to blame the other person.

Now that we have considered the components in different kinds of holding responsible, other terms can also be defined, and I start with blame. Blaming can be done either as an internal judgment or as an expressing of the internal judgment. This means that blaming is the same as holding responsible, but blaming is always a negative judgment, whereas "holding responsible" leaves it open whether the judgment is positive or negative. In the positive case, it would be praise. Blaming in the sense of internal judgment consists of components 1, 2 and 3. Blaming in the sense of external expressing of internal judgment consists of components 1, 2, 3, 4 and 5. One may blame a person in the sense of internal judgment in 1, 2 and 3, but withhold external expression of it because of point 9—one does not find that oneself is justified or entitled to blame the other.

What does it then mean to *be* responsible as opposed to *being held* responsible? In my view, a person is responsible for what he or she does or does not do in a situation if it is type physically possible for that person to act in a morally different way in a way which can be influenced by being held responsible. Being responsible is the requirement that makes it worthwhile to hold people responsible. In order for that to make more sense, I will now say more about the justification for the practice of holding responsible and go more into detail on the process of comparing what people do with a standard for what they should have done in that situation.

I agree with Vargas that even though the practice of holding others responsible can have different reasons and justifications, a main justification of it is that it is a general way of making people behave better.[345] He defends it well against the common types of critique,[346] but I shall look especially into the question of what makes blame fair, just or deserved on such an understanding of responsibility. But first, I must say more about comparing people's actions with a standard for that situation.

People usually have a capability of formal reasoning and a normal emotional life. Because they have this, other people expect that they will understand what is true and what it is right to do in various situations. We expect that they learn certain norms and that these norms are alternatives they consider when they make choices. As people grow older and become adults, we expect that

---

345 Vargas, *Building Better Beings*, 166, 86.
346 Ibid., 187–95.

they have had enough time to think and make their own experiences to have understood essentially what is true and right. Then we also expect them to act in accordance with that understanding.

But when it comes to holding others responsible, we make various adjustments. If a person's understanding of what is true and right or her emotional life have been destroyed, we tend to consider this as mitigating since these are important for the choice of action. For example, children may have had their emotional life destroyed by child abuse, or people growing up in sects may have been brainwashed, and so on. They have less responsibility in such cases, because their selves are less independent—for a *mind-external* reason. If they have made their selves into irresponsible selves from within, then we do hold them responsible, because the reason for their irresponsibility is *mind-internal*. The presupposition is that having a normal mind over time should lead to good and right choices and this is the default standard according to which we hold people responsible. But if there are mind-external reasons that have made it more difficult for them to behave according to the moral standard, we do find it mitigating, and rather blame those who have made it difficult for others to become good moral agents in the normal way.

It makes sense to focus on the cause of the behaviour we want changed. If a person has been hypnotized, or someone has made a person unable to act well, then we hold these other people responsible instead, since they have caused the person not to behave well, since it is best to change those who are the causes of something bad. That we focus on causes and use a default standard where people are allowed to make relevant experiences over time greatly reduces the problem of luck. The fact that luck plays a role is taken into consideration as a general rule, but in individual cases it will, of course, be difficult to know how large a role luck has played.

This actualizes the question of fair or deserved blame. My understanding of responsibility is in one sense the same and in another sense different from McKenna and Vargas. It is different in the sense that they are compatibilists, while I think that the world is not determined and that the practice of holding responsible is more important and more meaningful than what it is if the world is determined. If the world is determined, then every time I hold another person responsible for something, it was already determined before my birth that I should do so, and only one future is possible. If the world is not determined, then several futures are possible and concrete instances of holding others responsible can be the ultimate cause of why the future becomes A as opposed to B.

This is an important difference between my position and that of McKenna and Vargas. On the other hand, my position is quite similar, since I have said that although the world in general is not determined, in specific cases it may be the case that what the person does is the only thing that the person has token ability to do.

Galen Strawson has argued that that would be morally wrong to hold someone responsible if there is only one thing that a person has token physical possibility to do in a given situation.[347] I disagree, because the phenomenon of holding people responsible is part of what determines what the only token physical possibility is. There may be a situation A in which the only thing that Bob had the token ability to do was something wrong, and another situation B, very similar to A, but in which the only thing that Bob had the token ability to do was something right because he was held responsible for that kind of action. Perhaps he remembered having been held responsible before, or he saw the telling look from his father as he was about to act and this caused feelings in Bob that made him choose something else.

This would not be the case in a determined world, where it was determined before birth what Bob would do. But in an indetermined world, even if there is only one thing that is token physically possible for one person to do, an act of holding people responsible can change what that one token physical possible alternative is.

But if only one thing is token physically possible in a situation, how can holding someone responsible change what is token physically possible? If just one thing is token physically possible, how can it be changed? The question is relevant, so a more precise way of making my point would be to say that a situation in which one is held responsible and a situation in which one is not held responsible are two different situations. But this means that the act of holding others responsible is more important in an indetermined than a determined world, since it causes which future is actualized.

Could it still be that *holding people responsible* is a meaningful way of trying to influence their behavior, while *blaming* them is meaningless when only one thing was token physically possible? Well, blaming someone also influences what is token physically possible in a situation and the thought can arise in a person that "If I do this, people will blame me afterwards." So even blaming people is a meaningful attempt at influencing others to behave better.

---

347 Haji, in Kane, *The Oxford Handbook of Free Will* (1st ed.), 205–06.

Now it is time to ask if it is fair to blame someone if what they did was the only thing that was token physically possible for that person to do in a situation? Maybe it will influence them to behave better the next time, but is it fair? What is implicitly said when I blame a person who only had one token physically possible alternative is that the person should have changed her autobiographical self through earlier choices so that another alternative would have become the only token physically possible alternative now. Maybe the only token physically possible act a person could do in a situation was to hit someone. Then we can blame them for not having previously made themselves into a person who would not have hit someone in this situation.

But surely the earlier choices were also situations in which only one alternative was token physically possible. Is it ever fair to blame people then? If a person makes a series of bad choices throughout her life, when we pass judgement on that series of choices we say about the process that it is a bad one—that better choices should have been made—compared with the default standard of moral development. Since the world is not determined, practices such as holding people responsible and blaming are ways of influencing such series of choices to become better. The series of choices could have been different and how people become depends greatly on the responses they get from the context in which they grow up. Just think of the difference between growing up in the extreme context of warfare and growing up in a just society.

Given the fact that people grow up in different contexts and that luck plays a great part in our lives, what does it mean for blame to be fair, just or deserved? This is a big question that I will treat only briefly. I agree with Vargas both that the concept has many meanings and that basic desert is not so important as some philosophers seem to think. It seems to me that Neil Levy is correct in saying that, broadly speaking, desert and justice are overlapping concepts.[348] Justice can be thought of as either distributive (concerning how goods should be shared) or retributive (concerning how wrongs should be punished). Distributive justice could be understood so that it is just that all get the same, or that all get according to effort, or that all get according to need. Based on all these different understandings of distributive justice, some can say that people deserve to get the same, or according to effort, or according to need, and also that it is just or fair that they do so. For example all humans deserve to be treated with respect, the person who ran fastest deserved to win, or sick people deserve treatment—and it is fair and just that they do so. Concerning distributive justice,

---

[348] Levy, *Hard Luck*, 13.

some will say that criminals deserve punishment, and that it is fair and just that they do so.

What then is the relevant desert when it comes to praise and blame, and what, more specifically, is basic desert? It seems to me again that the basis for people's judgment of what is fair or deserved is a standard of justice that they use in different situations. People will use different standards, so those oriented politically to the left may judge that people deserve more according to need, while those oriented to right may judge that people deserve according to accomplishment.

Also, when holding others responsible in general, people use different ethical standards. Those who want people to change so that they make good choices on their own will often employ a standard of virtue or intentionality ethics. In that case, they will hold a person responsible for trying to do something wrong, even if the person did not succeed in doing it, because they want to change that person's character. In the legal system, on the other hand, it is difficult to judge people's virtues, so it is more common that people are convicted according to a standard of consequence ethics (although intention also plays a part). For example, you may go to prison for running over your daughter with your car, even if it was an accident, because the judges cannot know for certain in such cases whether it was on purpose or not.[349]

If there is an ethical standard for all situations which has truth value, then claims about responsibility in specific situations are objective facts about the world and then it is also true that people are responsible in those situations. If there is no ethical standard with truth value, then claims about responsibility in

---

[349] This understanding allows me to give the following answers to some problems on responsibility. John Martin Fischer puts forth one problem (Fischer, in Kane, *The Oxford Handbook of Free Will* (1st ed.), 284): A person sees a crime, but does not bother to call the police. However, his phone line has been cut, so even if he had tried, he would not have been able to reach the police. Was he responsible for not calling the police? I would answer: Yes, because according to a standard of intentionality ethics, he can be blamed for behaving irresponsibly in that he did not try to call the police. However, he will not be punished on the basis of any legal sanction. Another problem is the Kane/Widerker objection to Frankfurt-style examples. If the controller does not interfere, Frankfurt holds the agent responsible. Against this Kane and Widerker ask: What should the person have done instead? (See, for example, Widerker, in ibid., 329). My answer is that the person should have tried to act differently, which would have made the controller interfere, and then the controller would be the cause of what the person did. If the person does not try to do anything, but performs a bad act independently, we can blame the person for this according to a standard of intentionality ethics.

specific situations are not objective facts about the world, but rather a just matter of being held responsible by someone.

Back to the question of desert: if the basis for desert is people's standards, what are they specifically after when it comes to basic desert? Punishment and praise can be given different justifications based on their good consequences, but the point with basic desert is that it should not be warranted by such consequences. It seems to me that the basis for the idea of basic desert—that people deserve good or bad just for having done good or bad—is a (non-conscious) idea that good and bad should be evenly distributed. If you do bad to someone, you deserve punishment yourself and if you do good to someone you deserve something good (like praise) yourself because that maintains balance. If that is the case, this is also a case of comparing what happens with a standard (that all should be balanced).

If this is right, there is no special reason why basic desert is more important than other kinds of desert. And if it is wrong, it is not important for my understanding that basic desert should be included anyway.

4.6 Free Will and Responsibility in Various Cases

Thus far, I have shown how the definition of free will is fulfilled in cases in which the autobiographical self changes the initial desires, and I have presented my understanding of responsibility. As exemplified in the introduction to this chapter, however, there are many different kinds of deliberative process (see Figure 1). I now comment upon these different kinds and discuss to what extent they are examples of free will. I start with more general examples and then turn to typical problematic cases.

Rather than focusing on the divide between free and non-free choices, I argue that we should think of free will as existing along a continuum. Recall the definition of free will: It is up to us what we choose among alternatives and the source of the choice is in us. Kane has shown that the most important part of having free will is the second part, i.e., being the source of a choice. The definition of free will thus has a strong focus on *inner-directedness* by the claim that the source of the choice must be in us. When we see that free will is about inner-directedness, it is easier to grasp the claim about degrees on a continuum. People have different degrees of free will and they exert different degrees of free will in the different choices they make. This scale goes from un-free, in the sense that the person is not the cause of the choice, to (a little) free in the sense that the person—but not the autobiographical self—is the cause of the choice that is made (and the person can be more or less involved in the choice), to (more) free in the sense that the autobiographical self is the cause of the choice that is made (and the autobiographical self can be more or less involved in the choice), to (very) free in the sense that an independent autobiographical self is the cause of the choice that is made (and the autobiographical self can be more or less independent). This may seem strange, but I shall justify this continuum approach by showing how it fits with many well established intuitions (such as principles in the legal system), and solves various problems, so that it becomes a coherent solution to the problem of free will. I start by giving examples of the different stages mentioned above.

If a person is to be the cause of an act she performs, a desire in the person must cause the motor neurons to trigger the act. If a person is not the cause of an act she performs, meaning that a desire in the person is not the cause of the motion of her body, it does not constitute a free action. If I break a glass by accident it was not a free act. I might be held responsible for it, but then it must be indirectly in the sense that someone holds me responsible, perhaps for not rising more carefully from the table when I knew there were expensive glasses there. More often, people will not hold you responsible for breaking a glass that you did not break on purpose and no one will think of it as an act of free will when the person in no way chose to break the glass.

If a person has been hypnotized to do something, the act is not caused by a desire of the person but by the hypnotist's command and so it is not a free choice. There may be details about hypnotism I do not know—perhaps people must give subconscious consent so that they will not do certain acts even if hypnotized. But if there are cases in which someone else and not your own desires causes what you choose to do, then you are not exerting free will in such situations. If someone applies electricity to an area in your brain that makes your arm go up, it is not a free choice by you to raise your arm. If you have brain damage that gives you spasms, this motion is not something you have freely chosen to perform. All of this is obvious, but I mention it to show how my suggestion explains common sense opinions and to contrast them with similar but trickier cases later.

What if the cause of a choice is a desire in the person, but the desire is not a normal innate desire, but rather a desire caused by someone else or by a brain malfunction? I did say that at the end of the continuum close to no free will are choices where the person, but not her autobiographical self, causes the choice that is made. I can now state this more precisely that by this I mean that a normal and changeable innate desire causes the choice, for only in such cases will the person count as having a small degree of free will. If a person desires to eat chocolate and does so, it counts as an act of free will, even if the desire for sweet food is an innate desire, not caused by the autobiographical self. I shall return to cases where the autobiographical self either contains an approving or disapproving attitude of chocolate eating. But in general, eating a piece of chocolate is usually counted as an act of free will and should be since there is a degree of inner-directedness in it.[350]

If, on the other hand, a mad scientist has managed to create in a person a desire to kill dogs, then a choice to kill a dog is not an act of free will, as the cause of the desire is the scientist and not the person. The desire is the cause of the choice, but the scientist is the cause of the desire and I only consider normal changeable innate desires (or desires caused by the autobiographical self) as cases of free choices. The same would apply to a desire to kill dogs that was resulted from genetically caused schizophrenia. Again the cause of the desire is not a normal changeable innate desire (nor a desire caused by the autobiographical self), but rather a desire caused by brain damage or disease. There is no point in ascribing responsibility to the person if the desire to kill dogs is caused by a disease or a mad scientist. Since we want the desire to change, the best approach is to stop the scientist or treat the disease.

I said that a person can be more or less involved, even if the autobiographical self is not involved, so that the choice is more or less free. A person may act on a non-conscious desire, for example, when grabbing a handful of popcorn, which would still count as a free act (since it is your desire), but to a very small degree.[351] A conscious desire felt strongly and clearly, even for some time before the choice is made, is a clearer case of free will, even if the autobiographical self is not involved. So, if I non-consciously choose to shut a door I have been asked not to shut without ever thinking about the door shutting at all, I can still be blamed for shutting the door, but to a lesser degree than if I consciously chose to shut it.

Recall again the definition of free will: It is up to us what we choose among alternatives and the source of the choice is in us. If a person, but not her autobiographical self, is the cause of a desire which causes a choice, then "us" in the definition refers to the *person*, understood as a human body with a mind and a

---

350 I think this reflection helps to explain the debate about the Suzu Instant case: If Suzu Instant is created out of nothing, is she responsible when she makes her first act, or does responsibility require a history? (Michael McKenna, "Responsibility and Globally Manipulated Agents," *Philosophical Topics* 32, no. 1/2 (2004): 179–81). I would say that she has a very small degree of innerdirectedness, free will and responsibility, comparable to how small children develop their freedom and responsibility from scratch.
351 Below I justify including non-conscious choices as free.

core self; that the source of the choice is the *person* means that the cause of the choice that is made is one of the person's normal changeable innate desires. But the person did not choose to be born with those desires, so does it then fulfill the requirements of the definition of free will? It is much clearer that the requirements are fulfilled when the autobiographical self is the cause of the desire that is the cause of the choice that is made, because the autobiographical self can also be the cause of the desire, as shown above. But I have nevertheless chosen to include it as an example of free will when the person, but not the autobiographical self, causes the choice. Why have I done so?

Most people will count it as an instance of free will, for example, if one person hits another, even if her autobiographical self was not involved. The way in which such a scenario might happen is if a person gets a sudden desire to hit and acts immediately by hitting, without any memories from the autobiographical self being involved in the deliberation process. We hold people responsible for hitting others in such a situation, but why is that reasonable? It is reasonable because it is a changeable desire and so we hold such people responsible for not having gained control over the desire in the sense that their autobiographical self gets activated and changes the desire. Through life they have had the chance to think about hitting others and feel what is right and we expect that they should conclude that hitting others is almost always wrong and that this conclusion should be internalized in their autobiographical self so that when the desire to hit arises, the autobiographical self is activated and changes the desire. This is why we can blame people even for non-conscious choices, since it is their desires that cause the choices and we want them to change so that they do not act on such desires even non-consciously. When it comes to children, we blame them less than adults for things like hitting others since children have not yet had the chance to learn and internalize that hitting is wrong.

Some desires are easy to change, whereas others are not, and if a desire is difficult to change, a person is held less responsible for not having changed it.[352] Below, I provide examples of this, like the selection of ice cream topping and giving up an addiction. But there is a difference between consequentialist and non-consequentialist (or merit-based) views in terms of how much responsibility they will ascribe to others. A person with a merit-based view can think that it is mitigating if a person does something violent and has a mental condition which makes it more difficult for this person to control her temper. A person with a consequentialist view, in contrast, can say that those with such mental

---

[352] As Alfred Mele argues, a desire may even be irresistible, if it is impossible to change it intentionally (Mele, *Springs of Action*, 89).

conditions have a greater responsibility than others for making an effort to change their desires since these have negative effects.

But what does "changeable desire" mean, and what does it mean that it is easy or difficult to change a desire? By "changeable desire" I mean a desire that can change as a result of thoughts and feelings in the mind; it is easily changed if just a little and non-special mind activity is required, but it is difficult to change if much and special thinking and strong feelings must occur for a long time before the desire can be changed. For example, if I am to choose between ice cream toppings that I like almost equally well, it does not require much mind activity to make a choice or change the choice. Many different thoughts and feelings can make me change my preference. If I knew that I took the last topping that another person really wanted and it would have been easy for me to choose to take the other one, I could rightfully be blamed for that. The question of the extent to which a desire is changeable is relevant because we ascribe responsibility to people in order to change their desires. But some desires are very difficult to change, such as certain addictions where people are more often criticized for acquiring the addiction than for not stopping the associated behavior. I shall return to the question of addiction when I discuss problem cases.

The difference between changeable and non-changeable desires is not a difference between non-caused and caused desires—they are all caused. The difference is that changeable desires can change after a process of thinking and feeling, some easily, others not so easily. But they are all part of a causal process, and I have said that the causal processes in the mind happen as if the whole world were determined. How then can we have free will? Every change in your mind depends on earlier causes, but you are that causal chain! You are a person in the sense that you are a human body with a mind and a core self, and that core self is the conscious part of the causal process of the mind. When we select particular acts and ask for the cause, the particular cause in the causal chain is various desires that the person has. But does not freedom mean that we could have chosen something else? *Yes*, in the sense that several alternatives were type physically possible, but *no*, when it comes to the desire that caused the choice. You chose pizza because you desired pizza; other kinds of food were type physically possible to eat, but there and then you desired pizza, and free will does not require that you could just as well have chosen to desire to eat broccoli. Choices need to be caused by the person or the autobiographical self in order to be free, otherwise they are capricious.[353]

---

[353] What I say here is not contradicted by the fact that we can work to change our desires gradually, for if we do so, that is also caused by a desire to change the other desire.

It is common to say that we must be able to choose differently in the moment of choice in order to be free, but that is only sensible if it means that different alternatives are type physically possible, not if it means that you can easily change your desires. There are so many things that I might really want to do, where you could not ask me to suddenly want something else. If I really want to vote Democrat, I cannot suddenly choose to want to vote Republican. If I really want pizza, I cannot suddenly choose to want coffee instead, and so on. But it does not matter that I cannot want anything other than what I want. What matters is that the cause of my choice is a desire endorsed by my autobiographical self. It is not required that the mind produces a desire without a cause, because then this choice would be capricious. If that were the case, we would ask why the mind caused one desire as opposed to another and there would be no answer, nor free will.

But do we not feel that we can consider alternatives and think about what we feel like doing and then do that? Absolutely, but that is a causal process: Alternatives are imagined in the mind, different feelings are activated by the different alternatives, and the one with the strongest desire attached to it leads to action. That gives you a feeling of having made a free choice, even if it was a causal process where nothing else was token physically possible in that situation. But do we not also feel that we could have chosen something else? Yes, but there is always a cause for your change of mind—otherwise your mind is capricious. When you think "I want to do this instead," there was a cause for that change of mind, and that is good, for if changes of mind happen without a cause, our desires would be what they are for no reason.

It is very common to think that one could have chosen differently even in the moment of choice and this intuition is likely to be a driving force behind centered event-causal theories like that of Robert Kane. However, I have argued that this intuition is based on our feeling of having *type* physically possible alternatives. We feel that we could have done something other than drink coffee because we often do something else—we often drink tea—but maybe in a given situation the only thing that is token physically possible to do for the person is to drink coffee. He would still feel that it was possible for him to do something else, like drinking tea. The issue is that we cannot feel the difference between something that is *type* physically possible and something that is *token* physically possible. Therefore, we cannot trust people's intuition if they say: 'I really could have chosen tea instead, even in the moment of choice."

I have said that people are free when their autobiographical self is involved in the process of deliberation and changes their initial desires. Again, it is a causal process happening as if everything in the world were determined, for we do not choose when the autobiographical self becomes involved in a choice. This is confirmed in experience. We cannot choose whether or not to involve our autobiographical self, for if we start to think about that, the autobiographical self is already activated and involved. Memories and associations pop into our mind without us choosing that they should or not.[354] This does not mean that it happens as a result of indeterminism, only that it happens without being caused by a conscious choice. I shall return below to the question of what this element of luck means for free will.

Having considered free will in cases where the autobiographical self is not involved, I now present different cases where the autobiographical self is involved. I have already spent some time on cases where the autobiographical self changes initial desires and have argued that we are free in such cases. But I have also mentioned two other kinds of cases where the autobiographical self causes the desire that causes the choice that is made. The first case is of desires you are not born with but which the autobiographical self has acquired through life, like my example of a desire for rare stamps. Another example could be the desire for a certain football team to win the league. Such desires are often rooted in good experiences such as those which made you a fan of a certain football team. Deterrent desires, on the other hand, can be rooted in bad experiences so that, for example, you acquire a desire not to take drugs after a bad experience with cocaine.

With the knowledge we have today, it is difficult in many concrete cases to know what is an innate desire and what is an acquired desire. For one thing, it may be a matter of how precisely you describe the desire. We are born with a desire for sweet food, while a desire for a certain kind of chocolate (say, Snickers) is acquired. Another aspect is that even though we can say for sure that we are born with certain common desires, like the desires for food, sex and sleep, it is difficult to know whether more particular desires are acquired or largely genetically conditioned. Some findings in identical twins who have not grown up together show that they can have very concrete desires in common, which could indicate that quite specific desires can be genetically determined.[355] Thirdly, the interplay between genes and environment is very complex, as shown by epige-

---

354 We can indirectly influence what we think, but when we do, such attempts are also caused.
355 See a list of amusing examples in Steven Pinker, *The Language Instinct* (New York: W. Morrow and Co., 1994), 327–28.

netics, for example, where environmental aspects can determine which genes are "turned on or off" (rolled on or off histones).[356]

In any case, there are acquired desires that are caused by the autobiographical self and so are free, but it is not so important for the question of freedom whether they are acquired or innate. What is more important is whether the desire is endorsed by the autobiographical self or not, and this is the third kind of desire which I shall say is caused by the autobiographical self, even if it is more of an indirect causation. By "endorsed desire" I mean that some desires fit well with the autobiographical self, creating an approving attitude toward the desire which is stored in the autobiographical self, and the person is happy with having the desire. Other desires do not fit well with the autobiographical self, creating a disapproving attitude toward the desire, which is stored in the autobiographical self (this can give rise to a situation known as cognitive dissonance), and the person is not happy with having the desire. A woman who thinks of herself as moral and as someone who has certain opinions about what is right may be unhappy with feeling certain desires for something she considers immoral, whereas she would be happy with having a desire never to be unfaithful to her husband, for example. I call those desires that fit with the autobiographical self and which the person is happy to have "voluntary desires," while the desires that do not fit with the autobiographical self and which the person is not happy to have, I call "involuntary desires." Note then that "voluntary" and "chosen" are different terms in my terminology, since "voluntary" need not imply "chosen," but only "happy to have."

Here again the distinction between desires that are easy or difficult to change is relevant, for those desires that are easy to change are never involuntary. No one complains that they wish they did not desire to make their bed a certain way, for if you are unhappy with the way you desire to make your bed you automatically want to make it another way (unless you have some strange sort of compulsion). But people may be unhappy with their involuntary desires for sweet food, for married colleagues, that something bad should happen to someone, etc.—and these are desires that are more difficult to change. Voluntary desires are free, but how should involuntary desires be understood? Involuntary desires make people do things they do not want to do, and this is known as *akrasia*, or weakness of the will.

"Weakness of the will" is a term used for those who do something they do not want to do. For example, I may desire not to eat chocolate and yet I do, and

---

356 Amir Levine, "Unmasking Memory Genes," *Scientific American MIND* 19, no. 3 (2008).

that is called weakness of the will. That the will is weak seems to imply that there is something called the will, which can be strong or weak. I do not think that there is one entity deserving the name of "the will." Rather, I think that all there is are different desires of different strengths competing to be the one that finally triggers the motor neurons to make the person act. These different desires are what the person wishes to do, and the one that is actually acted upon is the one we say the person "wanted the most," or "willed." But sometimes we have contradicting desires; that is when it is relevant to speak of weakness of the will.

I find it useful to distinguish between different ways in which the term "weakness of the will" can be used. I concentrate on cases where people want to act in one way but do not do so. This can happen in situations in which a desire caused by the autobiographical self contradicts an innate desire, like an acquired desire to control aggression against enemies contradicting an innate desire to be aggressive against enemies. It can also happen in a conflict between desires that are both caused by the autobiographical self such as a recent desire versus an older desire, both caused by the autobiographical self. Perhaps you enjoyed drinking good wine before but after having children you have decided not to touch alcohol and now you feel contradicting desires regarding drinking wine. The term "weakness of the will" can also be used for competing desires where people think that one desire is morally good and the other desire is morally bad, and so when people act on their morally bad desires, they are said to have a weak will—not able to control their bad desires, for example, for too much alcohol. These may be desires caused by the autobiographical self or they may be innate desires.[357]

I shall disregard the moral examples and only consider the first two examples: where there is a conflict between desires caused by the autobiographical self and desires that are innate, and conflicting desires within the autobiographical self. How can such scenarios lead to acts of weakness of the will? I will start with the first case: a conflict between a desire caused by the autobiographical self and an innate desire. I have said that a person is freer (more inner-directed)

---

357 Richard Hare uses *akrasia* to denote lack of moral strength (Hare, quoted in Mele, *Irrationality*, 5). There are also other variables and distinctions concerning *akrasia* that I have chosen to omit since they are not important to my overall project. A person can show weakness of will in different areas at different times to different extents; it is a difference between weakness of the will in the moment of action and that concerning decisions about what to do later. Weakness of will can relate to control over thoughts, feelings, desires, and actions, but I focus on actions here. The distinctions in this footnote are from *Autonomous Agents*, 6, 8, 32, 121.

when the autobiographical self is the cause of the desire that leads to action than when it is not. This means that if the desire caused by the autobiographical self wins a conflict with an innate desire, then the person exerts more free will (and more self-control, as I argue below) in that choice than if the innate desire wins. If the desire caused by the autobiographical self is for a person not to eat sweets on a weekday and yet that person does because of an innate desire for sweet food, then that is a case of weakness of the will, which more precisely means that the desire caused by her autobiographical self was weaker than an innate desire.

The second case is when there is a conflict between desires that are all caused by the autobiographical self. If these desires are not sorted out, and the person does not know what she prefers, it is not right to speak about weakness of the will but rather confusion of the will. But if there is a new desire which the person now has as a voluntary desire, and an older desire that the person wants to get rid of, we can speak of weakness of the will when the person acts on the old (and now involuntary) desire she wants to be rid of. For example, this would be the case if a person joined a sect and there acquired some strange moral or religious views that influenced her desires, then left the sect and considered her views wrong, but was still unable to shake off some of the old desires. In this case, there is also weakness of the will if the old desire wins over the new desire since the new desire is a desire caused by a more independent autobiographical self than the old desire—this is a weakness of the will in this context. (The reason why the new autobiographical self is more independent than the old one is that it has changed at least one more desire than before.)[358]

Is it not strange that a person can say she wants one thing the most, and yet she does something else? Have I not said that the strongest desire leads to ac-

---

[358] Alfred Mele discusses the unorthodox case of a thief who thinks it would be best not to steal, but decides to do so anyway. Even if he is afraid, he steels himself and commits the crime. In this case, it seems normal to call it weakness of will if the thief did not steal, whereas it is self-control when he steals, even if he judges it best not to steal. Mele's own solution is to distinguish between an evaluative judgement and an executive judgement, and so whether the thief steals or not will be in accordance or not with his executive judgement (*Autonomous Agents*, 74). I interpret the story differently. If he does not steal because he is afraid, I would not think of it as weakness of will, but weakness of courage. If he steals, it may be a case of weakness of will, but this depends on the details of the story. Is his desire to steal in conflict with a newer desire not to steal, or is it not? This is what determines whether it is weakness of will, and not just that he thinks that stealing is not good, since if he desires to steal he must also think that stealing is good in one sense or another.

tion? How is weakness of the will then even possible?[359] It is time to consider, in more detail, what it means that one desire is stronger than another. I have already mentioned the consciously experienced side of strength of desires—that it has to do with the intensity and amount of pleasure or displeasure—but I have also said that, by definition, the strongest desire is the one that leads to action.[360] However, it seems that sometimes one desire can feel stronger than another and yet not be the one that leads to action. I can feel a strong desire for pizza yet eat fish, which I do not feel a strong desire for. Is there then a contradiction in what I am saying here?

One part of the solution to this problem is that a consciously felt desire may activate many strong contradicting desires in the mind, even if they are not consciously felt or consciously thought. Let us say a doctor suddenly feels a strong desire to have sex with a patient, yet does not act on this desire at all.[361] The desire probably activated many thoughts in the doctor's mind about scandal, prison, broken marriage, shame and so on, all with strong negative feelings connected to them (even if they were not consciously felt or thought), and so there was a stronger desire in the doctor's mind not to have sex with the patient even if not consciously felt. Mele mentions a problem raised by G. F. Schueler for those who think that the strongest desire leads to action; namely, how a person can intend to go to a school meeting even if he does not desire to do so.[362] My answer is that in the person's mind there are thoughts and desires concerning what people expect and what will happen if the person misses the meeting for no good reason, so the strongest desire is to go to the meeting even if it does not consciously feel that way.

Strength of desire then has to do with how good or bad the connected emotions are and how much they occupy the mind, but it may be both conscious and non-conscious. This determines the strength of the desire itself, but some

---

359 Some have argued that weakness of the will is impossible. Mele mentions, as examples, Socrates, Richard Hare, Gary Watson and David Pugmire (*Irrationality*, 8).
360 Supported by Singer, in Geyer, *Hirnforschung und Willensfreiheit*, 56–57. Mele discusses the critique that referring to the strongest desire does not explain an action. For example, if I ask why Bob threw the rock, the action is not explained by saying that he desired that the most strongly. Mele suggests that we do not think of it as an explanation because we already take it for granted that he desired it the most, but want to know why he desired to throw the rock (Mele, *Motivation and Agency*, 165). So, even if referring to the strongest desire does not explain a particular action, it does explain in general which desires lead to action when it is further explained what strength of desire means.
361 The example is from *Motivation and Agency*, 162.
362 Ibid., 29.

desires are more easily executed than others because of physical factors in the brain. In our brain, certain neural patterns have stronger synaptic connections than others. Every time a pattern is activated, its parts become more strongly connected to each other.[363] This is why negative thoughts you have thought many times easily come back and it is also why many psychologists tell you to repeat good thoughts many times. Synaptic strength cannot be experienced directly, but it can be experienced indirectly or inferred by how easily thoughts come to you, or how hard they are to get rid of. Synaptic strength is also part of the reason it is easier to jog if you engage in it as a regular habit than if you just have to decide at one moment between jogging and the sofa. If you are a regular jogger, you may feel a strong desire for the sofa and yet the desire to jog at the regular time makes you jog because of physical aspects of neural patterns in the brain. In that case, the desire for the sofa may in itself have been emotionally stronger than the desire to jog (at least that was how it felt consciously), but since the desire to jog had an easy path to be executed, it led to action, and was therefore strongest in the total sense where strongest means the one that led to action.[364]

However, it is even more complicated than that. There are several ways in which thoughts, feelings and desires influence each other, while physical factors also play a role, and this makes it difficult to set it all out in an easy formula. My aim here is only to point out the main contours of how it works. Many exceptions will not be treated, but I shall mention some here to indicate certain complicating factors. Alfred Mele presents the case of Ian, who most desires to sit and watch television although he should go out and paint the shed. After a while he shouts to himself: "Come on, get out!" And out he goes. How is that to be explained? Mele mentions several possibilities. One is that perhaps Ian has a habit of following orders and shouting to himself provides the necessary adrenaline boost to change what is the strongest desire. Furthermore, we can have several desires simultaneously, so even if painting the shed is not the strongest

---

[363] This is known as Hebb's rule, and is often summarized in the sentence "Neurons that fire together, wire together" (Bernard J. Baars and Nicole M. Gage, *Cognition, Brain, and Consciousness: Introduction to Cognitive Neuroscience*, 2nd ed. (Burlington, MA: Academic Press/Elsevier, 2010), 83–85). Synaptic strength does not make a desire stronger in the sense that it is connected with stronger feelings, but stronger in the sense that it more easily leads to action.

[364] Synaptic strengthening also explains why people over time develop more stable characters, habits, and preferences. At least I think so, and it fits very well with psychological research on personality, as shown in W. Mischel and Y. Shoda, "A Cognitive-Affective System Theory of Personality: Reconceptualizing Situations, Dispositions, Dynamics, and Invariance in Personality Structure," *Psychological Review* 102, no. 2 (1995).

desire, Ian may try a technique for making it the strongest desire, like shouting to himself. Other techniques for changing the strength of desire can be things such as imagining a piece of chocolate cake to be a piece of chewing tobacco.[365]

Thoughts influence desires. In my own experience, when a thought gives me a specific feeling or desire, I can change the feeling or desire by taking a meta-perspective: thinking about the fact that I am thinking about something which feels like that. It will often then feel different, since it is a new thought with a new feeling connected to it. This experience of mine supports Damasio's somatic marker hypothesis. Our thoughts about how likely something is to occur or when it will happen are thoughts that influence our desire for something. For example, I desire to have a million dollars, but that does not make me buy lottery tickets, because I think it so unlikely I would win.

What I am saying is that there are several things determining strength of desire, so that it is not strange that one desire leads to action even if a person has another contradicting desire, which may consciously feel stronger. This is a kind of conflict we have all the time and it is a life project to create an autobiographical self which integrates our desires in a coherent way that we like. I realize that my theory about the strength of desire is unfalsifiable, since I can always appeal to non-conscious desires or physical neural connections in order to defend my claim that the strongest desire leads to action. However, there is independent support for the claims and they do explain features that otherwise seem strange. I have already mentioned examples which clearly indicate a physical side of desire strength: The lateral hypothalamus can be stimulated electrically and make a person or animal feel compelled to eat and drink, whereas when it is destroyed, animals must be force fed not to die. Likewise, other areas of the brain could be stimulated to make people suddenly very sexually active.[366] These data fit very well with an understanding of desires having different strengths and causing action.

This concludes my discussion of the weakness of will. We have seen that we are free when our autobiographical self is the cause of the desire we act upon, either as a direct cause by changing initial desires or as an indirect cause by endorsing desires we are born with or acquire. We hold people responsible for

---

365 Mele, *Autonomous Agents*, 45–46, 179.
366 Joseph, *Neuropsychiatry, Neuropsychology, and Clinical Neuroscience*, 171–72, 87. Helen Steward claims that there is no empirical evidence of non-conscious decisions and that desire strength is an empty concept (Steward, *A Metaphysics for Freedom*, 159–60, 70–71), whereas I think that these examples show the opposite.

endorsing desires we think they should try to change, but we find it mitigating if the desire is very difficult to change (I shall return to the question of addiction).

The fact that we are freer when the autobiographical self causes the desire explains why we hold people more responsible for a planned criminal action than for a non-planned criminal action. If you see someone being rude to your spouse, you may immediately hit the rude person without having time to think about it. If you plan the attack, however, it is judged more strictly in a court of law than the immediate reaction. You are also responsible for the immediate action, since we think that your autobiographical self through earlier choices should have turned itself into an autobiographical self that immediately blocks an emerging desire to hit and that even prevents such desires from consciously occurring at all, but maybe your autobiographical self did not have time to react. If you plan the blow, however, your autobiographical self has had plenty of time to influence the choice to hit and clearly you have not changed your autobiographical self so that it prevents you from being violent, and then we hold you responsible to a greater extent.

Having now addressed the question of weakness of will, I have come to the last point on the scale of degrees of free will, which is when the desire that causes a choice is caused by an independent autobiographical self. I have already said that the autobiographical self becomes increasingly independent when it causes changes in initial desires and changes in itself, because it is then formed from within by the help of a general capacity for thinking and feeling. Early in life we do not have independent autobiographical selves, but we constantly face situations where we imagine alternatives, we make choices, and experience the consequences. When people have had many experiences and have had some time to think about different things, we expect them to reach certain conclusions about what is good and right. Holding them responsible for not doing what is good and right is a way of influencing them to do what is good and right.

In different cases, we ascribe less responsibility to people because they have been prevented from developing a normally independent autobiographical self. I have already mentioned children who have not yet had time to become independent. If someone grows up in a controlling and brainwashing sect it would also be mitigating, since this prevents people from having the normal opportunity to develop independence. It is the same if they are born with damage to the brain, which makes it impossible for them to think or feel in normal ways, and likewise, if they have been abused as children so that their mental or emotional life has been destroyed. The clue to understanding when we mitigate responsibility in these cases is that by ascribing responsibility we want to cause changes in bad behavior. This means that responsibility should be ascribed to the cause of bad behavior and that it is no use holding someone responsible for changing something which cannot be changed. So, even if people behave badly, I might instead blame the person(s) who had brainwashed or abused or hypnotized them. I also focus on changeable desires in ascribing responsibility, since the goal is to make them change, so I blame people less when the desire is more difficult to change and not at all if the desire is unchangeable by thoughts or feelings (I do not blame you for desiring food, drink and sleep).

I am freer, in the sense of being more inner-directed, in matters I have thought about a great deal than in matters where I just go with the flow, because the autobiographical self has been involved to a greater degree. I am also responsible for my acts when I go with the flow, for I could have taken time to think more about it. Lack of knowledge is mitigating in various cases, unless we think that the person should have known so that he or she can be blamed for the lack of knowledge. For example, I will not blame a person for not trying to save another person's life by use of an advanced technique that person has not heard of and few others know. But I might blame a person for not trying basic CPR to save a person and, even if the person does not know CPR, I might blame him or her for that, since I think that this is important knowledge that people should want to learn and actually do learn.

What I am saying is that free will lies on a continuum, where the degree of freedom has to do with the involvement of the autobiographical self—how strongly it is involved in the deliberation process and how independent it is by having been involved in earlier deliberation processes. The autobiographical self being the cause of a person's actions is, in my opinion, the content of the term "self-control." What it means to control one's actions is to cause one's actions, as argued by Mele, for how can you have control over something to which you are not causally linked? In order to have an effect on something, one must be causally linked to it.[367] Many who write about free will focus on control, but without answering in virtue of what it is that the agent controls her actions. Here I answer that what it means to control one's action is simply to cause it. The degree of control that we have over our actions is the different kinds of action I have described in this chapter, where we have most control when it is an independent autobiographical self that causes the choice. This detailed theory of free will is therefore also a detailed theory of self-control, and I have al-

---

367 Mele, *Autonomous Agents*, 10.

ready shown how it applies to the different cases of weakness of the will, which is lack of self-control.

I have said that sometimes our autobiographical self is the cause of our actions—and the cause of why that self is the way it is. Sometimes a person can find himself in an undetermined scenario and when we ask for the cause of the action, that person's autobiographical self may be the correct cause to select. The same applies to certain cases where the autobiographical self causes changes to itself by making a choice, having an experience and storing memories of that experience, which again will influence future choices: the autobiographical self gradually shapes itself from within by being the causes of changes in itself.

This may seem to lead to a regress problem, since as we move backwards in time, the causes of the changes will go back to before the person had any free will. It seems that external causes has shaped the way the autobiographical self became from the beginning, so that what happened was either a result of external causes or undetermined coincidences. But how could free will then arise in the first place?

I will now start in the other end and describe the way from a newborn and unfree human being on his way to getting free will. Let us call this person Willy, and see if we can free Willy. I assume here that Willy is born with a normal capacity for thinking and feeling, since these are the kind of persons I argue has free will. Willy has neither decided his genetic make-up nor the context he was born into. But when he is born, a new individual finds his place in the causal nexus of the world. And he is born into an undetermined world where different futures may take place.

There will be scenarios, not determined to happen, where it is the case that when we look for the cause of what happened, the answer will be that it happened because that was what the autobiographical self of Willy felt was best to do. In the beginning, if we ask why the autobiographical self of Willy felt that this or that was best to do, it will be caused by states of affairs other than the autobiographical self of Willy. But quite soon, when Willy acts in a scenario not determined to happen, he will make experiences that will feel good or bad, and these will be stored as memories.

Important memories are stored as part of the autobiographical self, and thus the memory stored causes a change in the autobiographical self. In a similar scenario next time, the changed autobiographical self may find another alternative to be the best—which again gives new experiences stored in memory and further changing the autobiographical self. This process here described is what I have called the development of a more and more independent autobiographical self, and I have said that a person is gradually more and more free the more his or her autobiographical self causes itself and the actions the person does. But this is a process where the autobiographical self does not determine what it finds good, it just acts on the basis of what it finds good. And the autobiographical self does not control the events that shape what it experiences or how it is shaped by them. So why is this free will?

It is free will because there is nothing more to free will than being the most important cause of actions. There is no possible control beyond being the cause, for what would such control amount to? If it should be more, it would require a detached soul or a meta-self, but why should the actions of such an entity be freer than what I have described here? From where did this detached soul get its criteria for choosing? The only way to build a person who can will what he wills is by a gradual process as I have described here, where experiences of what is good are made in an undetermined setting.

"What an autobiographical self found good" is the basis of free will and description of how free will is built step by step. In an undetermined world, there are many steps of what Willy's autobiographical self found good, which built Willy's autobiographical self and his free will. He did not cause the building blocks of his own body and brain or how they respond to experience or what he finds good. But he is the cause of every new reaction to scenarios in the world, and that is what is relevant.

Why is that what is relevant? Is this not too small a basis for holding people responsible? Surely where they were born, which experiences they had, etc., has influenced them greatly? It certainly influences them much where they were born, etc. But free will nevertheless deserves the name because it suffices to make responsibility meaningful. If the world is as I have described here, then holding others responsible and blaming them will influence what autobiographical selves find as good, which may cause better choices in the future. This is what we want from free will.

To sum up, free will lies on a continuum where different people have different degrees of freedom in different situations. This means that you can increase your freedom by learning about and thinking about alternative possibilities so that your autobiographical self can transform your desires and transform itself by use of reason and emotion.[368] I now want to test this understanding on vari-

---

[368] You can increase your freedom in several ways by taking time for reflection. One reason already mentioned is that reflective distance makes the alternatives feel differently, usually weaker, so that it is easier for your thoughts to change your desire. Let us say you have a bad habit of responding to your spouse rudely when you feel criticized, even if you know that you

ous difficult cases which have been discussed in the discourse on free will and which have been used to criticize various theories. If I can give coherent answers to these challenges, it speaks in favor of my understanding of free will.

---

often misunderstand and that it leads to pointless fights. You then say to yourself that the next time it happens you shall imagine yourself from the outside and weigh the reasons for and against responding rudely. The situation will feel different, and it will be easier not to respond rudely, which means that you have more control over the situation and you are freer.

Another example of how freedom can be increased by reflection is that you can come to realize that in certain situations you have several alternatives for action where you used to see only one alternative, so that you did not even think there was a choice to be made. By having new alternatives, you can change your autobiographical self from within in this area. For example, a person may be taking up much space in social settings and talking a lot, not reflecting over it, but just thinking that that is how social life works. Reflecting upon it, he may come to realize that he can choose either to take up space or give space to others. Reflecting upon it and involving the autobiographical self, the autobiographical self can now cause a new desire in the person, and so make the person more inner-directed and free to a greater extent than before.

Note that a person can then be smart, free and independent in one area of his or her life, but thoughtless and un-free in another area. An example could be a scientist who is very independent in his or her special field, but thoughtless and bound in relation to religious questions. Or the many people in Germany who were wise professors in one field, but at the same time thoughtless followers of Nazism.

5 Answers to Objections

In this chapter, I present common critiques and problematic cases to see how the theory I have suggested can solve these problems. I start by mentioning the problems of compatibilism and libertarianism that were summarized in chapter one. As problems for compatibilists, I mentioned the consequence argument, the manipulation argument and the zygote argument. As problems for libertarians, I mentioned the regress problem, the luck problem, the assimilation problem and the problem of the disappearing agent. I start now with problems for event-causal libertarians, since I define my theory as an event-causal libertarian theory.

5.1 Main problems for Libertarians

A recent book that lists several of these critiques is Helen Steward's *A Metaphysics for Freedom*. Her main objection is that the agent disappears in event-causal libertarianism, since choices reduce to desires, beliefs and bodily movement, and the agent disappears.[369] But the agent does not disappear in event-causal theories. Rather, what an agent is and what it is for an agent to make a choice is explained in a more finely-grained way. It is like explaining hardness by describing tension between atoms. The hardness does not disappear, it is just that what hardness is—and in virtue of what it is hard—is explained in a more finely-grained way.

In event-causal theories, the agent is reduced to a body and a set of processes within this body. Reduction here means that the same events in the world have been described in two different theoretical frameworks, whereas I would claim that the event-causal approach in this book is more coherent and finely-grained than a theoretical framework in which an agent acts by some irreducible kind of agency. The agent causationist may claim that something has been omitted in the event-causal framework. In my view, though, it has just been explained in a more detailed way, including that which agent causationists leave out; namely in virtue of what agents make choices. I often say that agents cause their actions, but then I use the language from the theoretical framework of agents and actions. This can then be described more precisely by referring to mind processes in a body. There is nothing wrong in talking about

---

369 Steward, *A Metaphysics for Freedom*, 62.

hardness, even if you think it can be phrased more precisely in terms of tension between atoms; likewise, there is nothing wrong in talking about agents acting although one thinks that it can be more coherently explained with reference to another theoretical framework.

I think that agent-causation is a normal assumption to start with. However, long reflection on all the examples of non-conscious thinking, feeling, desiring and choosing shows that adding some irreducible agent or agent causation is superfluous. Thus, while Helen Steward claims that there is no empirical evidence that people can make non-conscious choices,[370] I believe that I have shown many examples of how people can choose and act non-consciously in just the same way as when they choose and act consciously.

The critique that the agent disappears can also be formulated as a problem of regress. Since every event has a cause, it seems that we can follow the causal chain back to events that took place before the agent made a choice.[371] But I have explained why there is no regress problem in my account. Our autobiographical self develops through feedback from experience and influences future choices. This is an internal cyclical process within the agent creating the autobiographical self over time. In an undetermined world, there will then be many situations in which it is correct to select the autobiographical self as the cause, but are there not causes for why the agent became the way the agent is? Of course, but as shown in the chapter on causality in the example with the thunderstorm, we find the cause we are after by setting contrasts, depending on what we expect and are interested in. For all events, we can ask for causes back to the Big Bang, but the Big Bang is rarely the cause we are after. Rather, we ask for the cause in a given situation, given a long history before that. In questions of free will, the interest is usually why a person did A as opposed to B, and if the autobiographical self is the cause, the person is free. But why does the autobiographical self become the way it does? It does so through many choices in life, from an un-free start to becoming increasingly independent. It is all a causal chain, but it is the causal chain that is you, and the causal chain which is your life history was not determined to be the way it is. We do not have more freedom than that, but that is enough to fulfill the definition of free will and for it to be meaningful to hold people responsible.

In addition to the disappearing agent, Steward argues that there is another problem which is intractable for those who hold a causal theory of action, and

---

370 Ibid., 159.
371 Bok, *Freedom and Responsibility*, 201–05.

that is the problem of deviant causal chains.[372] The classic example is Donald Davidson's climber who holds another person on a rope and considers letting go of the rope. The thought makes him so nervous that his fingers start to shake and he loses his grip on the rope. We do not want to call this an intentional act of letting the other person fall. But if actions are mental states causing bodily movement, it seems we should call it an action, and so there seems to be a problem for those who defend an event-causal understanding of actions. Mele has a good answer with which I agree; here I extend it a little:[373] The climber does not perform a normal action, because then an intention to lose the grip sends a signal to the motor neurons to lose the grip. But in this climber's case, the idea of letting go causes a nervous feeling which causes the fingers to sweat and shake and thus lose grip. Since the climber's case is not that of an intention causing motor neurons to execute the intention, there is no problem for an event-causal approach to the mind to agree that this was not a normal action.

The remaining problems mentioned in chapter one were the luck problem and the assimilation problem. The problem of luck is considered by many the greatest, as with Neil Levy in his book *Hard Luck*. He defines luck as an instance of chance which is significant. Chance is not enough for something to be luck, since, for example, the number of trees in the forest is due to chance, but it is not a matter of luck.[374] Levy distinguishes between chancy luck and constitutive luck, where chancy luck are significant chance events in your life and constitutive luck is the luck involved in what kind of person you were born as.[375]

Levy argues that we do not have free will, not because of determinism or indeterminism, but because of luck.[376] Libertarians have a problem of luck because of indeterminism, but also compatibilists have a problem of luck, according to Levy, because so much of what happens in our mind and in our life is due to luck. For example, many external factors determine which ideas pop into our mind.[377] If one tries to solve the problem of luck by arguing that a person has a life history where the effects of luck can be cancelled out over time, this does not help, according to Levy, since every choice in history has been influenced by luck and one cannot solve a problem of luck by adding more luck.[378] Even

---

372 Steward, *A Metaphysics for Freedom*, 55–56.
373 Mele, *Motivation and Agency*, 59–60.
374 Ibid., 13.
375 Ibid., 29.
376 Ibid., 2.
377 Ibid., 90.
378 Ibid., 89.

when we change our character from within, such changes are based on our character which was either a result of luck now or earlier.[379]

I have three main responses to the problem of luck. The first is that we are born with a quite common capacity for thinking and feeling, and those who do not have these capacities are considered less free and less responsible. This basis is used as a standard when we ascribe people free will and responsibility, and luck is then taken into consideration in many ways. We find it mitigating if people are born in uncommon circumstances or with uncommon problems, and we find it mitigating if luck plays a strong role in specific situations.

We also give people time so that the effects of luck shall be cancelled out. So maybe you are more aggressive than normal, and maybe your parents were not that nice, but after a period of several years we think that given normal capacities for reasoning and feeling you should understand that it is wrong to steal, murder and lie. Especially in clear cases we expect that people understand what is right and wrong, whereas we can find it mitigating in more difficult ethical cases. So my first response is to accept that there is much luck involved in human action, but that this fact is included in how we evaluate people's free will and responsibility.

Is that a matter of solving the problem of luck with more luck, as Levy argues? No, it is a matter of letting reason and feelings find out over time what is right and wrong, even when disturbed by luck, and adjusting by the amount of luck involved. For example, a person growing up and traumatized in a war context may receive treatment and help instead of punishment to deal with his aggressive behaviour.

Against this one may argue that we cannot know to what degree people's choices have been influenced by luck, so we are not capable of taking the role of luck into consideration. I agree that we usually cannot know this to any exact degree. But that is not so important either when I consider responsibility to be something that has the goal of improving behavior. Holding others responsible, even those who have suffered much bad luck, can be a way of helping them to act better morally. It can also be a way of giving them more free will by making them aware of alternatives for actions that they can reflect upon and involve their autobiographical self in the process.

For example, by luck a person can have grown up in a family where they speak all at once, and he does not reflect over this behaviour, but finds it normal and interrupts other people all the time. When someone then holds him

---

379 Ibid., 92.

responsible and in some way communicates to him that this is not good behavior, he can realize that there is a choice to be made between talking all the time and letting other people talk, and realize that letting other people talk is a good choice. This makes the person more inner-directed than before and thus freer than before.

One could argue that it was a matter of luck that he was held responsible, but it was nevertheless his own thoughts, feelings and experiences which caused the response. Of course one can say that everything is luck, including that we have a capacity for reasoning and feeling at all. But then the concept of luck has become too broad to be a problem to worry about. As mentioned, we start off with a given basis as standard, and consider luck, freedom and responsibility in light of that. You may call everything luck, but that does not make it incoherent to continue thinking of free will, responsibility and luck in a narrower sense in the way I have done here.

Still, even if luck is taken into consideration, and holding others responsible can have good effects even when we do not know the amount of luck involved in a person's choice, we do not actually know whether that person has been so struck by bad luck that in effect he has no free will. That is true, but it does not threaten this theory of free will— this is my third main response— because of the fact that people have free will and responsibility to varying degrees in different contexts. People experience different degrees of good luck or bad luck in their lives, but people also have different degrees of free will and responsibility, and we may never know exactly how free and responsible a person really is.

But as I have argued, there are many cases where the autobiographical self is the cause of an action. And some people have had many chances to feel and think and make choices and change their autobiographical self from within to become more and more independent and free. Let us say my grandmother is about to fall off a cliff, but I rescue her. Why did I rescue her as opposed to push her off the cliff? If you answer that it was just a matter of luck, I answer that the concept of luck is used too broadly to be of interest. Then one has constructed a theoretical framework with a widely defined concept of luck within which everything can be defined as luck and every event explained by luck. Such a theoretical framework is too coarsely grained. We need a narrower concept of luck, in order to differentiate between free and responsible actions on the one hand and cases of luck on the other hand—with a lot of mixed cases in between.

The assimilation argument is a version of the luck argument. To repeat, Seth Shabo has argued a case where an indeterministic device in a person's brain determines her choices but sometimes it does not work, and then compared these situations in a rollback of histories. The argument then is that there is no relevant difference between a rollback of histories where the indeterministic device works or not—in any case there will be an undetermined outcome where the person sometimes chooses A and sometimes chooses B.[380]

When it comes to this argument, I deny that there is indeterminism in the moment of choice. History can therefore not be rolled back and give an exact same situation with different outcomes of the choice. In a rollback of histories, external indeterminism will give different worlds with different choices, and in the cases where the agent is the ultimate cause, the agent will have free will.

5.2 Main Problems for Compatibilists

Moving over to the arguments against compatibilism, I want to show how the theory I propose deals with these, since the theory is quite similar to compatibilism. Concerning the consequence argument, I do not control the past or the laws of nature, whether the laws are deterministic or indeterministic. So why does it help that the laws are indeterministic? Or as Manuel Vargas puts it: What does indeterminism add so that we get free will?[381] My answer is that indeterminism removes the past and the laws of nature as a cause that can be given for any event, sometimes leaving only the agent as the ultimate cause for a specific event. The past does not determine what will happen in the future. Several futures are possible and there will be specific situations not determined to happen where people will make choices that cannot be explained by reference to the past (when we ask why she did A as opposed to B), but must be explained with reference to the agent.

The manipulation argument is meant to show that there is no relevant difference between a determinism case and a manipulation case, and the challenge to the compatibilist is to show the relevant difference. One cannot argue that there is no relevant difference between a manipulation case and an ordinary case in my theory, since there certainly is. In a case of free action, the way I understand it, the agent is the ultimate cause, while in the manipulation case, the manipulator is the ultimate cause of the action. Pereboom shows that determinism and manipulation have similar effects, thus this argument supports

---

[380] Shabo, "Why Free Will Remains a Mystery," "Assimilations and Rollbacks: Two Arguments against Libertarianism Defended."
[381] Vargas, *Building Better Beings*, 79–80.

my claim that indeterminism is necessary for us to have free will in a strong sense of the term.

The same goes for the zygote argument. It cannot be used against my theory since a divine goddess cannot plan the life of a zygote in an indeterministic world. But again, the argument supports my claim that indeterminism is necessary for us to have free will in a strong sense of the term.

5.3 Other Problems

I have now commented upon the arguments from chapter one. In what follows, I shall consider some more detailed critiques against various models that have features in common with the theory suggested here. Ishtiyaque Haji has written a critique against the hierarchical mesh theories of Harry Frankfurt and Gerald Dworkin, and these theories are somewhat similar to mine since desires changed by the autobiographical self is a kind of second-order desire. I will here present the six criticisms from Haji to test how my own model solves the problems.[382]

The first critique looks at if someone has been made into a drug addict by no fault of their own, but identifies with his or her desire for drugs, then that person is responsible for being a drug addict according to Dworkin and Frankfurt. Haji disagrees.

The question of responsibility and addiction is a difficult one, often with strong feelings involved when the matter is discussed. I have the impression that many addicts and family members of addicts refer to the addiction as a disease that the addicted needs help to overcome rather than a vice that the addict is responsible for getting over. There are many differences between addiction and other diseases, but are there still enough similarities to make addiction deserve the term disease?

Epistemically possibly (=for all I know), there may be a genetic component making some people and groups more easily addicted. Drugs can also influence certain receptors in the brain that create withdrawal symptoms that are hard to resist, and as mentioned by Damasio, some drugs give a false impression of homeostasis which creates a strong desire for the drug in the brain. In addition to these physical aspects, social aspects are also important, such as childhood

---

[382] The six critiques are found in Haji, in Kane, *The Oxford Handbook of Free Will* (1st ed.), 211–12.

experiences, emotional development and the opportunity to develop into an independent person.

Concerning freedom and responsibility in the question of addiction, we should distinguish between (1) becoming an addict, (2) being an addict and using whatever the person is addicted to, (3) trying to quit, and (4) actually quitting. People should generally be held responsible for becoming an addict, although there may be special cases in which someone is forced into addiction. Then the one who did the forcing would be the cause of the person becoming an addict and so the one who exerted force would be blamed. There may be mitigating circumstances, such as a tough childhood and a social environment, so that it is more difficult to resist and the autobiographical self has had less opportunity to become independent. Some people have their emotional lives destroyed to such an extent that we should rather blame those who destroyed them emotionally.

When a person has become an addict, that person should be held responsible if he or she endorses the addiction as a voluntary desire. Remember that I argue that we should hold people responsible in order to change their behavior. We then think that they should—with their mind—realize that addiction is not good and so desire to overcome the addiction. As far as I know, we have no reason to think that drugs destroy the general capacity for reasonable thinking, even if they exert a strong emotional (conscious or non-conscious) influence on thinking. And so we claim that people have a responsibility to try to lose an addiction since we want them to come to the conclusion that they should try to overcome their addiction.

If they do desire to beat the addiction but cannot, we have a case of weakness of will. It is mitigating that an addiction is very difficult to overcome. So even if we blame someone strongly for becoming an addict, we may hold them less responsible for not managing to beat the addiction, since we know this to be very difficult. But in many cases, it is very important that they do overcome their addiction—they may be ruining a family—and then we may give them extra responsibility since the consequence is so important. This was the point I mentioned earlier that when people hold someone responsible according to a moral standard they may disagree on how blameworthy an act is depending on whether they focus on intentionality or consequences. Those who focus on intentionality will focus on whether the addict is trying to quit and blame the person depending on how hard she tries to quit, whereas those who focus on consequences may focus solely on whether the person actually manages to quit.

Are addicts then responsible for not quitting if they try to quit but cannot? In general, I think that they should be held responsible for what they can do as a result of normal thinking and feeling, even if I do not know in detail what that is. Not starting to take drugs in the first place is, of course, an important point, but as we have seen, there can be mitigating factors. Avoiding situations when you know you will be tempted or giving institutions the right to treat you by use of locked doors and force are examples of actions you may be responsible for not doing even if you are unable to resist a drug lying in front of you. But in general, addiction is a complex case with many parts where people can have more and less responsibility for the different parts. I think the policy on drug addicts should be that we hold them responsible in order to make them try to overcome the addiction and then, since it is difficult, help those who try as best as we can.

Haji disagreed with Dworkin and Frankfurt's view that if someone has been made into a drug addict by no fault of his or her own, but that person identifies with his or her desire for drugs, then that person is responsible for being a drug addict. The critique is too imprecise to make a judgement. I would say that such people are not responsible for becoming drug addicts, but that if they endorse their desire for drugs, we should hold them responsible in order to make them try to beat the addiction.

Haji's second critique is that if someone thinks that there is something he or she should not do, but nevertheless does it because of weakness of will (*akrasia*), then that person is not responsible according to Frankfurt; many critics disagree with Frankfurt on this. I agree with the critics; the reason that the critics are right is that in cases of weakness of the will, it is still a desire in the person that causes the choice that is made. When we hold people responsible, it is because they are the cause and we want to change the cause, so we should hold people responsible even in cases of weakness of the will.

Haji's third critique is that Dworkin and Frankfurt's theories seem to demand that second-order desires be approved by third-order desires, and so on, in an infinite regress. There is no such regress in my account, since initial desires are changed by the autobiographical self and the autobiographical self is changed in a dialogue between thoughts and feelings and the memories in the autobiographical self. The general capacity for new thoughts and feelings occurring as we have new experiences explains how new things can occur, so there is no regress at either higher or lower levels.

Haji's fourth critique of Dworkin and Frankfurt is that it seems strange to identify the self with second-order desires, thus hierarchical theories lack an account of what makes an action truly your own. With the aid of Damasio, I have explained in great detail what the self is and how it causes a change in initial (first-order) desires to become something like what Frankfurt calls second-order desires.

Haji's fifth critique of Dworkin and Frankfurt is that if the process creating first-order desires and then second-order desires is deterministic, why do second-order desires make you free? My answer is that when the world in general is not determined, it is often right to select the person or the autobiographical self as the cause, even if the process happening in the brain there and then happens as if the whole world were determined. In cases where an independent self changes an initial desire after imagining several alternatives, the definition of free will is fulfilled. The definition can also be fulfilled to different extents in different scenarios.

Haji's sixth critique of Dworkin and Frankfurt is that one could imagine a machine that would cause second-order desires in you. According to Frankfurt, you would then be free, which clearly is not the case. I agree, and I can explain why. If a machine causes the desire in you, it is not caused by the person or the autobiographical self and thus you do not have free will.

These were Haji's critical comments, but there are also other difficult cases, some of which have already been mentioned. The Frankfurt example has been explained: The person is responsible when the controller does not interfere, for then the person is the cause of the choice, independent of whether something else was token physically possible, whereas the person is not responsible when the controller interferes, since then the controller is the cause, not the person.

Are Frankfurt's examples even possible, or are they impossible and question-begging?[383] When does the controller interfere and is the world presupposed to be deterministic or not? The world is presupposed not to be deterministic. The controller can interfere at the moment just before he sees that the threshold will be reached where the strongest desire sends its signal to the motor neurons about to make the person act by then stopping that signal and putting another, stronger desire into the brain, which then triggers another set of motor neurons.[384] This is a coherent description of a thought experiment. It is not question-begging, for to beg the question is to presuppose (parts of) the conclusion you are arguing for without being or making aware of it. Here, I

---

383 Ibid., 291–95.
384 This means that the person has not yet completely made a choice, but would have done so if the controller had not interfered. Kadri Vihvelin distinguishes between the controller as bodyguard (stopping a person after her choice) or preemptor (stopping before her choice) (Vihvelin, *Causes, Laws, and Free Will*, 97–98), but this becomes something in between, since it would have been a choice had the controller not interfered.

explicitly stated my presupposition of indeterminism to make a point by showing the coherence of my position; that is not question-begging.

I have also mentioned in a footnote the example of the person who does not bother to call the police to report a crime, but as his telephone line is cut he would not have reached the police anyway. Is he responsible for not calling the police? According to a standard of intentionality ethics, he is responsible for not *trying to* call the police. According to a standard of consequence ethics, he is not responsible for not *actually having reached* the police.

An argument against theories of the kind I have presented is Peter van Inwagen's No-Choice Argument.[385] Consider a thief about to steal something when he suddenly remembers his promise to his dying mother that he will not steal anymore. The thief does not choose to remember his promise to his mother, but the remembered promise causes him not to steal. Thus, it seems that the thief has no choice but not to steal and so is not free. My reply to this would be that even if he does not choose what to remember, this memory alone is not the cause of him not stealing. If he hated his mother and thought that promise-keeping was for idiots, he would have stolen even if he remembered his mother. But if he loved his mother and made a sincere promise, these would be important memories and associated feelings would be triggered in his autobiographical self by the memory. So there is an important interaction between the memory and other memories in the autobiographical self that causes the thief not to steal; as his autobiographical self is the cause of his choice, he is free when he chooses not to steal.

According to Hilary Bok, libertarian theories of free will are impossible and cannot be understood causally since they inevitably lead to an infinite regress where it is impossible for the agent to end up as the cause.[386] Her point is that if we answer that the agent is the cause of something, we must keep asking for the cause of why the agent chooses as he or she does. This critique fails when it meets a nuanced theory about the agent and choices. The agent and the agent's mind, desires and autobiographical self can be understood as elements in a causal chain. The person is born with capacities for feeling and thinking what is good and right, and such thoughts and feelings shape her autobiographical self throughout her life as she faces experiences that were not determined to happen. But this process by which the autobiographical self shapes itself more and more in interplay with the mind in the meeting with undetermined events makes the autobiographical self into a more and more important cause when we

---

385 Van Inwagen, referred to in Clarke, *Libertarian Accounts of Free Will*, 97.
386 Bok, *Freedom and Responsibility*, 201–05.

want to explain choices. There are always other causes at play, so we can always keep asking and find out that we have certain genes and come from a certain family and that undetermined events have happened, and all of these play causal roles and influence our choices. But the point is that the autobiographical self is also one of the causes that should be selected as a cause and it can become quite important. It is not superfluous, since it is an entity with capacity to become what it does without being determined to become what it does, and so it is necessary in our causal explanation.

Robert Kane has some examples he often uses to support his view. First and foremost, there is the woman on her way to a meeting, struggling to decide whether to stop and help someone being assaulted or whether to proceed to the meeting. Kane says that whatever she does, she is free and responsible. I agree, but with a difference. In his view indeterminism in the woman's brain is necessary, but not in my view. I would say she is free because her choice is caused by her own desires. The desires are to get to an important meeting on time and to do what is morally right. If one of these desires is, to a greater extent, the result of independent earlier choices, we could call it a case of weakness of the will if she makes her choice based on the least independent desire. But in any case, she is free and responsible no matter what she does, since it is she as a person or her autobiographical self that is the cause of the desire that makes her choose what she chooses.

In two other examples, Kane describes a sniper who kills a man and a man who breaks a glass table top on purpose, and argues that they were responsible even if there were some indeterminism influencing the motion of their arms. I agree; the reason that they are responsible is that if we ask why the victim died as opposed to not dying, or why the table broke as opposed to not breaking, the cause is not indeterminism but the desire of the man who committed the act.

Another example mentioned by Kane is that of Martin Luther, when he said: "Here I stand, I can do no other." The point is that Martin Luther was free and responsible when he did that, but why was he free and responsible if he could do no other? The answer is that it was his autobiographical self that was the cause of the strong desire to do what he thought was right. Or at least he was free if it was his autobiographical self that was the cause of what he did.[387]

Chandra Sripada has argued that people actually are very concerned with which actions express our selves when we act, and that they ascribe intentionality and responsibility based on that. As a special case to support this, he de-

---

387 Kane, "Libertarianism."

scribes the so-called side-effect effect. In the most typical example, an assistant asks a chairman whether he wants to start a program that will give much profit but also harm the environment, and the chairman answers: "I don't care at all about harming the environment, I just want to make as much money as I can." People are asked whether the chairman intentionally harmed the environment, and roughly 80% say yes. Then they are offered an identical case, except that "harm" is replaced with "help". The chairman is asked whether he wants to start a program that will give much profit while also *helping* the environment, and the chairman answers: "I don't care at all about *helping* the environment, I just want to make as much money as I can." When people are asked whether the chairman intentionally helped the environment, roughly 80% say no.[388]

The challenge is to explain this asymmetry when the cases are so similar. According to Sripada, the solution is that people think that the chairman's negative attitude toward the environment expresses his deep self, and thus he intentionally harms it, while helping it does not express this deep self.[389] Rose, et. al., do not think that Sripada's explanation works, and argue that his own data undermines his claim.[390] My analysis of this case is that people consider the case and compare it with a standard for what the chairman should have done. Since he has a good reason not to start the program, many people will judge that he actively chooses to disregard this reason. "Starting a program despite its negative effect" is now considered one action, intentionally chosen. Compare this with a person who sits by the lake and does not sing "O happy day" and a person who sits by the lake and does not jump in to help a drowning person shouting for help. People will not judge that the person is intentionally not singing "O happy day," but they will judge that the person is intentionally not helping the drowning person. This is because we think there is a standard for what should be done in that situation, which is activated also in the mind of the person mentioned, so that it requires an intentional choice to disregard it.

Another common problem case is that of a man being threatened with a gun to hand over money. Is he responsible for handing over the money?[391] Yes, he is *causally* responsible for handing over the money, since he is the cause of handing the money over and because he had the type ability not to do so. However,

---

[388] Chandra Sripada, "The Deep Self Model and Asymmetries in Folk Judgments About Intentional Action," *Philosophical Studies* 151 (2010): 161.
[389] Ibid.
[390] David Rose et al., "Deep Trouble for the Deep Self," *Philosophical Psychology* 25, no. 5 (2012).
[391] Example taken from Berofsky, in Kane, *The Oxford Handbook of Free Will* (1st ed.), 188.

we do not hold him *morally* responsible, for in such a case we think he should have handed over the money rather than risking his life. Rather, we hold the gunman morally responsible because he should not threaten people with a gun. But if the gunman had threatened a man and instructed him to push a nuclear button that only he could push and that would destroy the world, then we hold the person being threatened morally responsible if he pushes the button (at least we do so for a very short while before we all die), because he had the type ability not to and we think he should not have done so.

5.4 Conclusion

This book has discussed the problem of free will, which consists of several problems: What is free will? Do humans have free will? How can it be explained coherently? I started in chapter two by discussing what causality is and found that we have to set up contrasts based on interest in order to find specific causes. This is important for explaining how persons can be the cause of their actions. In chapter three I presented a nuanced and empirical theory about the self, based on the writings of Antonio Damasio, which could be used to explain in detail how choices come about. Here I defined a person as a human body with a mind and a core self, and the core self is a series of conscious experiences while the autobiographical self is a neural pattern representing the main aspects of the life of the person. Desires arising in a person can be changed by activity in the mind and by influence from the autobiographical self. In this way, a person and her autobiographical self can be the cause of the desire that leads to the choice of A as opposed to B, and this fulfills the requirement for having free will.

I argued in chapter four that we have free will when the person or the autobiographical self is the cause of the desire that causes the choices that are made. Alternative possibilities need only be imagined by the person in order for the autobiographical self to be the cause of the desires that cause the choice that is made—the alternatives need not be token physically possible for the person to do in that situation. But the person is not the cause of why she chose A as opposed to B if the world is determined, so the theory presupposes that there is indeterminism in the world with undetermined effects at the macro level of humans. Whether the world is determined or not is something we are likely never to find out.

Moral responsibility is a matter of holding people responsible according to a moral standard for the situations they are in. Again, it does not matter that only one thing is token physically possible to do in a given situation, since the situation is different if someone is being held responsible, and then holding someone responsible can change what that one token physically possible thing is. The main reason for holding others responsible is to make them behave better.

Free will is a matter of inner-directedness, and exists on a continuum. People have a small degree of free will when their desires cause their choices without influence from their autobiographical self. They have more free will when their autobiographical selves are the cause of their choices and even more free will if they have independent autobiographical selves. This means that different people have different degrees of free will in different situations. It also means that you can attain more free will than you have now, and I hope that reading this book has been helpful in terms of making more freedom possible for you.

Bibliography

Armstrong, D. M. *The Nature of Mind, and Other Essays*. Ithaca, NY: Cornell University Press, 1981.
Armstrong, D. M. *Truth and Truthmakers*. Cambridge Studies in Philosophy. New York: Cambridge University Press, 2004.
Armstrong, D. M. *What Is a Law of Nature?* Cambridge Studies in Philosophy. Cambridge: Cambridge University Press, 1983.
Aronson, Jerrold R. "On the Grammar of "Cause"." *Synthese* 22, no. 3-4 (1971): 414–30.
Baars, Bernard J., and Nicole M. Gage. *Cognition, Brain, and Consciousness: Introduction to Cognitive Neuroscience*. 2nd ed. Burlington, MA: Academic Press/Elsevier, 2010.
Barsalou, Lawrence W. "Perceptual Symbol Systems." *Behavioral and Brain Sciences* 22 (1999): 577–609.
Beebee, Helen, Christopher Hitchcock, and Peter Charles Menzies. *The Oxford Handbook of Causation*. Oxford Handbooks in Philosophy. Oxford: Oxford University Press, 2009.
Bennett, Christopher. "The Varieties of Retributive Experience. " *Philosophical Quarterly* 52, no. 207 (2002): 145–63.
Bennett, M. R. *Neuroscience and Philosophy: Brain, Mind, and Language*. New York: Columbia University Press, 2007.
Bigelow, J., B. D. Ellis, and C. Lierse. "The World as One of a Kind: Natural Necessity and Laws of Nature." *The British Journal for the Philosophy of Science* 43, no. 3 (1992): 371–88.
Bigelow, John, Brian Ellis, and Robert Pargetter. "Forces." *Philosophy of Science* 55, no. 4 (1988): 614–30.
Bigelow, John, and Robert Pargetter. "Metaphysics of Causation." *Erkenntnis* 33 (1990): 89–119.
Bird, Alexander. *Nature's Metaphysics: Laws and Properties*. Oxford: Oxford University Press, 2007.
Blanke, Olaf, Stephanie Ortigue, Theodor Landis, and Margitta Seeck. "Neuropsychology: Stimulating Illusory Own-Body Perceptions." *Nature* 419, no. 19 September (2002): 269–70.
Bok, Hilary. *Freedom and Responsibility*. Princeton, NJ: Princeton University Press, 1998.
Boltzmann, Ludwig, and Brian McGuinness. *Theoretical Physics and Philosophical Problems: Selected Writings*. Vienna Circle Collection. Dordrecht: Reidel, 1974.
Budin, Itay, and Jack W. Szostak. "Physical Effects Underlying the Transition from Primitive to Modern Cell Membranes." *PNAS* 108, no. 13 (2011): 5249–54.
Carroll, John W. "Nailed to Hume's Cross." In *Contemporary Debates in Metaphysics*, edited by Theodore Sider, John Hawthorne and Dean W. Zimmerman. Contemporary Debates in Philosophy, 67–81. Malden, MA: Blackwell Pub., 2008.
Carruthers, Peter. *The Architecture of the Mind: Massive Modularity and the Flexibility of Thought*. Oxford: Oxford University Press, 2006.
Cei, Angelo, and Steven French. "Getting Away from Governance: A Structuralist Approach to Laws and Symmetries." *Methode - Analytic Perspectives* 3, no. 4 (2014): 25–48.
Chalmers, A. "Making Sense of Laws of Physics." In *Causation and Laws of Nature*, edited by H. Sankey. Dordrecht: Kluwer, 1999.
Clarke, Randolph K. *Libertarian Accounts of Free Will*. New York: Oxford University Press, 2003.

Clayton, Philip, and P. C. W. Davies. *The Re-Emergence of Emergence: The Emergentist Hypothesis from Science to Religion*. New York: Oxford University Press, 2006.
Damasio, Antonio R. *Descartes' Error: Emotion, Reason, and the Human Brain*. London: Penguin, 1994.
Damasio, Antonio R. *The Feeling of What Happens: Body and Emotion in the Making of Consciousness*. New York: Harcourt Brace, 1999.
Damasio, Antonio R. *Self Comes to Mind: Constructing the Conscious Brain*. New York: Pantheon Books, 2010.
Damasio, Antonio R. "Wie das Gehirn Geist erzeugt." *Spektrum der Wissenschaft (Digest: Rätsel Gehirn)*, no. 4 (2004): 6–11.
Davidson, Donald. "Actions, Reasons and Causes." *The Journal of Philosophy* 60, no. 23 (1963): 685–700.
Dawkins, Richard. *The Selfish Gene*. 30th anniversary ed. Oxford: Oxford University Press, 1976/2006.
Deheane, Stanislas and L. Naccache, "Towards a cognitive neuroscience of consciousness: basic evidence and a workspace framework," *Cognition* 79 (2001), 1–37.
Dennett, Daniel C. *Freedom Evolves*. New York: Viking, 2003.
Dowe, Phil. *Physical Causation*. Cambridge Studies in Probability, Induction, and Decision Theory. Cambridge: Cambridge University Press, 2000.
Earman, John. *A Primer on Determinism*. University of Western Ontario Series in Philosophy of Science. Boston, MA: D. Reidel Pub. Co., 1986.
Ehring, Douglas. "Causal Relata." *Synthese* 73 (1987): 319–28.
Espagnat, Bernard d'. *On Physics and Philosophy*. Princeton: Princeton University Press, 2006.
Fair, David. "Causation and the Flow of Energy." *Erkenntnis* 14, no. 3 (1979): 219–50.
Fernald, Russell D. "The Evolution of Eyes." *Karger Gazette*, no. 64 (2001): 2–4.
Fischer, John Martin. *Four Views on Free Will*. Great Debates in Philosophy. Oxford: Blackwell Pub., 2007.
Fischer, John Martin, and Mark Ravizza. *Responsibility and Control: A Theory of Moral Responsibility*. Cambridge Studies in Philosophy and Law. Cambridge: Cambridge University Press, 1998.
Frankfurt, Harry. "Freedom of the Will and the Concept of a Person." *Journal of Philosophy* 68 (1971): 5–20.
Fries, Pascal. "A Mechanism for Cognitive Dynamics: Neuronal Communication through Neuronal Coherence." *Trends in Cognitive Sciences* 9, no. 10 (2005): 474–80.
Gallagher, Shaun. "Philosophical Conceptions of the Self: Implications for Cognitive Science." *Trends in Cognitive Sciences* 4, no. 1 (2000): 14–21.
Gallagher, Shaun, and J. Shear. *Models of the Self*. Thorverton, UK: Imprint Academic, 1999.
Gazzaniga, Michael S. "The Distributed Networks of Mind (Gifford Lecture 2)." In *The Gifford Lectures*, 2009.
Gazzaniga, Michael S. "The Interpreter (Gifford Lecture 3). " In *The Gifford Lectures*, 2009.
Gazzaniga, Michael S. "What We Are (Gifford Lecture 1). " In *The Gifford Lectures*, 2009.
Geyer, Christian. *Hirnforschung und Willensfreihet. Zur Deutung der neuesten Experimente*. Frankfurt am Main: Suhrkamp, 2004.
Gieler, Uwe, and Bertram Walter. "Scratch This!". *Scientific American MIND* 19, no. 3 (2008): 52–59.

Ginet, Carl. *On Action*. Cambridge Studies in Philosophy. Cambridge: Cambridge University Press, 1990.
Gray, Jeffrey. "Mit den Ohren sehen." *Spektrum der Wissenschaft (Spezial: Bewusstsein)*, 2004, 62–69.
Hadjikhani, Nouchine, Arthur K. Liu, Anders M. Dale, Patrick Cavanagh, and Roger B. H. Tootell. "Retinotopy and Color Sensitivity in Human Visual Cortical Area V8." *Nature Neuroscience* 1, no. 3 (1998): 235–41.
Heathcote, Adrian. "A Theory of Causality: Causality=Interaction (as Defined by a Suitable Quantum Field Theory)." *Erkenntnis* 31 (1989): 77–108.
Heathcote, Adrian, and D. M. Armstrong. "Causes and Laws." *NOÛS* 25, no. 1 (1991): 63–73.
Hitchcock, Christopher. "Probabilistic Causation." Stanford Encyclopedia of Philosophy, 2010.
Hulswit, Menno. "Causality and Causation: The Inadequacy of the Received View." Article, *SEED* 4, no. 2 (2004). http://www.library.utoronto.ca/see/SEED/Vol4-2/Hulswit.htm.
Imbert, Michel. "Sehen ohne zu Wissen." *Spektrum der Wissenschaft (Spezial: Bewusstsein)*, 2004, 37–43.
Joseph, Rhawn. "Brain Mind Lecture 4 Parietal Lobes Body Image Phantom Limbs" (Sic). 2006. https://www.youtube.com/watch?v=X7hq47Rf2eY.
Joseph, Rhawn. *Neuropsychiatry, Neuropsychology, and Clinical Neuroscience: Emotion, Evolution, Cognition, Language, Memory, Brain Damage, and Abnormal Behavior*. 2nd ed. Baltimore: Williams & Wilkins, 1996.
Kahneman, Daniel. *Thinking, Fast and Slow*. New York: Penguin, 2011.
Kane, Robert. *The Oxford Handbook of Free Will*. Oxford: Oxford University Press, 2002.
Kane, Robert. *The Oxford Handbook of Free Will*. 2nd ed. Oxford: Oxford University Press, 2011.
Kaufman, Lloyd, and Irvin Rock. "The Moon Illusion." *Scientific American* 207, no. 1 (1962): 120–32.
Kim, Jaegwon. *Philosophy of Mind*. 2nd ed. Boulder, CO: Westview Press, 2006.
Ladyman, James, Don Ross, David Spurrett, and John G. Collier. *Every Thing Must Go: Metaphysics Naturalized*. Oxford: Oxford University Press, 2007.
Lange, Marc. *Natural Laws in Scientific Practice*. New York: Oxford University Press, 2000.
Levine, Amir. "Unmasking Memory Genes." *Scientific American MIND* 19, no. 3 (2008): 48–51.
Levy, Neil. *Hard Luck: How Luck Undermines Free Will and Moral Responsibility*. New York: Oxford University Press, 2011.
Lewis, David. "Causation." *Journal of Philosophy* 70, no. 17 (1973): 556–67.
Lewis, David. "Counterfactual Dependence and Time's Arrow." *Nous* 13 (1979): 455–76.
Lincoln, Tracey A., and Gerald F. Joyce. "Self-Sustained Replication of an RNA Enzyme." *Science* 323, no. 5918 (27 February 2009): 1229–32.
Lowe, E. J. *A Survey of Metaphysics*. Oxford: Oxford University Press, 2002.
Mandik, Pete. "Mental Representation and the Subjectivity of Consciousness." *Philosophical Psychology* 14, no. 2 (2001): 179–202.
Markowitsch, Hans J. "Neuropsychologie des menschlichen Gedächtnisses." *Spektrum der Wissenschaft (Digest: Rätsel Gehirn)*, no. 4 (2004): 52–61.
Matthews, Gary G. *Introduction to Neuroscience*. 11th Hour. Malden, MA: Blackwell Science, 2000.
Maudlin, Tim. *The Metaphysics within Physics*. Oxford: Oxford University Press, 2009.
McDowell, John Henry. *Mind and World: With a New Introduction*. 1st Harvard University Press paperback ed. Cambridge, MA: Harvard University Press, 1996.
McKenna, Michael. *Conversation & Responsibility*. New York: Oxford University Press, 2011.

McKenna, Michael. "Responsibility and Globally Manipulated Agents." *Philosophical Topics* 32, no. 1/2 (2004): 169–92.

McLaughlin, Brian P., Sven Walter, and Ansgar Beckermann. *The Oxford Handbook of Philosophy of Mind*. Oxford Handbooks in Philosophy. Oxford: Clarendon, 2009.

Mele, Alfred R. *Autonomous Agents: From Self-Control to Autonomy*. New York: Oxford University Press, 1995.

Mele, Alfred R. *Free Will and Luck*. New York: Oxford University Press, 2006.

Mele, Alfred R. *Irrationality: An Essay on Akrasia, Self-Deception, and Self-Control*. New York: Oxford University Press, 1987.

Mele, Alfred R. *Motivation and Agency*. New York: Oxford University Press, 2003.

Mele, Alfred R. *Springs of Action: Understanding Intentional Behavior*. New York: Oxford University Press, 1992.

Mele, Alfred R. *Surrounding Free Will*. New York: Oxford University Press, 2015.

Mischel, W., and Y. Shoda. "A Cognitive-Affective System Theory of Personality: Reconceptualizing Situations, Dispositions, Dynamics, and Invariance in Personality Structure." *Psychological Review* 102, no. 2 (1995): 246–68.

Monti, Martin M., Audrey Vanhaudenhuyse, Martin R. Coleman, Melanie Boly, John D. Pickard, Luaba Tshibanda, Adrian M. Owen, and Steven Laureys. "Willful Modulation of Brain Activity in Disorders of Consciousness." *New England Journal of Medicine*, no. 362 (2010): 579–89.

Mumford, Stephen. "Laws and Lawlessness." *Synthese* 144, no. 3 (2005): 397–413.

Mumford, Stephen, and Rani Lill Anjum. *Getting Causes from Powers*. Oxford: Oxford University Press, 2011.

Nagel, Thomas. "What Is It Like to Be a Bat?" *The Philosophical Review* 83, no. 4 (1974): 435–50.

Parfit, Derek. *Reasons and Persons*. Oxford: Clarendon Press, 1984.

Paul, L. A., Edward J. Hall, and John David Collins. *Causation and Counterfactuals*. Representation and Mind. Cambridge, MA: MIT Press, 2004.

Pearl, Judea. *Causality: Models, Reasoning, and Inference*. New York: Cambridge University Press, 2000.

Penrose, Roger. *The Road to Reality: A Complete Guide to the Laws of the Universe*. London: Jonathan Cape, 2004.

Pereboom, Derk. *Free Will, Agency, and Meaning in Life*. New York: Oxford University Press, 2014.

Pinker, Steven. *How the Mind Works*. New York: Norton, 1997.

Pinker, Steven. *The Language Instinct*. New York: W. Morrow and Co., 1994.

Puntel, Lorenz B., and Alan White. *Structure and Being: A Theoretical Framework for a Systematic Philosophy*. University Park, PA: Pennsylvania State University Press, 2008.

Redhead, M. L. G. "Explanation." In *Explanation and Its Limits*, edited by Dudley Knowles. Royal Institute of Philosophy Lectures, 135–54. Cambridge: Cambridge University Press, 1990.

Rescher, Nicholas. *The Coherence Theory of Truth*. Clarendon Library of Logic and Philosophy. Oxford: Clarendon Press, 1973.

Rescher, Nicholas. *Free Will: A Philosophical Reappraisal*. New Brunswick, NJ: Transaction Publishers, 2009.

Rescher, Nicholas. *Process Metaphysics: An Introduction to Process Philosophy*. Suny Series in Philosophy. Albany: State University of New York Press, 1996.

Rose, David, Jonathan Livengood, Justin Sytsma, and Edouard Machery. "Deep Trouble for the Deep Self." *Philosophical Psychology* 25, no. 5 (2012): 629–46.
Rowlands, Mark. *Externalism: Putting Mind and World Back Together Again*. Chesham, Bucks: Acumen, 2003.
Salmon, Wesley C. *Scientific Explanation and the Causal Structure of the World*. Princeton, NJ: Princeton University Press, 1984.
Sampaio, Eliana, Stéphane Maris, and Paul Bach-Y-Rita. "Brain Plasticity: 'Visual' Acuity of Blind Persons Via the Tongue." *Brain Research*, no. 908 (2001): 204–07.
Saunders, Nicholas. *Divine Action and Modern Science*. Cambridge: Cambridge University Press, 2002.
Scanlon, Thomas. *Moral Dimensions: Permissibility, Meaning, Blame*. Cambridge, MA: Belknap Press of Harvard University Press, 2008.
Schachter, S., and J. E. Singer. "Cognitive, Social, and Physiological Determinants of Emotional State." *Psychological Review* 69, no. 5 (1962): 379–99.
Schaffer, Jonathan. "Causation by Disconnection." *Philosophy of Science* 67, no. 2 (2000): 285–300.
Schaffer, Jonathan. "Causes as Probability-Raisers of Processes." *Journal of Philosophy* 98 (2001): 75–92.
Schaffer, Jonathan. "Contrastive Causation." *Philosophical Review* 114, no. 3 (2005): 327–58.
Schaffer, Jonathan. "Contrastive Causation in the Law." (2010). http://rsss.anu.edu.au/~schaffer/papers/CCLaw.pdf.
Schaffer, Jonathan. "The Metaphysics of Causation." Stanford Encyclopedia of Philosophy, 2007.
Schmidt, Richard A. "Motor Schema Theory after 27 Years: Reflections and Implications for a New Theory." *Research Quarterly for Exercise and Sport* 74, no. 4 (2003): 366–75.
Schmidt, Richard A. "A Schema Theory of Discrete Motor Skill Learning." *Psychological Review* 82, no. 4 (1975): 225–60.
Searle, John R. "Biological Naturalism." In *The Blackwell Companion to Consciousness*, edited by Max Velmans and Susan Schneider, 325–34. Malden, MA: Blackwell, 2007.
Searle, John R. *Consciousness and Language*. New York: Cambridge University Press, 2002.
Searle, John R. "The Mystery of Consciousness Continues." *The New York Review of Books* (2011). http://www.nybooks.com/articles/archives/2011/jun/09/mystery-consciousness-continues/?pagination=false.
Searle, John R. "Why I Am Not a Property Dualist." *Journal of Consciousness Studies* 9, no. 12 (2002): 57–64.
Shabo, Seth. "Assimilations and Rollbacks: Two Arguments against Libertarianism Defended." *Philosophia* 42, no. 1 (2014): 151–72.
Shabo, Seth. "Why Free Will Remains a Mystery." *Paficic Philosophical Quarterly* 92, no. 1 (2011): 105–25.
Sher, George. *In Praise of Blame*. New York: Oxford University Press, 2005.
Shermer, Michael. "Aunt Millie's Mind." *Scientific American* 307, no. 1 (2012): 84.
Singer, Wolf. "Ein Spiel von Spiegeln." *Spektrum der Wissenschaft (Spezial: Bewusstsein)*, 2004, 20–25.
Sklar, Lawrence. *Philosophy of Physics*. Dimensions of Philosophy Series. Boulder, CO: Westview Press, 1992.
Smith, Angela M. "Control, Responsibility, and Moral Assessment." *Philosophical Studies* 138, no. 3 (2008): 367–92.

Sripada, Chandra. "The Deep Self Model and Asymmetries in Folk Judgments About Intentional Action." *Philosophical Studies* 151 (2010): 159–76.
Sripada, Chandra. "Self-Expression: A Deep Self Theory of Moral Responsibility". http://sites.lsa.umich.edu/sripada/philosophy/ (Under review).
Stanovich, Keith E. "Rational and Irrational Thought: The Thinking That IQ-Tests Miss." *Scientific American MIND* 20, no. 6 Nov/Dec (2009): 34–39.
Sternberg, Robert J., and Jeffery Scott Mio. *Cognitive Psychology*. 4th ed. Belmont, CA: Wadsworth, 2006.
Steward, Helen. *A Metaphysics for Freedom*. Oxford: Oxford University Press, 2012.
Stickgold, Robert, and Jeffrey M. Ellenbogen. "Quiet! Sleeping Brain at Work." *Scientific American MIND* 19, no. 4 (2008): 23–29.
Strawson, Galen. "The Impossibility of Moral Responsibility." *Philosophical Studies* 75, no. 1/2 (1994): 5–24.
Strawson, P.F. "Freedom and Resentment." In *The Philosophy of Free Will: Essential Readings from the Contemporary Debates*, edited by Paul Russell and Oisín Deery, 63–83. New York: Oxford University Press, 2013 (1962).
Søvik, Atle O. "A Critique of Robert Kane's Theory of Free Will." (Under review).
Van Inwagen, Peter. *An Essay on Free Will*. Oxford: Clarendon Press, 1983.
Vargas, Manuel. *Building Better Beings: A Theory of Moral Responsibility*. 1st ed. Oxford: Oxford University Press, 2013.
Velmans, Max, and Susan Schneider. *The Blackwell Companion to Consciousness*. Malden, MA: Blackwell, 2007.
Viaud-Delmon, Isabelle, and Roland Jouvent. "Zwischen Virtuell und Real." *Spektrum der Wissenschaft (Spezial: Bewusstsein)*, 2004, 70–75.
Vihvelin, Kadri. *Causes, Laws, and Free Will: Why Determinism Doesn't Matter*. New York: Oxford University Press, 2013.
Wandell, Brian. "Colour Vision: Cortical Circuitry for Appearance." *Current Biology* 18, no. 6 (2008): 250–51.
Watson, Gary. "Responsibility and the Limits of Evil: Variations on a Strawsonian Theme." In *Responsibility, Character, and the Emotions: New Essays in Moral Psychology*, edited by Ferdinand David Schoeman, 256–86. New York: Cambridge University Press, 1987.
White, Benjamin W., Frank A. Saunders, Lawrence Scadden, Paul Bach-Y-Rita, and Carter C. Collins. "Seeing with the Skin." *Perception and Psychophysics* 7, no. 1 (1970): 23–27.
Wolf, Susan R. *Freedom within Reason*. New York: Oxford University Press, 1990.
Woodward, James. "Scientific Explanation." Stanford Encyclopedia of Philosophy, 2009.

Name index

Anjum, R. L. 39
Aquinas, T. 96
Aristotle 96
Armstrong, D. 38, 41
Aronson, J. 24
Aspect, A 36

Baars, B. J. 150
Bach-Y-Rita, P. 67
Barsalou, L. 95
Beebee, H. 27
Bennett, C. 128
Bennett, M. R. 57
Berofsky, B. 169
Bigelow, J. 25, 38
Bird, A 39
Bishop 2
Blanke, O. 87
Bok, H. 167
Boltzmann, L. 43
Budin, I. 59

Carroll, J. 39
Carruthers, P. 97, 102
Cei, A. 39
Chalmers, A. 39
Clarke, R 8
Clayton, P. 42, 59

d'Espagnat, B. 50
Damasio, A. 56
Davidson, D. 31, 96, 159
Davidson,D 6
Davies, P. C. W. 42, 59
Dawkins, R. 59
Deacon, T. 42, 59
Deheane, S 94
Dennett, D. 53
Dijksterhuis, A. 90
Dowe, P. 24, 34
Ducasse, C. J. 28
Dworkin, G. 163

Earman, J. 116

Ehring, D. 31
Ellis, B. 25

Fair, D. 24
Fernald, R. D. 66
Fischer, J. M. 138
Fitzgerald, S. 76
Fraassen, B. v. 23
Frankfurt, H 3
Frankfurt, H. 163
French, S. 39
Fries, P. 60

Gage, N. M. 150
Gallagher, S. 66, 87
Gazzaniga, M. 65, 67
Gazzaniga, M. S. 70
Ginet, C 6
Gray, J. 66

Hadjikhani, N. 63
Haji, I. 163
Hare, R. 147, 149
Hart, H. L. A. 49
Heathcote, A. 25, 38, 41
Hirstein, W. 66
Hitchcock, C. 23, 33
Hobbes, T. 96
Hodgson 2
Honoré, A. M. 49
Hulswit, M. 21
Humphreym, P. 30

Imbert, M. 65

James, W. 96
Joseph, R. 63
Jouvent, R. 66
Joyce, G. F. 59

Kahneman, D. 104
Kane, R 7, 116
Kane, R. 139, 144, 168
Kant, I. 96

Kaufman, L 67
Kim, J. 31

Ladyman, J 16
Ladyman, J. 40
Lange, M. 40
Levy, N 9
Levy, N. 137, 159
Lewis, D. 23
Lincoln, T. A. 59
Locke, J. 96
Lowe, E. J. 50
Luther, M. 168

Mackie, J. L. 22, 28
Mandik, P. 83
Markowitsch, H. J. 78
Matthews, G. G. 79
Maudlin, T. 40
McDowell, J. H. 95
McKenna, M. 136
Mele, A 5
Mele, A. 96, 98, 104, 120, 150, 159
Menzies, P. C. 32
Mill, J. S. 50
Mischel, W. 150
Monti, M. M. 80
Mumford, S. 39

Naccache, L. 94
Nagel, T. 80

O'Connor, T 6
O'Connor, T. 52

Parfit, D. 88
Pargetter, R. 25, 38
Pearl, J. 47
Penrose, R. 38
Pereboom, D 3
Pereboom, D. 127, 162
Pinker, S. 75
Prigogine, I. 36
Pugmire, D. 149
Puntel, L. 89
Puntel, L. B. 18

Ramachandran, V. S. 66, 79
Redhead, M. L. G. 36
Rescher, N 17
Rock, I. 67
Rose, D. 169
Roskies, A. 112
Rowlands, M. 68
Ryle, G. 96

Salmon, W. 25
Saunders, N. 2
Scanlon, T. 15
Schachter, S. 75
Schaffer, J 21
Schmidt, R. A. 103
Schueler, G. F. 149
Searle, J 84
Searle, J. 70
Shabo, S. 161
Shear, J. 66
Sher, G. 127
Shermer, M. 64
Shoda, Y. 150
Singer, J. E. 75
Singer, W. 65
Sklar, L. 116
Smith, A 60
Sobel, J. H. 2
Socrates 149
Spinoza, B. 96
Sripada, C 15
Sripada, C. 102, 168
Stanovich, K. E. 92
Sternberg, R. J. 67
Steward, H 13
Steward, H. 157
Strawson, G. 124, 136
Strawson, P. F. 126
Szostak, J. W. 59

van Inwagen, P. 167
Vargas, M. 128, 134
Viaud-Delmon, I. 66
Vihvelin, K. 54

Watson, G. 127, 149
White, A. 18, 30

Widerker, D. 138
Wittgenstein, L. 96

Wolf, S. R. 3
Woodward, J. 35

Subject index

Action 106–110
    as cause of desire 111–113
Addiction 163–165
Agent 86
Agent-causation 158–159
Akrasia, *See* Weakness of will
Alternative possibilities 114–116
    type vs token 114, 144–145
Assimilation argument, the 8, 161

Basic Argument, the 124
Blame, *See* responsibility
Blindsight 70

Cause 21–55
    absences as cause 34–35, 46–48
    as contrastive 22–23, 33, 49–53
    connection to effect 22–27, 34–49
    downward 42
    formal 42
    grainedness of 54
    most important 48–49, 51–52
    relevant 48–49
    selection of 28–29, 49–53
    transitivity of 55
Causality, *See* Cause
Causation, *See* Cause
Choice 12
Coherence 17–18
Compatibilism 2–5
Concepts 29–31, 44
    definitions of 29–31
    fuzzy 44
Consciousness 78–81, 89–94
    caused by brain activity 63–64
    core and extended 81
    function of 89–94
Consequence argument 3, 53
Control 155–156

Daring soft libertarianism 9
Deep Self theories 15
Deliberation processes 108–110
Desire 97–106
    caused by agent/person 110–112
    changeable 143
    strength of 100–105, 150–153
    voluntary and involuntary 107, 148
Determinism 2, 115
    defined 2
Deviant causal chains 159
Disappearing agent 9, 157–158
Dispositions 60

Emotion 72–76
Event, concept of 31–33

Feeling, *See* Emotion
Free will 1–10, 106–157
    defined 1
    in different degrees 139
    the problem of 1

Homeostasis 62

I 88, 125
Indeterminism 6
    agent-internal 10
    agent-external 10
    as condition for free will 118, 162
    at macro-level 116
Inner-directedness 139

Laws of nature 36–41
Levels 35–37
    of description 36–37
    ontological 36–37
Libertarianism 5–10
    agent-causal 5–6
    centered event-causal 6–8
    deliberative event-causal 8–9
    event-causal 6–9
    non-causal 5–6
Luck, the problem of 8–9, 159–163

Manipulation argument, the 3–4, 163
Memory 76–78
Mesh theories 3

Mind 62–105
    as event-causal 62–67, 95–96
    as non-conscious 67–72

Naturalism 19–20
Neurons 60
No-Choice argument 167

Person 89
    as cause of desire 111–114
Perspective 57, 69–72
    first-person and third-person 57, 69–72

Qualia, *See* Conciousness
Quality of will theories 15

Reasons-responsive theories 3
Reduction 30, 37–43
    of macro to micro 37–43

Regress problems 7, 124, 158, 169
Representation 61

Self 81–89
    as cause of desire 112–114
    as ultimate cause 125–127
    autobiographical 84–85
    core 82–84
    independence of 122–127
    proto 82
Self-forming action 7
Side-effect effect 169
Subjectivity 83–84

Thinking 95–97

Weakness of will 148–153

Zygote argument 5, 164

www.ingramcontent.com/pod-product-compliance
Lightning Source LLC
Chambersburg PA
CBHW030655230426
43665CB00011B/1099